IAN MALCOLM, from Lurgan in
years in journalism before returnii
mature student at Queen's Universi
was inspired by a lifelong fascination with Irish.

Three years as a journalist-by-night, a student-by-day and a
single parent in between paid off when he graduated with first
class honours, enabling him to undertake doctoral studies with
funding from the prestigious Arts and Humanities Research
Council.

Ian works as a translator/interpreter and freelance language
consultant. His specialist lectures on the Irish language from a
Protestant perspective have taken him all over Ireland and beyond.
A regular commentator in the Irish language media, he served as
a member of the RTÉ Authority for three years.

Ian has two children, Ian Óg and Tara.

Lá breithe sona duit a dhaidí

le grá

Gráinne, Connla,

Lola.

xr

☞ TOWARDS INCLUSION

PROTESTANTS AND THE IRISH LANGUAGE

IAN MALCOLM

Ian Malcolm

BLACKSTAFF PRESS

BELFAST

In association with Iontaobhas ULTACH / ULTACH Trust

Faigheann Iontaobhas ULTACH tacaíocht ó
Fhoras na Gaeilge.

Foras na Gaeilge

First published in 2009 by
Blackstaff Press
4c Heron Wharf
Sydenham Business Park
Belfast BT3 9LE

in association with
ULTACH Trust
6–10 William Street
Cathedral Quarter
Belfast BT1 1PR

Typeset by CJWT Solutions, St Helens, England

Printed in England by Cromwell Press Group

ISBN HARDBACK 978-0-85640-844-1
ISBN PAPERBACK 978-0-85640-848-9

www.blackstaffpress.com
www.ultach.org

To preserve anonymity, the names of the students who participated
in the author's research have been changed.

Do

Mo mháthair, a thug crógacht domh
agus mé ag tosú ar an
aistear fada seo.
Fosta do mo chol ceathrair Gavin,
ar dheis Dé go raibh a anam. Is é
ár mbua bua ár dteanga.

CONTENTS

7 Learning the lessons

ACKNOWLEDGEMENTS

So many people to thank and so little space. But I shall try. Firstly, my dear friend Professor Dónall Ó Baoill of Irish and Celtic at Queen's University Belfast has been an inspiration since the beginning of this project. Dónall, undoubtedly one of life's true gentlemen, was never more than a quick phone call and a staircase away. There are many others at QUB I must thank, among them Professor Liam O'Dowd of Sociology and Social Policy for giving such valuable advice on my questionnaire and checking over my stats.

I am forever grateful to the lecturing team, past and present, in Irish and Celtic Studies who guided me effortlessly through my undergraduate studies. Dr Rhian Andrews, Dr Mícheál Ó Mainnín, Dr Nollaig Ó Muraíle and Bn. Máire Uí Bhaoill all helped lay the foundations for this project. Many other teaching staff outside the School were also very helpful, with insightful lectures which opened up new vistas for me in statistics, data-handling and analysis techniques. I cannot name everyone, but am particularly grateful to Professor Bob Miller for making the science of data management approachable and enjoyable.

The Arts and Humanities Research Council made it possible. Taking the leap from a full-time paid job into the uncertainties of post-graduate life was made much easier by AHRC sponsorship. I hope it's been a worthwhile investment. And I should like to thank Queen's University for taking a chance on me in the first place.

I must not forget the most important people of all in my work – the pupils in the schools who shared their opinions with me. They were fascinating to listen to. Similarly, my gratitude goes to the teachers, who not only allowed me access to their students at a busy time (all time seems to be busy in schools today) but facilitated me in every possible way, giving freely of their energy and interest. The same is true of the staff at Gael-Linn, particularly Réamonn Ó Ciaráin.

On a personal level, my good friend Gordon McCoy was a fount of useful advice (he'd find obscure papers I could not have imagined even existed), while Stiofán Ó Direáin ensured I never lost my sense of perspective. The same is true of the Ultach Trust's Aodán Mac Póilin and Róise Ní Bhaoill. Indeed, the Ultach team as a whole helped me take my initial vague notion of 'a book about Protestants and Irish' from ill-defined concept to hopefully readable reality. Thanks also to Penny Pollard for her many words of encouragement on my 'beautiful journey'.

Nor can I forget my long-suffering family, who have had to endure me talking about paradigms, axioms, neologisms and Chi-Square. If nothing else, their vocabularies have been enriched. But they have provided so much encouragment, even if they cannot understand why I get excited by little things like a 0.05 p value. To Ian Óg, Tara, Lewis and Paula, I say this: 'Love youse all.' To my Dad, I say: '"*Go mbeannaí Dia Duit*" is four words, not one!'

Of course, there are many others I have not mentioned. To them, too, I offer my heartfelt gratitude. And as for any errors? I'm afraid to say I must claim full responsibility . . .

Go raibh maith agaibh uilig.

INTRODUCTION

In Northern Ireland the Irish language is something with the power to enrage and enthral, seen by many as a symbol of nationalism and republicanism, yet viewed by others as a harmless expression of a cherished culture. There is little common ground between the two viewpoints and for most unionists and Protestants the language is rarely seen in a positive light.

As the language revival in Northern Ireland gathers pace, boosted by the recognition and associated commitments outlined in the Good Friday/Belfast Agreement of 1998, many unionists and Protestants still firmly believe that the language is an important element in the political armoury of an increasingly confident nationalist and republican community. They perceive the language as a political weapon used as part of an overall strategy for the diminution and dilution of 'Britishness' in Northern Ireland.

On the other hand, it can be demonstrated that the Protestant people of the north-eastern corner of Ireland have had an association with the language at different levels for centuries. Indeed, some argue that Irish – a minority language on the west European fringes – would be in a far less healthy state today had it not been for Protestant interest. The association has ebbed and flowed, but nevertheless continues in that some Protestants in Northern Ireland still identify strongly with Irish. Indeed, I am one.

The number is small and it is true that the vast majority of Protestants have no meaningful understanding of or contact with the language. Irish is something that most are only likely to encounter in the media and, when they do, the context is generally negative. If column inches in the newspaper letter pages and broadcast minutes on the local phone-in radio shows devoted to the language debate are anything to go by, Protestants and unionists remain hostile towards Irish. But is this an accurate way to measure their views? Do the letter-writers and phone-in contributors genuinely indicate the strength of unionist feeling about the language?

Given that so much has changed in Northern Ireland since the end of the Troubles, a reassessment of this stereotyped view is overdue. The belief that Protestants and unionists treat the language with suspicion and distrust remains broadly unchallenged, in that opinions which were taken for granted during the Troubles are still accepted as the prevailing position. The time has come for a fresh look at the issue and in doing so it seems appropriate to move to a new constituency.

Young people have most to gain in the long-term from cultural rapprochement and they are the focus of this book. My primary aim, therefore, is to explore contemporary Protestant perspectives on the language, specifically those of young people in the 16–18 age group: by establishing their views we may be better equipped to find out if Irish can become a shared and inclusive part of our heritage, rather than something seen as exclusive and divisive. The Gael-Linn Enrichment Programme in Gaelic Studies (EPGS), which takes the language and culture into second-level colleges, where it has never been previously available, provided a convenient platform for such research, and the cooperation of participating schools meant it was possible to achieve a sample comprised of two groups – those who had been 'exposed' to Irish and those who had not.

A substantial part of this book is based on research that I conducted in a number of Protestant grammar schools and it is important to identify the techniques used in the fieldwork. These included a questionnaire to provide quantitative data, while focus groups and one-on-one interviews offered a qualitative perspective. In writing a book aimed at a general audience, however, I have had to make a number of judgements and the best way to do this – I feel – is to let the young people themselves speak out. Priority is consequently given to the focus group material, although the statistical perspective is not entirely overlooked.

A history of the Protestant engagement with Irish over the centuries is a logical starting point, as I feel we need to understand the past before we can move on. Whether it advances the contemporary debate or not, I'm not too sure, but I hope the opening chapter provides a comprehensive yet succinct summary of the role that the Irish language has played in the Irish Protestant experience.

A summary of more recent arguments shows the various ways in which both proponents and opponents of the language frame their viewpoints. This is a synthesis of the many factors, attitudes and perceptions which help to explain why Protestants in general tend to have a negative view of Irish. An appreciation of the reasons why Northern Ireland Protestants regard the language with suspicion has to be a sensible prelude to further enquiry.

Northern Ireland's segregated school system has been detrimental to cross-community understanding, contact and dialogue. Young Protestants have little or no direct engagement with the Irish language or those who speak it and this possibly reinforces negative views; at the very least, it does nothing to dispel them. However, the Gael-Linn EPGS has made the language accessible for some young Protestants. A detailed background on Gael-Linn and – more importantly – its course reveals how it has succeeded in achieving its goal. There is a certain bitter-sweet irony in that segregated education actually made my enquiries easier, for it meant I could access predominantly Protestant cohorts in all schools.

A background to the schools surveyed, augmented by interviews with the teachers who facilitate the Gael-Linn programme, sets the scene for the in-depth exploration of the attitudes of young people themselves towards the language. This provides a comprehensive snapshot of teenagers' opinions, not just in terms of Irish but in terms of the wider cultural context in which they believe it is situated. Given the freedom to talk at length in a series of focus groups, they spoke with a refreshing candour about the language and associated issues.

Results of the questionnaire completed by the pupils are included in a summarised form. Data were subject to a variety of statistical tests but these are omitted in this book and I have abridged the findings so that readers can get a broad flavour of the students' views, categorised by, for example, gender, religion and age. The focus groups provide a greater 'richness' of information, but the statistics are still important and of course the questionnaire captures the views of many pupils not involved in the round-table sessions.

So what can we learn from the young people? Is there sufficient evidence to indicate that any attempt to re-engage Protestants with

Irish will work? With an eye on the future, I assess the possible effects of a range of other factors on the language issue in Northern Ireland. Globalisation, for example, is something that could impact heavily on efforts to broaden the appeal of Irish more generally.

At the outset, I should like to make it clear that this work is, strictly speaking, concerned with the attitudes of young Protestants (or those of Protestant background) to the Irish language. It is not meant to be a treatise on the education system in Northern Ireland, but schools offered a realistic research arena as it was only within the classroom context that I could access a viable sample of young people from Protestant backgrounds who had been given the chance to become acquainted with Irish. The multi-strand approach used could equally have been applied to church groups or youth clubs, but finding sufficient numbers with any knowledge of Irish would have been impractical.

It was not initially my intention to explore students' views on Ulster-Scots but after pilot-testing the research model it became clear that the matter would arise at some point during the fieldwork. I decided to anticipate this and added a sub-section on Ulster-Scots, primarily to avoid potential accusations of bias in that my 'language survey' only covered one language. Unexpectedly, this strand provoked some of the most heated debate in the focus groups. Findings in relation to Ulster-Scots are not analysed in depth but I feel that those interesting points which did emerge are at the very least worth recording, even if they are essentially a by-product of the main research.

A little about my own background is necessary at this point because I write as a more-than-interested observer. Coming from the Protestant/unionist tradition I can understand why some who share my background feel uneasy about the Irish language and view it as a cultural extension of nationalism and republicanism. On the other hand, as an Irish speaker I can readily understand the appeal, beauty and relevance of the language. As subsequent chapters will show, reconciling the two interpretations is something that Protestant Irish speakers have often struggled with.

On a personal level, I ought to admit that learning Irish did initially cause some difficulties for me. Not all friends and family readily accepted my interest in what was often summarily dismissed as 'the ould Garlic'. Eventually, most realised that Gaelic had not changed my core values as Protestant, unionist and British. Speaking – and loving – Irish did not mean I became a rabid republican, subscribing to *An Phoblacht*, sleeping under a Tricolour bedspread and voting Sinn Féin. My core values remain exactly the same. My politics and religion have not changed in any way because I speak Irish. And why should they?

Some, though, have remained unable to understand my 'Gaelicisation' and interpret it as a rejection of my 'Protestant' heritage. I was once even advised by a staunch unionist with a very Irish surname that if I wished to speak 'that foreign language' I should go 'and live down south'. Other responses have been less gently argued! Yet it would be disingenuous to make too much of these negative reactions, for others have expressed surprise and even delight that a 'Prod' should be a fluent Irish speaker. The typical response falls somewhere between the two extremes. Indifference might well be the most accurate description. And I really ought to add that a few republicans too have made clear to me their doubts about an Irish-speaking unionist! In answer to them, I solemnly declare that I am not and never have been a member of MI5.

Irish is often perceived by unionists and Protestants as not being 'neutral'; as being a 'republican' language. This in itself is a complex sociolinguistic issue. Any language can be used in a way that is not neutral. After all, one can excoriate the Queen in English just as readily as one can calumnify the Pope in Irish. A language provides the nuts and bolts of self-expression and the speaker is free to mix and match whatever elements he or she chooses. I refuse to accept that a language itself can be 'political', but agree that the way in which it is used can be and this, in turn, means that it can become 'politicised' – through no fault of its own. That, I believe, is what has happened in the case of Irish.

However, the word 'depoliticisation' is a different concept entirely. This familiar but clumsy term is something I explore in the final chapter. It is used frequently by sources and respondents in this book but I believe the time has come for robust evaluation of a concept which may suggest different things to different people.

My personal view of Irish meant that I had to exercise caution during my research, as I did not want outcomes to be influenced by my own fondness for the language. I might personally hope to see Irish become more acceptable to people who share my background but it would be unforgivable to allow that desire to intrude on the fieldwork. Consequently, I made sure that I was at all times independent, using a reflexively self-critical approach to put distance between my research aims and my personal opinions. Only when the questionnaires/focus groups had been completed was I able to reveal that I was a Protestant Irish speaker. During the interviews, students sometimes made remarks about Irish which I found unpalatable or inaccurate but, given my remit, I could not allow myself the luxury of active participation in the debate.

I believe, then, that as far as possible I avoided 'giving anything away'. It was vital not to offer any sort of sign that one comment was 'right' while another comment was 'wrong'. There is a tightrope of sorts to be walked when one has a deep interest in what one is investigating but this is not unusual in research of this nature. The important thing is to be able to create the space, create the distance, to allow the research to develop as an independent entity.

One key point which should be fully understood at this stage is that of labelling. The terms 'Protestant' and 'unionist' are frequently interchanged in Northern Ireland. One is religious, the other political. They often merge but it is possible for a Protestant to be a republican, in the same way as it is possible for a Catholic to be a unionist, even if those who 'cross-pollinate' are tiny minorities. While I don't hesitate to use these labels freely as they provide a useful shorthand, the nuances outlined above should be kept in mind.

Finally, I believe that, in terms of Protestants and the Irish language, it is not a question of changing the debate but opening it. Young people represent the future and those who see Irish as being a force for inclusivity must take steps to ensure that it belongs to all, especially the young. I hope that this book will demonstrate that there is real reason for optimism that the language can become the intellectual property of all, regardless of politics or religion.

Essentially, this book is the voice of the young people I met. They have spoken – and I believe that their voices are worth listening to.

1

HISTORICAL PERSPECTIVES

INTRODUCTION

In his autobiographical short-story collection *Nuair a Bhí Mé Óg* (When I Was Young) the celebrated County Donegal writer Séamus Ó Grianna offers some interesting observations about Protestants and Irish at the turn of the nineteenth/twentieth century. In 'Albanaigh An Phointe' (Protestants of the Point) he looks at his neighbours in the Rosses area of west Donegal:

> Is dóiche gur iaróibh na hAlban a bhí sa chéad dream a tháinig. Ach sa tír s'againne anois is ionann Albanach agus Protastúnach, is cuma cén tír arb as é. Agus is ionann Gael agus Caitliceach ... Tá na hAlbanaigh ar an Phointe le trí chéad bliain. D'fhoghlaim siad an Ghaeilge ar an Phointe. Agus ní labhradh siad ach í go dtí cupla scór bliain ó shin ... Ní raibh mioscais ar bith riamh eadar na Gaeil is na hAlbanaigh fá ghnoithe creidimh san áit s'againne. Ach bhíodh siad amuigh ar a chéile ó am go ham de thairbhe polaitíochta. (repr. 1979:143)

> It's probable that the first group which came was from Scotland. But in our area now 'Scot' and 'Protestant' mean the same thing, whatever country he's from. And Gael and Catholic are the same ... The Scots have been on the Point for three hundred years. They learned Irish on the Point. And they spoke nothing but it [Irish] until around forty years ago ... There was never any disagreement between the Gaels and the Scots about religious matters in our area. But they used to fall out now and again because of politics. [my translation]

In a way, Ó Grianna's words provide an apt introduction to this brief history of Protestant engagement with the Irish language. He demonstrates, firstly, that for centuries there was nothing unusual about Irish-speaking Protestants and, secondly, that disagreements over politics are certainly not new on this island. Ó Grianna mentions that the way the 'Scots' spoke Irish was a source of gentle amusement for the 'Gaels' but, in general, paints a picture of an area where people lived and traded in harmony most of the time. And Irish was simply an integral part of that picture – free of controversy and free of politics. Indeed, in County Donegal some Protestants still use Irish as a daily language.

Loyal Belfast subjects welcomed Queen Victoria to the city with banners carrying Irish mottoes in 1849. The phrase *Érin go Brágh* (Ireland for ever) appeared outside a specially constructed pavilion to accommodate almost twelve thousand delegates at the Ulster Unionist Convention of 1892 in Botanic Park in Belfast. These undisputed facts, which now merit mere footnotes in the pages of history, do seem to show that 'as late as the turn of this century [the twentieth] unionists were not unhappy with reference to the native tongue' (McGimpsey, 1994:11). The Convention, after all, was effectively the genesis of modern unionism.

So what has changed, at least in terms of Northern Ireland?

EARLY ENCOUNTERS

Over the centuries, many Protestants have enjoyed a close affinity with the language and have been to the fore in groups and movements concerned for its welfare. What is important is to try to discover what began the process of Protestant alienation from the language. The issue might not, after all, be one of inherent hostility, but one of gradual separation, leading to virtually total detachment from a language that was once shared to some degree. Mac Póilin (1990:1) observes that the Planter[1] and Gael stereotypes ignore the inter-mingling of the people of Ulster and Scotland for about a thousand years before the Plantation: he adds that, between about 500 and 637 AD, the kingdom of Dalriada encompassed north-east Ulster and western Scotland. This, of course, was a mingling not just of people but of language, and the interplay continued so that '... Antrim and Down had been so extensively settled by the beginning of the seventeenth century, largely from Scotland, that they were never part of the plantation of Ulster' (ibid).

Exploration of the pre-Plantation movement between Ireland and Scotland is not necessary but Mac Póilin has successfully drawn attention to an East–West dimension in terms of early language and culture. The Gaelic tradition continued even when the Plantation began because a significant proportion of the Protestant incomers were speakers of Scots Gaelic, although the numbers are a hotly contested subject of debate.

This movement of people and culture has echoes even today, for unionists in general look fondly on links with the 'mainland', and Scotland has a special place in unionist hearts. The East–West dimension is a matter of pride for Northern Ireland Protestants, while the North–South axis is often viewed with suspicion.

There were two elements to the Plantation, in that some of the incomers were English and others Scots. Dealing with the latter group, attempts have been made to quantify the number of Gaelic speakers among the settlers. Mac Póilin (1990:1) points to indicators that many of them had a Gaelic background, given that western Scotland, in particular, 'was still largely Gaelic speaking in the seventeenth century, and many settlers came from there'. He adds that Gaelic speakers from Scotland moved to Ulster after the eighteenth-century Scottish rebellions 'and there are records of settlers arriving in Ulster unable to speak English'. That said, there is not much solid evidence about the language of the Planters for most of the 1600s and it is only towards the end of that century and the beginning of the next that a clearer picture begins to emerge.

Nonetheless, Ó Snodaigh (1995:30) believes that the Gaelic-speaking contingent of the Scottish Presbyterians who came to Ulster in the seventeenth century was large in number, possibly forming the majority. Undoubtedly, many Gaelic-speaking Scots made the journey, but it is difficult, even perhaps ill-advised, to speculate on percentages or proportions.

Coslett Quinn might be on more solid ground when he refers to a better-documented period (1994:30):

In the eighteenth century Galloway was Gaelic speaking. I imagine wider areas of Scotland were Gaelic speaking of course. McSkimmin says they spoke some sort of queer Gaelic in the Scotch quarter in Carrickfergus until about 1800, and the local Irish-speaking people could not understand it.

The 'traffic' between Protestant Planter stock and the Catholics who lived amongst them was, Ó Glaisne suggests (1981:34), perhaps 'almost always greater than might be inferred from school histories'. Mac Póilin (1990:2) reminds us that the extent to which the incomers and the natives mingled is often ignored, for English speakers often found themselves in minority situations and consequently learned Irish. Inter-group marriage took place and many Gaels converted, 'either from conviction or to maintain their property: seventeenth-century jury lists, restricted to members of the established church – the Church of Ireland – show plenty of Gaelic surnames'.

THE ESTABLISHED CHURCH AND IRISH

In post-Plantation Ireland there was tangible Protestant engagement with the Irish language in various ways. One was the complex battle for the hearts and minds of Ireland's Catholics in which the language was used as a weapon of proselytism on this new evangelical battleground. At the same time, the old Gaelic order was crumbling.

The Church of Ireland's efforts to evangelise through Irish offer some valuable insights into the traumatic collision between Gaelic Ireland and the new Protestant order. Ó Snodaigh (1995:35) notes that debate on the use of Irish within the Established Church was 'long and sometimes sharp'. This debate is explored in some detail by Barnard (1993), who says that enthusiasm for using the Irish language for Protestant instruction waxed and waned during the seventeenth century. The interest in the language shown by the Church of Ireland was 'fitful'.

It is frequently noted that, in 1570, Queen Elizabeth provided a Gaelic typeface to enable the printing of religious material to facilitate the dissemination of 'the Word' among the native population but

Barnard detects a certain tardiness in systematic evangelising in Irish and contrasts this with the haste with which Protestants used Welsh to proselytise: 'Irish, in contrast, was despised as the barbarous language of a backward people: at once the source and conduit of error' (1993:245). Such ambivalence characterised the Established Church's attitude to the language.

The Church appears never to have achieved a meaningful consensus on promoting the faith through the indigenous tongue and some of those who favoured such an approach added the codicil that, by doing so, the Irish language would eventually be eradicated and the native population brought around to the virtues of English. John Richardson, for example, a cleric at Belturbet in County Cavan in the early eighteenth century, saw the need to win over Catholics by teaching them in their own tongue. But, says Barnard (1993:254):

He reassured his critics that this concession need not last long, because the Irish, once converted to Protestantism, would forsake their distinctive customs, including their language. Accordingly, he could predict, 'in time the Irish language may be utterly abolished'.

Not all were so cynical. William Bedell (1571–1642), a provost of Trinity College in Dublin and, later, bishop of Kilmore, wanted clerical graduates to be able to minister in Irish. While at Kilmore, he oversaw the translation of the Old Testament into Irish (it was published after his death), 'seeking to redefine the objectives of the Church from an exclusive mission to the English and Scots colonists to the creation of an indigenous Protestantism' (Ford, 1999:41). He did, however, engender hostility amongst his fellow Protestants, 'largely a product of his implicit rejection of the essentially Anglicizing assumptions of the Protestant Reformation in Ireland' (ibid).

Another example of favourable Protestant views towards the language is Patrick Dunkin (Prebender of Dunsfort in County Down in 1640), who used verse in Irish to lambast the 'Roundhead thugs' who forced him to flee to the Isle of Man, 'destroyed St. Patrick's faith' and invented a 'religion without authority' (Mac Póilin, 1990:2). That he chose to excoriate his opponents in Irish is noteworthy but possibly just an interesting aside.

In reality, it appears that Church of Ireland efforts in respect of the Irish language were weak and poorly focused. Saving souls might have been the primary mission but saving the language was feared by some as a potentially unpleasant by-product of evangelism in Irish. On the other hand, it must be remembered that the seventeenth century was a turbulent time of war, rebellion and suspicion between 'old' and 'new' Ireland, so the question of mission through Irish may not have received the priority it might have in a settled society free of conflict. Consolidation was probably more important than conversion.

Some genuinely believed in the language's own worth but, whatever the motives, the balance sheet shows that prayer books and catechisms were printed to little real effect. Ultimately, 'The Church of Ireland collectively lost interest in evangelising in Irish', says Barnard (1993:260), who suggests that the Church of Ireland Gaelic lobby's failure may be proof that institutional inertia and theological determinism were too strong and that the lasting interest in the language, 'if not dismissed as more eccentric than important, speaks rather of a relaxed antiquarianism than of evangelical zeal' (ibid:265).

THE PRESBYTERIAN CHURCH AND IRISH

Since many of the Planters were Scots Presbyterians whose language was Gaelic, their Church had an advantage over its Established counterpart. Despite the differences between the sister languages of Scots Gaelic and Irish, there was a linguistic bridge between Gaelic-speaking Presbyterians and the native population. It could be argued, therefore, that the Presbyterian Church had a more natural affinity with the language.

Ó Snodaigh (1995:47) and Mac Póilin (1992:1) cite a 1712 pamphlet in which one J. Maguire is quoted by Richardson as saying:

I met many of the inhabitants, especially in the baronies of

Glenarm, Dunluce and Killconway, who could not speak the English tongue; and asking them in Irish what religion they professed, they answered they were Presbyterians, upon which I asked them further, how they could understand their minister preaching; to that they answered, he always preached in Irish.

Blaney (1996:17) says that the pool of Irish-speaking Presbyterians was swelled by conversions from the native Irish, their Celtic origins disguised by anglicisation of their names. The 'O' – a Celtic marker – was frequently dropped but 'Mac', or 'Mc', remained extremely common. He says it is clear that there were Presbyterian congregations where Irish/Gaelic was the majority language: 'The only ones for which information has survived are North Antrim, Dundalk, and Rademon. It is reasonable to assume there must have been others': indeed, 'conservative estimates suggest that at least half of all the early Presbyterians in Ulster were Irish/Gaelic speakers' (ibid).

Setting the tricky business of numbers aside, the Church undoubtedly needed preachers for some of its own congregations but also turned its attention to missionary activity. Synod minutes of the early eighteenth century indicate a great enthusiasm for this work, as well as a number of Irish-speaking ministers. Further, those whose Irish was not up to the mark for preaching were exhorted to improve their command of the language. After 1720, however, the Synod's energies were taken up by weighty doctrinal matters and it was more than a century before the Presbyterian Church again focused seriously on the language issue.

Fitzsimons (1949:257) argues that the aims of the Church's Irish Catechism were to proselytise and anglicise. Extracts from the preface of the Irish Section of *The Church Catechism in Irish* (1722) indicate that 'the nature and motives of the proselytising campaigns ... were intended in reality, not for the propagation of religion, but as a means of completing the conquest of the Irish nation'. Instruction to the Irish natives in their own language did reappear as a part of Presbyterian missionary policy at the 1833 Synod of Ulster (Fitzsimons, 1949:258). Indeed, the Church took steps to make it incumbent on its clerical students to study at least some Irish.

Schools providing education through the medium of Irish were a key part in this new outreach and the project apparently flourished before a decline that coincided with the Great Famine. An interesting footnote to the work of the 'Home Mission' schools campaign is the war of words in the Glens of Antrim which began when a local priest attempted to discredit its work by alleging that school numbers and activity were fabricated. The complex and bitter battle – the so-called Glens Bible War – is well covered by Blaney (1996:110–118) and sheds some light on the tensions that existed in areas where the Catholic Church resented proselytising Protestants. Presbyterians appeared happy to use Irish for evangelical advantage and it may have stung the Catholic hierarchy that they had done little to encourage or preserve the language up until that point.

Protestant clerics, says the British and Irish Communist Organisation (BICO) (1973:35), 'just made use of Irish for missionary purposes while it was the living language of the mass of the Catholics'. Ultimately, attempts at conversion (using Irish as the medium) met with little success. MacDonagh (1983:109) says '... the drive to proselytise among the Irish-speaking peasantry did not long survive the Great Famine ... partly because of scandals and widespread relapses among the converted, and partly because of the dwindling of British financial support', while McCoy and Scott (2000:4) put it this way:

Despite some successes, a movement which changed the cultural scene in Scotland was dissipated in Ireland amid political and sectarian strife. In the nineteenth century the Catholic Church perceived the Irish language to be an impediment to the temporal advancement of its congregation; the hostility of the church to the language rendered Protestant proselytism in Irish a futile endeavour.

THE 'OTHER' ENGAGEMENT

There was more to Protestant association with Irish than just proselytising, and over the centuries other people with no vested interest in converting Catholics valued the language in other ways. This tradition represents a strong strand in the Protestant linguistic engagement that involved members of the main denominations and puts prosleytism into context. Some of those to the fore were churchmen, but their interest in the language was not based on the conversion imperative.

Mac Póilin (1992:2) cites Arthur Brownlow, who died in 1710, grandson of an English Planter and the forebear of Lord Lurgan, 'as a fascinating example of the political, religious, and cultural cross-fertilisation of the late seventeenth century'. From a Gaelicised Norman family, he was a collector of Irish manuscripts. Among his collection was material which would not have otherwise survived (Ó Buachalla, 1982:25). Brownlow was patron to the south-east Ulster scribe Eoghan Mac Oghannain and it seems possible that future generations of the family also lent their support to Irish bards, among them Peadar Ó Doirnín. Sims (1964) speculates that Irish may have retained a tiny foothold in areas close to Lurgan until the time of the 1911 census.

Ó Buachalla supports the theory that 'the presence of such a culturally permissive landlord ... must have contributed to the retention of Irish in the area' (1982:26), adding 'it is said that he himself [Brownlow] translated Irish poems into English':

That the High Sheriff for County Armagh and one of the principal landowners in the county should interest himself in Irish literature is in itself revealing and interesting: more significant, however, are its implications for any comprehensive sociocultural analysis of post-Plantation Ulster. It suggests that the simplistic monolithic view of life in Ulster usually presented to us by our politicians (one in which all natives are Catholic Gaelic and republican and all Planters are Protestant English and loyalist) does not stand up to objective scrutiny ... (ibid:25)

Proof that Protestant clerical interest in Irish was not all about conversion is provided by the example of the Reverend Moses Neilson (1739–1823), a Presbyterian minister (sometimes referred to as

Nelson) who established an academy at Rademon in County Down. Magee (1988:64) says that the school quickly won a reputation not just for the quality of the tuition but for the liberality with which it was conducted, adding: 'Thus, in addition to the sons of his own congregation, Moses Nelson prepared young men intended for the Catholic priesthood in Latin, Greek, English, French and many other subjects.' Indeed, one of his students, Father Luke Walsh, later the priest in north Antrim who sparked the Home Mission controversy, wrote of his warmth for Neilson 'a man of as great moral worth and sterling integrity as Ireland could boast of …' (1844:146).

One of Neilson's seven sons, William (1774–1821), went on to become one of the most significant figures in the nineteenth-century Protestant engagement with Irish and appears to have shared his father's values. By all accounts a gifted linguist, he was, after training for the ministry in Glasgow, ordained minister of the Presbyterian congregation in Dundalk in 1799 – his facility in Irish apparently securing his appointment – and soon started a school similar to his father's, again catering for all religions (Magee, 1988:72). Subjects included Latin, Greek, Hebrew and Irish. A clearly formidable academic, he compiled an English grammar as a youth, as well as a textbook on Greek. His *Introduction to the Irish Language*, published in 1808, is, however, the work for which he is best remembered. Says Seery (1991:7):

It was creditably printed for P. Wogan, 15 Lower Ormond Quay, Dublin, and dedicated to the Lord Lieutenant, Philip Earl of Hardwicke. Written by a Presbyterian, dedicated to an Anglican and published by a Roman Catholic, its hundred-and-twelve subscribers embraced all creeds and classes … We may safely say that William Neilson's most enduring monument is his Irish grammar.

Mac Póilin (1990:2) views the *Introduction* (repr. 1990) as an important repository of County Down Irish, now extinct, pointing out that it contains the first folktale ever printed in the language, as well as dialogues in the speech of the people, with an English translation.

Neilson became Professor of Irish, Greek, Latin, Hebrew and Oriental Languages at Belfast Academical Institution in 1818 and died in April 1821, having just been offered the post of Professor of Greek at Glasgow University.

Neilson was a member of the Belfast Literary Society, the Belfast Society for Promoting Knowledge and was 'actively associated with the revival in 1819 of the Harp Society for blind harpists in Belfast' (Seery, 1991:9). This is a significant point for, by the nineteenth century, Belfast was blossoming culturally and 'the town seems to have been full of talented people busily reshaping the politics, science, industry and culture of their time' (Mac Póilin, 1990:2). Interest in Gaelic seems to have been a strong component of this development and Ó Neill (1966:60) traces its origins to around the time of the publication of Charlotte Brooke's *Reliques of Irish Poetry* in 1789. As a result of this, he claims, the famous harp festival of July 1792 was staged in Belfast – at a time when political ferment, in the run-up to the 1798 rebellion in which Ulster Presbyterians played so central a part, was growing.

Not all Protestants with an interest in Irish, however, subscribed to the fever of rebellion. Neilson's politics, for example, were liberal but not revolutionary and it should be noted that he spent most of 1798 preparing a shortened version of an English/Irish dictionary. Blaney points out that he was loyal to the British connection (1996:41). The Antrim Glens Protestant, Dr James McDonnell, born in 1763 – a leading medic of his day, a member of many of Belfast's learned societies, a lifelong language enthusiast and an avid collector of Irish manuscripts – kept a 'prudent distance' from the United Irishmen but was a key organiser of the Belfast Harpers' Festival (Mac Póilin, 1990:2). Blaney writes (1996:41/2):

> … it would be difficult to identify any individuals at that time who were both republicans and lovers of Irish language and culture. Thomas Russell, who was executed in Downpatrick for being a United Irishman, had gone to Irish classes, but was never proficient in the language. If one were to list the prominent United Irishmen – Wolfe Tone, Russell, Jemmy Hope, Henry Joy

McCracken etc. – their lack of involvement with Irish would be immediately apparent. Nevertheless, the attitude of the *Northern Star* was an exception. It was the organ of the United Irishmen, and published *Bolg an tSoláir*, the first (albeit short-lived) Irish language magazine.

At this time, then, we see the Irish language not as a clearly defined strand in emerging nationalist or republican ideology but as something to be admired and cherished in its own right by educated Protestants, a tradition that was to continue throughout the nineteenth century. Ó Neill (1966:61) does make a link between political and cultural nationalism in this period but adds that, while the Dissenters' 'revolutionary spirit' vanished after the Rebellion of 1798, 'an interest in Irish culture survived among many of the Northern Protestants'. This interest had Belfast as its epicentre and the energy gradually became channelled into revival activity, leading in 1830 to the formation of the Ulster Gaelic Society (Cuideachta Ghaeilge Uladh), an organisation which published several works in Irish. It was different from its predecessors because it showed more interest in the contemporary language (Ó hAilín, 1969:93) than was common for the period.

Many names feature in the Protestant engagement with the language in the nineteenth century, among them James McKnight, one-time editor of the *News Letter* and leader of the Ulster Tenant Rights Movement, and John McCambridge, who played a prominent role in efforts to preserve the language in the Glens of Antrim. Many more could be listed but two examples perhaps best sum up this phase of Protestant interest in Irish. The first, Samuel Bryson (1776–1853), was the son of a Presbyterian clergyman of apparently liberal views on Catholic emancipation.[2] Mac Póilin (1990:3) describes him as an important scribe and collector whose efforts led to the preservation of significant material that would otherwise have been lost. Between 1803 and 1810 he wrote eight Irish manuscripts, including sagas, romances, his brother's sermons and 'a unique late version of the story of *Deirdre and the sons of Uisneach*' (ibid).

An apothecary in Belfast and a former military assistant surgeon, Bryson involved himself in the Belfast Harp Society, the Natural History Society and the Literary Society. Praising Bryson's diligence and energy in saving manuscripts, Blaney (1996:52) says he 'pointed the way' towards our second example, Robert Shipboy MacAdam (1808–1895), perhaps the most significant Protestant figure in the broader Irish-language movement in nineteenth-century Belfast. MacAdam, indeed, is honoured today in the name of the renowned Irish-language centre, Cultúrlann MacAdam-Ó Fiaich, on the Falls Road in west Belfast. Yet his legacy is little known outside Irish-language circles, and perhaps not even well known within (Craig, 2007:9, 40).

MacAdam, an industrialist whose foundry at one time employed more than 250 workers, spoke fourteen languages and was involved in many of the city's learned societies. His primary passions, however, were the language, music and archaeology of Ireland. In common with Bryson, he was fascinated by Irish, collecting manuscripts, folktales and proverbs, even 'employing scribes from all over Ireland', people who were famous in their own right. Says Mac Póilin (ibid):

> MacAdam's achievements have never been properly recognised. He was the prime mover in introducing a question on knowledge of Irish in the 1851 census. In 1852 he organised a major exhibition for the British Association for the Advancement of Science, to '… enable strangers from other countries to judge for themselves the nature and extent of our ancient civilisation' … he founded *The Ulster Journal of Archaeology* … he compiled a large English/Irish dictionary … in 1849 he prepared – in Irish – mottoes to welcome Queen Victoria on a visit to the city …

Blaney asserts that MacAdam has left a significant and lasting imprint on the story of Irish in east Ulster (1996:123), adding that he was completely apolitical. With his death in 1895, 'Belfast lost one of the great Irish-language and antiquarian figures of the nineteenth century', says Hughes (1998:59), who adds that he should be remembered not just for his 'monumental' achievements as industrialist and businessman, as archaeologist and antiquarian but 'also as a champion of the cultivation of the Gaelic language and its broader culture, old and modern'.

The year of his death – 1895 – is significant in that it also marked the arrival of the Gaelic League in Belfast. As will be seen, the League's ultimate politicisation represents a watershed in the history of Protestant involvement with the language. In MacDonagh's words (1983: 108): 'for almost the entire length of the nineteenth century the bulk of the pioneering work for the preservation or restoration of Gaelic culture is attributable to Protestants'. However, we see clearly that even in the course of MacAdam's own lifetime the nature of the engagement was already changing. In his childhood, Irish would have had few negative overtones (other, perhaps, than its association with poverty), but towards the end of the century it had become 'part of the whole Catholic/nationalist package, to the chagrin of some of its Protestant upholders' (Craig, 2007:9).

A NEW APPROACH

Mac Póilin (1990:4) reminds us that the identification of Irish with a political ideology is a fairly recent development: overt politicisation did not happen until the twentieth century. The process, however, has clear origins in the mid-nineteenth century. Firstly, however, MacDonagh (1983:105) puts the extent of Protestant involvement in language preservation and revivalism into perspective:

> ... generally speaking the primary drives and work, down perhaps even to the formation of the Gaelic League in 1893, were Protestant. This is not to suggest of course that Gaelic sympathisers among Irish Protestants ever constituted more than a tiny minority. But all pre-League Gaelic movements were minute in scale; and in such lilliputian bodies, it was easy for Protestants to predominate, most of all in leadership.

Cronin (1996:131) describes the nineteenth century in Ireland as a period of accelerated political change, pointing to the success of the Land League, the emergence of Parnell, the conversion of British politician Gladstone to Home Rule and the foundation of the Gaelic Athletic Association (GAA) as indicators of 'growing political and cultural confidence'. The confidence in question was Catholic confidence, but Protestants, too, played their part in the construction of a national identity. My concern, however, is not with the broader political picture but with its effects on Protestant involvement in the Irish-language field.

In purely northern terms, several observers see the growth of Belfast as a factor in changing Protestant opinions. Andrews (2000:49) writes that, until 1850, Protestants in the city had no difficulty in accepting the language as a normal part of cultural life but, 'as polarisation continued, the areas where Irish speakers were concentrated became Catholic, and so did the language by association'. Consequently, Protestant solidarity with Irish began to wane because it was seen as Catholic and, therefore, suspect. Hughes (1998:61) reminds us that, in MacAdam's lifetime, the city's population increased tenfold, while sectarian divisions became more marked. Ó Neill (1966:66) notes:

The increasing indifference to the language and literature may be attributed to two causes, first to the utter failure of '98 which brought in its train a disillusionment with revolutionary ideas, and ultimately a rejection even of liberalism; secondly to the pressure of industrialization which changed Belfast from the pleasant enlightened town it had been into a mass of dark Satanic mills where there was little room for culture of any kind.

Meanwhile, the likes of Samuel Ferguson and Standish O'Grady were sifting through the corpus of early Irish poetry and legend. Belfast-born Ferguson, for example, decided 'that the Anglo-Irish must save themselves by identifying thoroughly with the Irish past' (MacDonagh, 1983:109). While still antiquarian in outlook, they do appear to represent a new consciousness, but it was the mid-century

Young Irelander Thomas Davis – himself 'practically ignorant of Gaelic' – who 'redefined the concepts of "nationality" and "liberation", riveting nationalism to cultural separation and cultural separation to the Gaelic "heritage" in general, and to the Gaelic language in particular' (ibid:111). Davis, 'convinced that it was vital to reverse the anglicisation of Irish culture, argued for the revival of the Irish language, and attempted to foster a nationality of the spirit uniting the Irish of all religious traditions' (Gray, 1999:137).

Much has been made of Catholic 'indifference' to Irish and it seems that the Church's concern for the welfare of the language was 'comparatively slight until late in the nineteenth century' (MacDonagh, 1983:107). It has even been described as one of the most effective anglicising influences in the country, in some cases actively discouraging the use of Irish. Politically, Daniel O'Connell's exhortations to his followers to learn English are frequently cited and Ó Fiaich (1969:109) picks up on an intriguing contradiction:

> The contrast between the attitude of O'Connell and that of Davis towards Irish – O'Connell, of Gaelic and Catholic stock, with a fluent knowledge of the language, seeking to promote English, and Davis, of Anglo-Irish and Protestant stock, with only a smattering of the language ... calling for the spread of Irish – has been looked on as one of the great paradoxes of nineteenth-century Irish history. Davis's voice was that of the pioneer, destined to influence later generations more than his own.

Barnard (1993:271) says that 'most orders, other than the Franciscans, failed ... to publish in Gaelic, which they sneered at as the demotic of a plebeian, unruly and degenerate society'. But times had changed and Catholic clergy – post-emancipation – were now the leaders of a new and powerful political force (Andrews, 2000:47). Protestants, meanwhile, began to withdraw from the Irish-language scene as the Home Rule debate gathered pace and many feared becoming involved in the political struggle (Ó Neill, 1966:66).

CHANGING THE GUARD

As MacDonagh notes above, Protestants took the lead in 'lilliputian bodies' which were to the forefront in the preservation of Irish. While the interest of antiquarians in the language might often have been nothing more than inoffensive dabbling, a new and dynamic force was to change the ground rules by explicitly making the link between language and nationalist politics. The beginnings of Conradh na Gaeilge (the Gaelic League), however, echoed the past in that once again a Protestant was a prime mover in its establishment. Indeed, the organisation, founded in 1893 in Dublin, was carefully steered clear of politics for more than twenty years by Douglas Hyde, later the first president of the Republic of Ireland. That it did ultimately succumb to political pressure may have been interpreted by Protestants and unionists as a clear message that the time when they could engage with the language on their own terms had passed.

The League's foundation had been prefaced by that of the Society for the Preservation of the Irish Language in 1876, a body whose composition was altogether more Catholic than anything that had gone before. Says MacDonagh (1983:114):

> ... Irish Catholics had become, by the late nineteenth century, sufficiently self-assured and practised to dispense with the traditional Anglo-Irish leadership, hitherto so common even in 'native' causes. Although essentially Protestant in inspiration, it [the Society for the Preservation of the Irish Language] elected a Catholic archbishop, MacHale, as Patron, and included a Catholic priest, Nolan, among its leading members. Clerical participation was still more evident and significant in the Gaelic League.

Maguire (1991:24–26) attributes the 'shift in emphasis from scholarly or antiquarian pursuits to the promotion and propagation of Irish as a living language as most dramatically and effectively realised by the Gaelic League'. Connolly (1999:215) says: 'Unlike earlier movements concerned with antiquarian and folkloric studies, the league sought to revive Irish as a spoken and literary language.'

Running language classes, organising the Oireachtas – a national festival similar to the Eisteddfod of Wales – and publishing its own newspaper, *An Claidheamh Soluis*, the League brought Irish-language debate to a new and mainly Catholic audience. Kiberd (1993:74) suggests that it was the formation of the Gaelic League that genuinely brought about the revival of the Irish language.

Yet to understand the League, at least in its early stages, we must understand Hyde, the County Roscommon Protestant who was its president from inception until the catharsis of 1915, when republicans effected a takeover. Hyde's seminal 1892 lecture on 'The Necessity for De-anglicizing the Irish People' called for action to arrest the language's decline and denounced the imitation of English manners (Connolly, 1999:253), thus setting out his cultural stall. However, a year later he was insistent that the League should remain above politics and this was to remain his touchstone. Hyde believed that it was 'essential to include people from all political persuasions in the revival movement' and attempted 'to bring together all shades of nationalist and unionist opinion behind the common cause of the Irish language' (O'Reilly, 1998:36).

Hyde even attracted a small number of unionists – among them the head of the Independent Orange Order and the Grand Master of the Belfast County Lodge – to League ranks in the early years. The novelist George A. Birmingham (the Reverend J.O. Hannay in his clerical role) described himself as a loyalist, felt secure as part of the League's Protestant minority and in 1906 wrote warmly of the 'welcome' for those who shared his beliefs (cited Mac Póilin, 1992:6). Protestants were members from the beginning in Belfast and Ó Snodaigh (1995:85–92) lists many of those involved, recording that the first Belfast branch meeting took place on the Beersbridge Road: membership soon stood at 120 and activities included Gaeltacht visits. The League's campaign, at the end of the century, to improve the status of Irish in schools received support from Protestant and normally unionist sources in, for example, Monaghan County Council and the Larne Board of Guardians (Nowlan, 1969:45).

However, Irish Protestants were no longer in the ascendancy and even in Ulster the membership was largely Catholic. Most Protestants were suspicious. The often-quoted words of O'Byrne (1946:175) are worth repeating:

... the language in Belfast came, at least partly, into its own. But the League was never considered quite 'respectable' – that awful Belfast word – by the Planter. To be a Gaelic Leaguer was to be suspect always. The League might shout at its loudest and longest that it was non-political and non-sectarian. The slogan did not impress Belfast. With the League's membership ninety-nine per cent Catholic, what could one expect? 'Scratch a Gaelic Leaguer and you'll find a Fenian' was the formula in the old days ...

Birmingham (Hannay), a year after extolling the warmth of the League welcome for a 'loyalist' like himself, expressed disquiet at its direction, seeing 'the Sinn Féin position to be the natural and inevitable development of the League principles'. So, where did Hyde stand? Mac Póilin says the Gaelic League co-founder's appeal to nationalism to support the language revival 'inevitably implicated much of the League's work in the nationalist project' (1992:4):

Hyde's ambiguous attempt to use nationalist political sentiment to underpin what he hoped would be a non-political movement ultimately became impossible to sustain.

Greene (1972:18) agrees that the 'revolutionary' nature of Hyde's de-anglicisation policy, combined with his desire to keep politics out of the League, suggests a 'strange and complex' individual. However we interpret Hyde, unionists clearly became less and less able to maintain their involvement in the League (Mac Póilin, 1992:4).

Accusing Hyde of being unrealistic, MacDonagh (1983:112) contends that, far from avoiding politics, his de-anglicisation agenda, so clearly stated in 1892, was unviable without slipping into anglophobia. Hyde, by turn described as 'advanced nationalist' and 'politically agnostic', presided over an organisation that was 'deliberately infiltrated and exploited by extremists' (ibid), becoming a school for rebellion instead of uniting unionists and nationalists.

Nowlan (1972:44) argues that a movement which stressed the individuality of the Irish people was naturally bound to find it hard to avoid becoming embroiled in contemporary politics: the militant Irish Republican Brotherhood saw the League's potential for furthering its own aims and Seán T. Ó Ceallaigh, business manager of *An Claidheamh Soluis*, recounted how he recruited young people around Ireland into the IRB while on League business (cited Ó Huallacháin, 1994:57). Arthur Griffith's Sinn Féin also found it a convenient vehicle for political advancement.

Greene (1972:19) suggests that the Irish language was secondary in this hidden agenda as the Gaeltacht's decline continued while the new political parties used the League 'as a recruiting ground and paid lip-service to its policies'. With Sinn Féin and the IRB gaining a hold on the organisation at grass-roots level, and the activities of the Irish Volunteers, led by League co-founder Eoin Mac Neill, it was only a matter of time before the takeover was complete and at the Ard Fheis of 1915 in Dundalk, Hyde resigned after the proposal of a motion which committed the League to working for a free Ireland. According to Dunleavy and Dunleavy (1991:327) it was no snap decision for, aware that those who wanted 'activist plots in the League's programme' were in the majority, Hyde had made his decision several weeks earlier. Perhaps he had helped undermine himself by becoming 'the archetype of the Catholic-Protestant, cunning, subtle, cajoling, superficial and affable' (Kiberd, 1993:134).

The link between the language and nationalism/republicanism was effectively made and Patrick Pearse, leader of the 1916 Easter Rising, stated proudly in 1914 (cited Mac Aodha, 1972:23): 'I have said again and again that when the Gaelic League was founded in 1893 the Irish revolution began.' As mentioned above, Ó Snodaigh's 1995 edition of *Hidden Ulster* includes a very impressive list of Ulster Protestants who were involved in the League – but the author makes no reference to the decisive 1915 Ard Fheis or Hyde's predicament.

The events of 1915 in Dundalk can only have confirmed Protestant fears that the language movement offered no place for unionists – as did the involvement of prominent Gaelic Leaguers in the 1916 Easter Rising – but, while Dundalk represented a watershed, the drift had started years before. Dunleavy and Dunleavy (1991:251) record that in 1905 the *Church of Ireland Gazette* had attacked Hyde and the League 'for activities inimical to the interests of Irish Protestants'. Most telling, perhaps, are the thoughts of Hyde himself, spelt out in his private memoir of 1918 in which he conceded that, by the time of the takeover, it would have been difficult to attract more unionists to the Gaelic League in any event (Ó Huallacháin, 1994:74). In Hyde's own words: 'I think we had won over the best of the unionists who were inclined that way, and I doubt that many more would have come in to us' (ibid).

What MacDonagh (1983:116) describes as the 'role-reversal' was already complete by 1914, so that Protestants, north and south, not only felt alienated from the Gaelic movement but even threatened by it, 'as much perhaps for its Catholicisation as for its extreme politicisation'. That League doctrines were largely incorporated into the policy of Sinn Féin (Ó hAilín, 1969:99) can hardly have been an encouragement to them. The League, as Ó Fiaich (1969:110) puts it, had proved to be the greatest political force in the nationalist ranks during the period, while Ó Cuív believes that its success was not in language revival but in re-awakening the national consciousness (1969:128–129). Mac Póilin (1992:8) observes that events in Dundalk confirmed Protestant suspicions: 'The overt politicisation of the language in 1915 resulted in the almost total alienation of unionists from the language, and is still relevant to the attitudes of unionists in Northern Ireland.'

MAKING SENSE OF HISTORY

In a rigorous disassembly of the arguments put forward in Padraig Ó Snodaigh's *Hidden Ulster* pamphlet – a precursor to his book of the same name, cited earlier in this chapter – BICO was scathing about his work. BICO was Stalinist in outlook and believed in the 'two-nations theory'; i.e. that Ulster Protestants represented a nation in their own right. This, in turn, made BICO not unattractive to some left-leaning loyalists and it is believed that there were links between the organisation and some paramilitary elements. Indeed, its response to Ó Snodaigh is underpinned by anti-nationalist/republican sentiment.

While ostensibly a direct attack on Ó Snodaigh, BICO's 1973 pamphlet 'Hidden Ulster' Explored is also a defence of the two-nations theory and a thorough examination of the Planters' engagement with Irish. The squabbles over numbers are too convoluted to explore here, but essentially BICO minimises the number of speakers while writers more favourable to the language maximise the figures.

BICO goes on to deal with some of the Protestant Irish speakers and enthusiasts listed in this chapter. Patrick Dunkin is dismissed as 'an Anglican Royalist reactionary … [whose] Gaelic reflected no Protestant tradition … In respect to Gaelic he was not a representative man but an eccentric' (BICO, 1973:20). Charlotte Brooke, BICO suggests, might well have written *Reliques of Hindu Poetry* had it been the case that her ancestors had gone to India instead of Ireland (ibid:34). A main thrust of BICO's argument is that Protestant interest in Irish was romantic or antiquarian in nature and not concerned with revival. A more recent Protestant advocate of Irish, Canon Coslett Quinn (cited above), was dismissed by BICO as 'an antiquarian eccentric' (1973:6).

BICO's attacks aside, there is still reason for a cautious approach to the issue of Protestants and Irish in the historical context. Given my own personal perspective as a Protestant speaker of Irish, it's initially comforting to think that my co-religionists in centuries past have had a close affinity with Irish. But there are questions to be asked. Adair (2000:146) rightly warns against ignoring the 'complex and various' nature of 'the interplay between communities in Scotland and the north-east of Ireland'. It is often tempting to opt for easy over-simplifications.

Regarding proselytism, was it right to use the Irish language to win converts to the Protestant faith? Some in the Church of Ireland, after all, appear to have hoped that, once converted, the 'natives' would forget Irish and embrace English. Was Irish just a weapon of convenience in this war of 'the Word', something to be dumped as fast as humanly possible once the initial objective was realised? There seems even to be a touch of guilt in the observation by Ó Glaisne[3] that:

> Christians of varying shades have, alas, acted very strangely in the name of their religion and love. In Ireland, Protestantism has too often been used as a weapon to suppress, to exploit and to exclude rather than something to comfort and enlighten. Protestants have traditionally been particularly given to the use of vernaculars in worship. But look at the Irish case. (1981:34)

It seems to be the case that neither the Established Church nor the Presbyterian Church seriously contemplated the promotion and maintenance of the language for its own sake, although some individuals may have valued Irish as more than a tool of conversion. It is worth adding that proselytism has become a 'dirty' word in the contemporary language debate and those trying to promote the language for Protestants rarely use the term because of its negative connotations.

Coming to the nineteenth century, how inspirational are figures such as Robert Shipboy MacAdam? After the Famine, the language was dying all over Ireland, yet Irish clung on in the remote Gaeltacht areas of the West. It is doubtful that the efforts of the Belfast Protestant enthusiasts had any significantly positive effect on preserving the language in remote places where Irish was synonymous with poverty. Collecting Gaelic songs and 'reliques' may have been a diverting pastime for the better-off in Belfast, but did these activities actually 'save' the language or make a difference to the lives of those who spoke it?

Then we have Douglas Hyde, often held up as a shining example for potential Protestant Irish speakers. But do his credentials bear closer scrutiny? True, he was keen to win over unionists to Irish and, given his reaction to the Conradh na Gaeilge Ard Fheis of 1915, it is clear that he was not a physical-force republican. But, as a nationalist, his appeal to modern-day unionists vis-à-vis Irish is very limited. Some who try to promote the Protestant Irish (language) identity make an exemplar of Hyde, boasting of his Protestant origins but neglecting his ultimately nationalist outlook. It might even be considered surprising that, in view of his 'de-anglicising' speech in 1892, he was able to entice any unionists into the League at all.

There is another, as yet academically unexplored, element to the equation. In 1915 Britain was at war with Germany. Did the war itself accelerate the process of detachment, as a heightened sense of nationalism on the part of 'British' Protestants and 'Irish' Catholics magnified perceived differences?

CONCLUSIONS

Essentially, our appreciation of the historic Protestant engagement with the Irish language has been lost in the maelstrom of more contemporary arguments. The evidence does show that many Planters who settled in Ireland would have been no strangers to Gaelic, and the Churches' need to preach to them in the language reinforces the point. But we must be careful not to imply that the language was embraced by all Protestants. Later came the revival and again there was significant Protestant input – but the warning note sounded in the previous sentence remains equally valid in respect of this phase of engagement with Irish.

It is fascinating to speculate how Protestant involvement with the language might have evolved had it not been for the metamorphosis of Conradh na Gaeilge from cultural organisation into a breeding ground for political activism and insurrection. The League's change of direction seems to mark the point at which it became no longer generally acceptable – or comfortable – to be Protestant and an advocate of Irish. The withdrawal process may well have started earlier, but it accelerated as republican politics and the language coalesced. Sadly, we shall never know what would have happened had the League stayed close to its original aims and objectives.

The past cannot and should not be ignored, but one must never forget that it can be used arbitrarily. Some nationalists may talk up the interaction of Protestants with the language in the past, hoping to encourage present-day (re)engagement, while some unionists may make little of previous encounters for the opposite reason. My work relies on a more contemporary analysis of the language issue in Northern Ireland and I hope that it – rather than events and personalities from centuries past – can provide a viable starting point for debate.

2

LANGUAGE ON THE FRONTLINE

INTRODUCTION

As was seen in the previous chapter, a selective approach can be used to justify a particular stance or argument in terms of Protestant interaction with the Irish language. One observer might choose the nineteenth-century revival to demonstrate how Protestants took a leading role in understanding, nurturing and even reviving Irish, while another might choose the twentieth century as the basis for an argument that unionists have always looked upon the language with suspicion and hostility.

History is important and should be understood, especially as many use it selectively for their own ends by carefully ignoring what does not fit their 'perfect picture'. That's fine. I have no argument with those who wish to interpret history in a particular way, as the practice of revisionism is as old as history itself. The important point is that we understand the history, so that we can see where particular arguments or trains of thought began.

This chapter looks closely at Protestant and unionist attitudes towards Irish since the foundation of Northern Ireland in 1921. The Stormont government's negative attitude towards Irish is examined, while a variety of research explores not only the 'republicanisation' of Irish but Protestant and unionist reactions to that process. Data from the 2001 census and other studies help to present an overall picture of prevailing attitudes. Language, of course, is just one component of a complex sociocultural equation that has created the Northern Ireland of today.

LANGUAGE SENSITIVITIES

Why is Irish viewed by many Ulster Protestants and unionists as a cultural weapon wielded freely by 'the other side' (a euphemism used by both Protestants and Catholics in Northern Ireland to describe those not of their own religion)? In an ideal world, for example, the Protestants of the Shankill (a loyalist 'heartland' in west Belfast) would have no difficulty in accepting Irish, as the name of their area is, in fact, Irish. Such acceptance, however, does not exist in any general way.

Mac Póilin (1990:1) refers to the question of cultural identity as one of the 'fundamental divisions of our society':

> Catholic nationalists speak easily of 'our language', whether they speak Irish or not, while most of the Protestant and unionist community regard that language as alien, even when they have obviously Gaelic surnames …

Even the terminology causes trouble, adds Mac Póilin, as the term 'Irish' involves a cultural and political context which means that unionists 'often find themselves choking on the political package that goes with the word' (ibid).

Dealing as it does with questions of language, perception and identity, part of this work sits between the domains of sociolinguistics (the study of language in relation to society) and sociology of language (the study of society in relation to language). Whatever the definitions, it is clear that the interface between language and society can be highly fraught and sociolinguistics fieldworkers have to tread carefully.

Crystal (1994:34) observes 'that language is often the primary outward sign of a group's identity', with a real probability of conflict when different languages are formally associated with the concepts of national and state loyalties. The resultant conflicts can be 'bitter and violent' and Crystal identifies awakening (or reawakening) of cultural identity as one reason for their development. The growth of the Frisian Movement in the early twentieth century as an expression of cultural difference between Friesland and Holland is just one of many European examples from the period: efforts to recover a disappearing culture/identity revolved around language. So there was nothing unusual when Conradh na Gaeilge (see Chapter One) explicitly linked language and a nationalist movement. As Ó Murchú (1972:23) notes, 'the cultivation of distinctive ethnicity usually involves as its most significant element the question of language'.

Culture, and how it is presented, can exert a powerful influence on how people think and live, becoming a potent source of division, something that is clear in the Northern Ireland setting. Language becomes 'an arena where political and cultural allegiances are fought out' (Kramsch, 1998:77). Yet, it is only one ingredient in the mix of flags, parades, colours and music that plays such an important role in the constitution of community identities. Even the 'Protestant' Lambeg drum and the 'Catholic' bodhrán have adopted symbolic status, although there is no historic reason to connect either instrument with just one tradition. 'Irish' music embraces both communities, and many young Protestants enjoy Irish dancing as much as their Catholic counterparts.

The linguistic schism is more clear-cut. Crystal adds that choosing one language over another provides an immediate and universally recognised badge of identity. Language also provides a particularly clear link to the past. While dialect is determined by many different variables (locality, class, education, etc.), using a different language can be a way of making a definitive cultural statement. In Northern Ireland there is no pressing necessity to use Irish, as everyone, with the possible exception of some recent immigrants, speaks English. The days of the monoglot Gael are long gone.

Modern Europe is characterised by cooperation and integration, but the importance of diversity and respect for difference is a keystone of its core values. Today, issues of language and ethnicity are coming to the fore in the various republics of the former Soviet Union, as well as some of its former partner nations in the Warsaw Pact, emerging from situations where they were pressurised by dominant 'imperialist' languages. As Novak-Lukanovič (2006:113) puts it:

> In almost every society, there is an overlap of different cultures, traditions and values – something that can enrich an individual culture but has the potential to result in conflict.

English as cause for division

If language is more than a means of communication, in which words are imbued with 'undertones, shades of meaning and nuances'

(Rosenberg, 2002:41), we might briefly consider the position of English in Northern Ireland. Its use can require caution to avoid giving offence and it is sometimes deliberately used incautiously for that purpose. Northern Ireland's 'second city' is officially called 'Londonderry', favoured by Protestants/unionists;[4] Catholics and nationalists prefer the pre-Plantation name 'Derry', dropping the 'London-' prefix, which carries overtones of conquest. Broadcasting organisations are adept at overcoming the difficulty of pleasing an audience from both communities: in news reports the BBC will refer to 'Londonderry' in the first instance and 'Derry' subsequently. (One radio presenter maintains a long-running joke with his audience by pointedly calling the city 'Derry-Stroke-Londonderry', while even the academic Kevin McCafferty titled his 2001 work *Ethnicity and Language Change: English in (London)Derry*).

Alternative names by which Northern Ireland is known can also be dangerously loaded. 'The Province' is often used to refer to six-county Northern Ireland by unionists and loyalists, but nationalists and, especially, republicans despise the term because, for them, 'Province' means the original nine counties of Ulster and not the post-Partition six. Similarly, 'Ulster' is Protestant/unionist shorthand for Northern Ireland, while the Catholic/nationalist 'Ulster' is again the historic nine counties. Unionist references to 'the mainland' or 'GB' mean 'Britain', but these are descriptions that nationalists are unlikely to use. Not a few politicians have been left red-faced by using the wrong term. Additionally, the Republic's state broadcaster RTÉ rarely refers to Northern Ireland in news programmes, instead calling it 'the North' but outside of news 'Northern Ireland' is used freely.

Despite a strong sense of ethnic distinctiveness between the communities and culturally codified ways, Milroy (1987b:113) does not believe these include systematic linguistic differences and notes that there appears to be no clear difference in language use where the two groups live together, as in working-class east Belfast. Differences which have been observed 'are probably best characterised as regional *differences*, since for example east and west Belfast *Protestants* each perceive the accents of the other group as distinctive'. An east Belfast accent, to a point, is associated with Protestants and a west Belfast accent associated with Catholics[5] but oft-touted 'shibboleths' such as how Protestants and Catholics pronounce the letter 'h' differently lie outside the phonological system and probably result from segregated education (Milroy and Gordon, 2003:113).

Lack of contact between the communities in Belfast has not led to a form of English that is distinguished either phonologically or grammatically along religious lines. McCafferty does suggest that Protestants in mainly Catholic (London)Derry adopt innovative phonological features from Belfast and the predominantly Protestant eastern part of Northern Ireland earlier than Catholics but adds that it is possible Catholics merely lag behind in adopting them (2001:212). Whether or not there exist in Northern Ireland definitively 'Protestant' and 'Catholic' forms of English has been a matter of debate and requires further sociolinguistic investigation, with ethnicity as a key variable. Although worth noting, issues of English in Northern Ireland are an interesting aside: the starting point for this chapter is the indisputable ethno-religious divide between the communities over Irish.

ATTITUDES TO IRISH AFTER PARTITION[6]

Protestant engagement with the Irish language – even if it was already limited to a small number of enthusiasts – turned to mistrust, and the process of withdrawal continued in the years after Partition in 1921, developing into outright hostility on the part of some. This is not to say that all Protestants in Northern Ireland stopped speaking Irish: small numbers who were not nationalists continued to be involved. However, if the notion of a link between Irish and militant republicanism had been implanted into the mainstream unionist mindset by Conradh na Gaeilge's non-language activities, the years of Stormont rule that followed added to the damage. Unionist politicians, ruling without effective nationalist opposition, made no secret of their animosity towards Irish.

Stormont's stance on Irish has been described by a modern-day unionist as one of 'malevolent neglect' (McGimpsey, 1994:9).

Andrews's research into official papers provides some measure of the hostility towards Irish. He focuses on how the administration handled the language issue in relation to education[7] from 1921 to 1943, but the tenor of debate gives us an idea of overall attitudes. The government came under pressure from outside bodies, among them the Orange Order, to downgrade the teaching of Irish in Catholic schools. Such pressure was probably unnecessary given the hostility to the language of many unionist MPs who were themselves in the Order. Even though the government made teaching of Irish extremely difficult, it was still described as wasting public money by a unionist senator who argued that Irish teaching was part of a long-term republican plan to drive the English language and English speakers out of Ireland. Andrews recounts the fierce debate over the place of Irish on the curriculum and, over a period of years, it was reduced to the level of a 'foreign language' (1997:82).

In reality, the government was pushing Irish to the fringes but, wary of any criticism from the Orange Order and organisations such as the 'Loyalty League', trumpeted its success in reducing facilities. Some politicians even wanted to abolish Irish teaching altogether. Andrews concludes that stalemate had been reached in that 'Irish was grudgingly tolerated as a foreign language … but, unlike other languages, was subject to periodic abuse from unionist politicians' (ibid:87).

The cultural rights of an ethnic minority were therefore ignored as a ghost from the past which did not officially exist (Maguire, 1991:27, 41). Then again, bigotry ran both ways. Northern Ireland was for many years a place where even doing something as simple as buying a loaf of bread could have implications unimaginable in a 'normal' society (Craig, 2007:40).

The Stormont debates give a flavour of broader Protestant views on the language (after all, the MPs and senators were representing their electorates, though it could be contended that they, rather than their voters, were setting the agenda) and anti-Irish sentiment continued when the parliament was prorogued in 1972, replaced by Direct Rule. As cross-channel MPs, appointed by Westminster, took on Northern Ireland portfolios at the height of the Troubles, addressing language issues was a low priority when compared to tackling the murderous actions of republican and loyalist paramilitaries.

The Northern Ireland Gaeltachts

At the time of Partition, there were several Gaeltachts[8] in the new Northern Ireland, among them the Sperrins in County Tyrone, the Antrim Glens and Rathlin Island, off the north coast. Another tiny Gaeltacht clung on in south Armagh. There had been other small Gaeltachts and pockets of Gaelic speakers just a few years earlier, but many had already disappeared. Nevertheless, Padraig Ó Baoighill, a County Donegal native speaker, recalls his first visit to the Tyrone Gaeltacht in 1956:

> I called into McCullagh's pub in Greencastle and was advised to go to see Johnny Bán McAleer of Muin na Míol, 'a good Irish speaker', they told me. There he was in the doorway and, when I addressed him in Irish, he welcomed me heartily in the native tongue … Johnny Bán had very little English until he went to school, his mother Bidí Mhór being a native Irish speaker. (2000:684)

Ó Baoighill met up to twenty native speakers in the Tyrone area between 1956 and 1959, proof that Irish, while limited to a handful of elderly people, had somehow survived despite Stormont's policies. One would not have expected, of course, that Irish would be nourished in 'a Protestant state for a Protestant people' which saw Irish as subversive. It should be added, however, that some of the smaller Gaeltachts in the Republic suffered a similar fate, despite state 'support' for Irish, Omeath in County Louth being an example.

Southern overtures

In contrast with Northern Ireland, the new Free State set out an ambitious programme of national Gaelicisation. There was a degree of wishful thinking on the part of a handful of post-Partition Protestants who felt that the language could be a unifying force. The two discussed here, Ernest Blythe (or Earnán de Blaghd) and Risteárd Ó Glaisne, far from being unionists 'stranded' in the new state wholly embraced nationalist Ireland and believed the language could help bridge the gulf between Belfast and Dublin.

MacDonagh (1983:118) describes Ernest Blythe as 'the last of the great Protestant Gaelicisers'. Blythe, from near Lisburn, County Antrim, joined the Gaelic League and the Irish Republican Brotherhood while working in Dublin. Jailed during the 1916 Rising, he rose to prominence in the Free State as minister for finance from 1922 to 1931. Connolly (1999:49) describes Blythe, who published poetry and memoirs in Irish as Earnán de Blaghd, as 'a rare example by the early twentieth century of an Ulster Protestant embracing cultural and political nationalism'. It appears that he had Irish-speaking Presbyterian relatives in the south County Down area and eventually became a fluent speaker. As an important player in Dublin politics, he set about using his offices to further the language (Blaney, 1996:207):

The Irish language was his first love ... Many, especially politicians, find Irish useful for other ends, but for Blythe Irish was an end in itself. One of his monumental achievements, as a cabinet minister, was the foundation of *An Gúm*, the government publishing house for the printing of hundreds of books in Irish.

According to MacDonagh (1983:113), Blythe dominated the Gaelicising movement of the 1920s by virtue of his office, but he adds that the Protestant 'kingship' of Gaelicisation ended with Douglas Hyde (see Chapter One). Where the two differed was that Blythe was an Ulster Presbyterian, not a southern Anglican. Blaney (1996:208) claims that, as a northern Protestant, Blythe 'understood perfectly' the unionist position, maintaining that, if they were to be persuaded to rejoin the rest of Ireland, they should be offered a common Irish identity 'demonstrated principally through the Irish language, a proof that culture and not religion was the distinguishing feature of an Irish person'. This is disputable: his argument was not a compelling one as far as Ulster Protestants were concerned. Most unionists were not looking for a 'common Irish identity'. He might have 'understood' Protestants, but he clearly did not understand the principal tenets of unionism.

In later years, the County Cork Methodist Risteárd Ó Glaisne[9] – a prolific writer whose works included a biography of Ian Paisley in Irish – also looked wistfully northwards in the hope that fellow Protestants might embrace the language he loved. His 1965 pamphlet, *The Irish Language: A Protestant speaks to his co-religionists*, was a plea to Northern Irish Protestants to engage positively with the language, in which he drew heavily on history and the nineteenth-century revival. He hoped that wider use of Irish would lead to a deeper understanding of Ireland and possibly bring about a decisive change of political attitudes in some Protestants. This is a manifestation of the nationalist belief that unionists can be won over to the virtues of their ideology, examined later in this chapter.

Ó Glaisne understood the need to bring Protestants into his 'national' mainstream and founded the magazine *Focus*, an all-Ireland monthly review of arts, literature and current affairs. Articles in Irish featured, but Ó Glaisne, aware of his predominantly Protestant and cross-border audience, took a careful approach, ensuring that *Focus* did not include 'too much Irish' (Ó Glaisne, 2005:268).

One letter-writer, a Church of Ireland minister from Mallow in County Cork, complained about an issue which contained two Irish articles instead of the usual one (ibid). Another incensed correspondent – this time from Belfast – described Irish as 'peacefully-moribund' and not 'fit for revival', adding: 'Your policy regarding the Irish language will hardly commend *Focus* to many Protestants in British, though Irish, Ulster' (ibid:270). He felt that the only reason for a Protestant to learn Gaelic (apart from interest and sentiment) was to 'obtain a better hearing for his faith from nationalist contemporaries' (ibid).

Ó Glaisne denied in *Focus* that the magazine had any official policy on Irish but admitted in his memoirs that, unknown to most of its readers, he deliberately took a stand on its behalf in its pages. *Focus* was a relatively specialist magazine, aimed at Protestants who could weigh arguments carefully rather than react in knee-jerk fashion, so it is interesting that a number of its presumably well-read readership found the inclusion of articles in Irish so unwelcome even in the early 1960s, before overt politicisation by republicans.[10]

The southern belief that greater understanding of the Irish language and their innate Irishness can help persuade Ulster Protestants of the benefits of a united Ireland effectively died with Ó Glaisne in 2003. Few Dublin politicians or language activists would now think of using Irish as a way of extolling the Republic's virtues. More compelling recent arguments have been based on the so-called 'Celtic Tiger' economy, which transformed the country in the 1990s and 2000s. Forging stronger business ties and proclaiming the advantages of an all-Ireland economy became more relevant than notions of harmonisation through language. Mutual financial benefit, not cultural enrichment, was the new cross-border currency, albeit itself subject to the vicissitudes of global economics. Indeed, the financial downturn which began in 2008, hitting Ireland hard, perhaps countered the 'mutual benefit' argument, as shoppers from the Republic flocked across the border to take advantage of a euro–sterling exchange rate strongly in their favour.

THE BELFAST RE-ENGAGEMENT WITH IRISH

Despite Stormont's maltreatment of Irish and the demise of the Northern Ireland Gaeltachts, the language was never extinguished, so even as the 1970s dawned, Belfast *Gaeilgeoirí*[11] were able to tap into the combined resources (linguistic, not financial) of the relatively nearby Donegal Gaeltacht and still-fresh folk memories of 'real' Irish speakers in the city. The proximity of native speakers, traditionally prized as embodying language authenticity and representing the original cultural context, offered added value. These ties with the past contained Fishman's 'link to greatness as well as the substance of greatness itself' (1972:44).

Irish offered a separate ethnic identity which could be a source of pride. The conditions were right for the maintenance and advancement of the language, the primary requisite of which is being able to use it on a regular basis. The creation of the Shaw's Road Gaeltacht in Belfast and the opening of an Irish-medium primary school ensured that this requisite was being met from the 1970s. 'Identity' provided a powerful incentive and the raw materials were already there.

Unionist hostility, however, had not diminished. As Mac Póilin (1999:113) maintains: 'Modern unionist perceptions of the language movement were formed in the first two decades of the twentieth century and have changed little since.' During the 1970s and 1980s, says Goldenberg (2002:25), this was seen, for example, in the refusal of grants for an Irish-language group's classes, accentuating 'the resentment felt by Catholics/nationalists and ensuring that Irish language classes were made a priority in their political agenda'. There were many skirmishes over the language during this period, quite a few relating to the unionist-dominated Belfast City Council's reluctance to fund Irish-language projects.

Republicans, Sinn Féin and Irish

Sinn Féin's experiments with culture as a new dimension to the IRA's armed struggle brought Irish up the political agenda during the 1981 hunger strike in the Maze prison, when republicans attempted to win political – rather than 'standard' criminal – status. The first hunger striker to die, Bobby Sands, was a republican prisoner who spoke Irish. This appears to have had an inspirational effect and the revival blossomed in the years that followed, led by republicans. O'Reilly (1998:54) was told by a Sinn Féin activist informant that Irish-medium schools were 'packed' with republicans' children and that the language movement was being driven by republicans. The revival of Irish was now an important plank in the republican 'struggle'.

Another informant told O'Reilly that being 'involved militarily' was 'the best you could do for your country' but others 'would say that teaching Irish was the best thing you could do' (1998:60). As Sapir

(1957:102) observed, a healthy culture is not just passive acceptance of past heritage, 'but implies the creative participation of the members of the community'. Even among outsiders, there was a perception that during the Troubles young nationalists had a choice: get involved in the IRA or get involved in the language (Nic Leoid, speaking on BBC Scotland, *Eorpa*, 19/11/2002). Such a choice, though, could not be described as Sapir's 'healthy culture'. Little wonder, then, that Sinn Féin's energetic approach to language activities helped to create the impression that Irish was only for republicans.

Even though there was 'only a handful' of serious *Gaeilgeoirí* in the republican movement, the political conflict led to the assumption that the Irish language revival was confined to the Catholic/nationalist minority. O'Reilly continues:

> In Northern Ireland the discourses have developed in the context of a direct political relationship between Irish people in the North, the unionist population and Britain. A segment of the nationalist population in the North believe that learning and speaking Irish underlines their distinct identity in open contrast to British cultural and political hegemony. (1998:160)

The appearance in republican areas of murals in Irish again seemed to throw down a gauntlet to unionists and underpin suspicions about the language. '*Tiocfaidh Ár Lá*' (Our Day Will Come) is ingrained in the unionist mind as a 'Provo slogan', although it is just one of many examples. Nic Leoid (BBC Scotland, *Eorpa*, 19/11/2002) stated that murals like '*I ndíl chuimhne na gcimí Poblachtánacha a fuair bás i ngéibheann i rith na coimhlinte reatha seo*' (In loyal memory of the republican prisoners who died behind bars during this current struggle) 'tie Irish to republican terrorism in Belfast's Catholic areas'. Irish, she declared, was seen by Protestants as the language of the enemy and represented the spread of nationalism.

Probably the most heavily loaded and controversial republican remark about the Irish language came in a 1980s statement on the language, in which the writer described every phrase in Irish as 'a bullet in the freedom struggle ... every phrase you use is a brick in a great building, a rebuilding of the Irish nation' (Sinn Féin, 1984:4).

This, unsurprisingly, has been frequently used by unionists as an argument against Irish, which became the proverbial 'double-edged sword', simultaneously providing a new focus for many in the nationalist/republican community and incensing unionists. Many demands were for civil rights in Irish. To unionists, 'civil rights' were already available through English and did not come into the equation: they viewed the campaign simply as an unwelcome new front in the intensifying battle with republicanism. Of course, culture and language require resources and resources are obtained politically, something the Ulster-Scots[12] movement now well understands in its own drive for parity of esteem.

One west Belfast mural proclaims: '*Cearta Teanga, Cearta Daonna*' ('Language Rights are Human Rights'). Even today, despite huge advances made by the Irish language movement, the 'rights' issue is still high on the agenda, as seen in a 2006/07 court action in which a Belfast *Gaeilgeoir* charged with disorderly behaviour demanded that her case be heard in Irish. Dunbar (2005:8/9) describes the prohibition of Irish in Northern Ireland courts as '*An Péindlí Deireanach*' ('The Final Penal Law'). City *Gaeilgeoirí* have also formed links with other minorities whose demands for civil rights have been built around the core of language, most notably Catalans and Basques, with cultural days often held in west Belfast. It's possibly worth noting that Sinn Féin and Basque separatists had another thing in common: a military wing.

Sometimes the rights agenda was taken to extremes. Fitzduff (2000:76) claims that when nationalists gained control of a particular council for the first time, they decided that phones would be answered in Irish as well as English – until it was pointed out that at the time there were more speakers of Chinese languages than Irish in the area. Another anomaly was the provision of expensive simultaneous translation equipment for conferences. But this was often abandoned after minutes as the concept of pure communication – i.e. talking to each other – took precedence over linguistic assertions of identity (ibid:77).

PROTESTANT RESPONSES AND 'RECLAIMING IRISH'

Despite broadly negative attitudes towards the language, some unionists and loyalists have argued that Irish culture belongs to everyone. It is an argument based on the concept of 'reclaiming' a lost heritage and the legendary Irish warrior Cú Chulainn has been commandeered to service the thesis. We should note that many of those who believe in 'reclamation' look not to relatively recent times when Protestants engaged with the language in 'real life', but to a dim pre-Christian past to provide inspiration and a foundation for the argument. Others, though, are more pragmatic but historic reasons still seem to be the driving force.

The loyalist engagement with Irish

Ó Glaisne (1981:39) cites a 1974 edition of the magazine *Combat*, linked to the Ulster Volunteer Force, in which 'Ulaid' states that Ulster Protestants have as much claim, 'if not more in some cases', to the Gaelic culture as Catholics. The writer argues that 'the Protestant people gave their culture away to the Roman Catholics'[13] and stresses the influence of music, poetry, song, dance, stories and folklore on contemporary Ulster. 'Ulaid' concludes that there is no contradiction in being British 'and at the same time wishing to enjoy and preserve our own distinctive culture'.

This was an early political reinterpretation of the relevance of Irish culture for Northern Ireland Protestants by an extremist organisation but others not aligned to loyalist paramilitaries refined the argument during the 1980s, using Cú Chulainn as a motif for Ulster standing alone against the rest of Ireland. The Ulster Young Unionist Council (UYUC) – youth wing of the mainstream Ulster Unionist Party – embraced the mythological hero (whose statue in Dublin commemorates the 1916 Rising) in a 1986 discussion document which opines that 'neglect of an ancient heritage resulted in republicans being able to steal the legend of Cuchulain from us' (UYUC, 1986:1). The document constructs a 'separate' Ulster identity with strong historical roots and seems to be based on Ian Adamson's 1974 revisionist theory of the Cruthin as Ireland's earliest inhabitants. Adamson speculates that the Cruthin were displaced by the Gaels and migrated to Scotland, before returning to the land of their birthright as Planters in the seventeenth century.

These and similar documents of the mid-1980s deal with cultural 'reclamation' generally, but, in truth, rarely touch on the language issue, although it is possible that they provided a context for some who went on to vigorously argue that Irish belongs to all. Ó Glaisne, while finding encouragement in *Combat* magazine, was perhaps a little too enthusiastic in believing that unionism and loyalism were coming to an accommodation with Irish. In the same 1981 essay he notes the dedication of a Belfast Orange Lodge's new banner by Grand Master the Reverend Martin Smyth, later an influential Ulster Unionist MP. The Gaelic motto '*Oidhreacht Éireann*' ('Ireland's Heritage') appeared on the banner and was 'the first such emblem to have a motto printed in Gaelic'. Unfortunately, the lodge (LOL 1303) suffered because of the paedophile senior member William McGrath, who was involved in the Kincora boys' home sex abuse scandal of the early 1980s. McGrath was also the leader of a shadowy loyalist paramilitary group called Tara but, after Kincora, LOL 1303 sank without trace.

In the 1990s, a group called Ulster Third Way urged Protestants to learn Irish. It advocated an independent Ulster, 'a bold, self-confident civilisation based in large part on its cultural and ethnic Ulster-Scots roots, without ignoring the contribution of Ulster-Gaels' (*Ulster Nation*, 1990). Its founder David Kerr, responding to a row over funding for an Irish-language group, attacked a Belfast Sinn Féin councillor for using Irish as a political weapon to 'wind up those Protestants silly enough to let them' (ibid). Nevertheless, he went on to outline the history of the language, concluding that Protestants should feel comfortable with Irish and accusing republicans of using 'pidgin Gaelic' for political and sectarian reasons:

Don't be afraid to quote gaelic, use gaelic names and speak the language if you wish. Don't allow the Provos and their ilk to hijack the language and transform it into a weapon against all Ulsterfolk.

Don't listen to ignorant unionist politicians who brand it a 'foreign language'. Reclaim this vital part of these islands' common British heritage! (Kerr, D., *Ulster Nation*, 1990)

The reclamation discourse has also recently been espoused by John Coulter, the son of a prominent unionist politician in the Ulster-Scots heartland of Ballymena, who suggests that Protestantism should concentrate on 're-taking' cultural items which have been 'paraded' by republicanism as part of 'Irish nationalism's supposedly unique ethnic identity'. At the same time, he rubbishes those who are 'making fools of themselves' by trying to repackage the Ulster-Scots 'accent' (Coulter, 2004):

… some unionist activists in the Irish-speaking community believe the time is now right to launch a linguistic counter offensive against Irish nationalism's stranglehold on the island's own language.

Coulter, however, does not explain exactly who those 'unionist activists' are.

The loyalist 'Jailtacht'[14]

Some 'mainstream' loyalists engaged positively with the Irish language during the 1970s and 1980s, and in a very unlikely setting. At one stage, Ulster Volunteer Force (UVF) and Red Hand Commando[15] prisoners in Long Kesh prison started learning Gaelic. Gusty Spence, a founder member of the reconstituted UVF in the 1960s, was Commanding Officer of the groups in the jail while serving a life sentence for murder.

It was – and still is – widely believed that Spence became fluent in the language, but he later set the record straight when he admitted to gaining only a smattering. Nonetheless, in a meeting after his release he was able to exchange initial pleasantries in Irish with the leader of Ireland's Catholics, Cardinal Tomás Ó Fiaich, a cleric renowned for his nationalist views. The press was rather excited by the notion of hardened loyalist paramilitaries learning Gaelic and exaggerated the extent of this strange engagement. In 1977 Spence said that five of his men – 'proud loyalists, UVF men' – had attained the Fáinne.[16] He continued: 'I also have sixteen other men studying the Irish language and who hope to attain their proficiency badges in the near future' (Garland, 2001:222).

A footnote to Spence's encounter with the language was the attempt to recreate on the outside a 'downtown office' of the Camp Council, a prison forum where loyalists and republicans cooperated on matters of mutual concern. Spence, while in prison, became an advocate of advanced loyalist thinking (he was an architect of the loyalist ceasefires of the 1990s which gave breathing space to the fledgling peace process). In attempting to stimulate dialogue on the outside, paramilitaries could not be seen talking to each other because of 'hypersensitivities'. States Spence:

There would be a coordinator trusted by all the groups – Elizabeth Kennedy. She happened to be a Protestant who spoke Irish, which she deliberately learned so she could speak to the IRA in their own tongue. Some prisoners made smart-ass remarks to her in Irish, but Elizabeth was no pushover. She made a couple of remarks in Irish that left them smarting. Elizabeth was to be the first coordinator of the downtown office in Belfast but unfortunately she died very soon [after]. (Garland, 2001:222)

Other loyalist Jailtacht 'graduates' have shed light on its development: curiosity seems to have been a factor. William Smith, an inmate in the early 1970s, says the proximity of the segregated compounds meant that loyalists heard republicans speaking to each other in Irish. Smith, from Belfast's Shankill Road, was affected because 'I was listening to a language that I couldn't understand, that I had never heard before; but it was not a foreign language. It was my own native tongue' (1994:17). He built bridges with the 'enemy' while acquiring the recipe for poteen (illicit liquor brewed from whatever is at hand) and asked one of the republicans to teach him Irish. Smith learned Irish, sitting on a chair at his perimeter fence, from a republican in the adjacent compound. He achieved some fluency before the authorities, realising he was serious, allowed an Irish teacher into the loyalist compounds to conduct classes. Smith notes an ironic twist (ibid:18):

> The republican prisoners barred the teacher from their compound because they said he was teaching Fianna Fáil[17] Gaelic. We had the oddest of situations in that we had an Irish language teacher coming into the loyalist compounds but he wasn't allowed into the republicans. And of course, I had a problem because I was learning from both a learned republican prisoner, and the Irish language teacher, and one would say that that was wrong, and the other would say that this was wrong.

Smith left prison with a positive view of language and Irish culture, even lobbying the GAA to consider promoting its sports within the Protestant community. He envisaged an Ulster Culture Centre in the Shankill area, where Protestants could learn the language, Irish dancing or music without having 'to sneak away'. In 1994 he described Irish as belonging to 'all people of this country, Protestant, Catholic, Dissenter, loyalist, republican' and confidently predicted a new era when the language would find a Protestant community wanting to learn the culture, wanting to be educated in their history. His vision has yet to be realised.

McCoy (1997a:114) notes that those with proven loyalist 'credentials' had acquired 'symbolic capital' in working-class Protestant communities and could learn Irish without fear of censure: 'Loyalist prisoners and ex-prisoners could publicise their interest in Irish without fear of being vilified for betraying the unionist cause.' Protestant learners with less symbolic capital could expect to become the object of suspicion and possible community punishment. He offers the example of a unionist who found it politic to display a portrait of the Queen in his parlour to restore his symbolic capital after his cleaner had noted his collection of 'strange' Gaelic books.

'Fluent unionists' and urban myths

Occasionally, prominent unionist and loyalist figures are hailed as fluent speakers and exemplars of an inclusive approach to Irish. Gusty Spence is a perfect example of the perceived fluent speaker whose linguistic ability has been over-reported. As noted, he learned 'only a smattering'. When I started learning Irish as a Protestant I was often told by other students – all Catholic – that I 'should go and speak to Gusty Spence: he's really fluent'. Similarly, John Robb, a retired surgeon, was often hailed as a 'fluent unionist'. Dr Robb is indeed fluent and Protestant, but his political views as a 'New Irelander' would win over few unionists. The Catholic desire to over-report the fluency of senior unionist/loyalist figures probably centres on the notion that they – if they actually existed – could lend credibility to the argument that Irish belongs to all. The same goes for efforts to over-report the unionism/loyalism of those who are genuinely fluent.

Ian Adamson (mentioned earlier), proponent of the Cruthin theory, is regarded as a multi-linguist of note: he is said to have ten languages, including Sioux and Swahili. While he has some Irish expressions at his command, his facility is largely untested and unquestioned in the public arena. As with most urban myths, however, there is usually some factor that leads to the impression of unionist/loyalist fluency. Another example is former Belfast Ulster Unionist councillor Chris McGimpsey. Often cited as fluent, his grasp of the language is, he admits, 'rudimentary' but he has eloquently made the case for wider Protestant participation in the language.

Catholic speakers often seem to think that the mention of the odd unionist or loyalist politician's name might help make a stronger case, probably with the aim of reassuring Protestants and trying to make them feel more at home in what can be a strange environment for someone who is new to the language. In reality there is no 'big name' to help sell Irish to unionists and even those that are mentioned might not have the level of proficiency that is suggested. Irish can be a 'hard sell' and it is little surprise that Catholic/nationalist speakers do try to use the names of those they think that potential Protestant/unionist speakers can identify with.

THE CONSEQUENCES OF NEGATIVITY

Negative views towards Irish among Protestants occasionally surface in violent ways. In 2005, for example, the house of a young Protestant woman living in a loyalist east Belfast estate was petrol-bombed. She believed this was because her first name was Róisín, a 'Catholic/Irish name' (BBC, 2005a).

A less violent example of hostility towards Irish was seen in 2004 on BBC Northern Ireland's prestigious *Talkback* radio show. For a week, politicians from the main parties were guest presenters and the SDLP's Bríd Rodgers (who had been Agriculture Minister in the Stormont Assembly) opened her programme with the Irish greeting '*Go mbeannaí Dia daoibh*', which simply means 'May God bless you'. These four words sparked a flood of complaints. One caller hoped it was 'the first and the last time that *Talkback* would be introduced in that way'; another described 'Irish gobbledygook as deeply offensive to Northern Ireland Protestants' and several suggested that Mrs Rodgers go 'down South' where she could use 'that language' as much as she wanted (BBC Radio Ulster, *Talkback*, 7/9/2004).

Rodgers, a native Irish speaker from County Donegal and a leading nationalist politician in Northern Ireland for decades, was taken aback by the reaction. While explaining that the BBC has a bilingual policy, she nevertheless apologised on several occasions for having offended some people but could not understand how she had provoked such hostility:

It does annoy me that people think that speaking Irish is something offensive to them. Sure, most of our place names in Northern Ireland are Irish. It's part of all our heritage; it's not just mine. I think it's a pity people see it in that light but ... I'm sorry if I've offended anyone, but I certainly don't think it should be an offence to use my own language. (ibid)

While many callers were highly critical, several who claimed to be Protestants or unionists praised Rodgers for using Irish and said they had not been offended. 'Thomas' from North Belfast was one, but he added that Rodgers should have known that speaking in Irish 'would have caused a bit of a stir'. Many Protestants do feel offended by Irish and it is argued that some manifestations of the language are designed to cause as much offence as possible to unionists. An informant told McCoy (1997b:161) that every time Sinn Féin leader Gerry Adams opened his mouth 'he puts a nail in the coffin of the language for Prods'. It is clear that Rodgers did not use Irish to offend and in spite of her fluency used it only rarely during her Assembly term.

The impact of politicisation

Politicisation of the language and the link between Sinn Féin and Irish helps explain why most unionists are perceived to have little interest in what they view as a cultural weapon or even 'a stick to beat Protestants with'. Despite republican protestations to the contrary, the language question had undeniably become a non-violent component in the broader anti-British 'struggle' as far as unionists were concerned. This made Irish even more unpalatable to the majority in that community.

Even though some Protestants engage with Irish on their own terms, the perception that it belongs only to Catholics is long-standing. Many Protestants allege that Irish was hijacked by republicans; a few think that it was 'surrendered'. (The tenor of the Stormont debates suggests that there was never any unionist empathy for Irish, although Andrews (1997:87) does point to evidence that, in the years immediately after partition, some 'influential unionists' had accepted that it 'deserved a special place in the education system'.) In truth, most do not care how it happened and care even less for the language itself. Hume (1990:19) confirms this lack of attachment to Irish among his fellow unionists when he says Protestants regard Irish as irrelevant and alien. What has happened, effectively, is that the inability of most Protestants to speak Irish and their lack of desire to know it has established an 'us versus them', 'Irish versus British' dichotomy (O'Reilly, 1998:98).

DUP politician Sammy Wilson's notorious dismissal of Irish as a 'leprechaun language' in the 1980s/90s has been quoted *ad nauseam* since as a one-line putdown. In a later television interview, however, he placed the remark in a fuller context:

I'm not interested in speaking the Irish language. I'm British. If people want to speak in the language of leprechauns, that's up to themselves. I don't want to make Irish language more popular. I don't see what use it is in improving communication between people in Northern Ireland. (BBC Scotland, *Eorpa*, 19/11/2002)

When asked by the presenter if the strength of the language was causing tension between the two communities in Northern Ireland, he continued:

I have absolutely no doubt that's what it is designed to do. Maybe some individuals genuinely wish to speak Irish: I have no difficulty with that. My difficulty comes when it is used as a battering-ram.

Wilson's remarks appear to be part of a DUP anti-Irish agenda that labelled the language as a cultural weapon. In an article in the *Lurgan Mail*, Northern Ireland Assembly Member Stephen Moutray (2004a:6) roundly condemned Irish, but placed Ulster-Scots in the same category – a 'hobby' language. Intriguingly, Moutray returned to the same newspaper the following week (2004b:6) with a robust defence of Ulster-Scots as a language which had 'confounded its critics and defied the cultural imperialism of the Gaelic lobby to take its place as an integral part of the community'. Mr Moutray, having 'seen the light', believed Ulster-Scots was a language which had shown itself 'able to meet every demand and overcome every obstacle'.[18]

The DUP's de facto status as a stanchion against all things Irish did take an interesting twist when one of its councillors – Ruth Patterson – welcomed participants to the World [Irish] Dancing Championships in Belfast with a greeting in Irish in 2004. Patterson was happy to admit that, in her youth, she had learned a few Irish dancing steps. She would have been, she said, happy to extend the same welcome in any language and, indeed, did so again *as Gaeilge* several years later at a 2006 Irish-language event in Belfast City Hall.

From a republican viewpoint, however, Wilson's 'leprechaun language' jibe was a gift which seemed to sum up unionist intolerance and cultural paucity. Many years after Wilson first made the statement during a debate in Belfast City Council, former Sinn Féin councillor Máirtín Ó Múilleoir admitted in a 2006 radio interview that his party used the comment 'as a club to beat the unionists with after that' (BBC Northern Ireland, *Good Morning Ulster*, 1/8/2006). Both remarks offer a concise and depressing commentary on how contentious Irish had become. For some republicans, Irish was a method of getting at unionists. And unionists, for their part, obliged by taking the bait.

The result has been language-based prejudice, not based on how a particular language is used or spoken, but on *what* language is used. Of course, it is wrong to assume that everyone who shows interest in Irish is equally interested in republican politics. Many Catholic Irish speakers do not identify with republicanism in any way, but this distinction is generally lost on unionist politicians.

MEASURING UNIONIST/PROTESTANT ATTITUDES

Some qualitative and quantitative data is available to help examine contemporary unionist/Protestant attitudes towards Irish. A survey in the mid-1990s, commissioned by a (London)Derry Irish-language group to discover why unionists repeatedly turned down invitations to its events, showed the depth of hostility towards Irish among Protestants (Kerr, E.:1994). The conclusions (summarised) were:

- Negative attitudes ranged from 'total abhorrence to personal dislike, mixed with an overt mistrust of [Irish] users'. The language was described as a facet of political insurrection but overall there appeared to be a total ignorance of, and to a lesser degree, a lack of interest in anything 'Irish'.

- Some respondents felt there was a close correlation between use of Irish and militant republicanism.

- The recent growth of the use of the language mirrored the growth in republicanism – particularly stressed was the emergence of Sinn Féin as a political party.

- A common response was the general dislike, and mistrust, of anything Irish, whether it was language, music, dance, sport, drama or the like. Respondents felt it was 'foreign'.

- There was little understanding of previous Protestant/unionist involvement in the Irish language and cultural movement.

- Many respondents displayed a blockage towards all things 'Irish', perhaps suggesting an innate dislike of all that is not 'British'.

The researcher stated:

> The use of the Irish language is seen [as] a flagrant recognition of being 'disloyal'. In other words, to speak Irish is to make a public and bold statement by an individual that they are not British. The dislike of all things Irish could be described as the kernel of the problem. The language has, in the eyes of the respondents, all the negative connotations attached to militant republicanism.

The study made sobering reading,[19] underlining negative Protestant perceptions. The researcher believed that the implication of embracing Irish as a unionist/Protestant was a perceived lessening of one's Britishness. The responses were predominantly negative, even among those who did not express outright hostility to the language. Most felt that it would be impossible to 'sell' Irish to unionists/ loyalists or to introduce it into Protestant schools. Only one respondent's views could be described as vaguely positive. The report was never published.

Other data

Research by the Northern Ireland Life and Times Survey (ARK, 1999) asked several language/education-related questions. Results showed an expected schism. Only 1 per cent of Catholics claimed that Irish was the main language in the home (Protestants registered 0 per cent). Asked if they themselves could speak Irish, 3 per cent of Protestants replied yes, but 20 per cent said they knew someone who was an Irish speaker. The corresponding figures for Catholics were much higher: 29 per cent claimed to be able to speak Irish and 56 per cent knew an Irish speaker. Of Protestants, 80 per cent opposed the introduction of bilingual road signs, but 67 per cent of Catholics were in favour.

Of Catholics, 61 per cent agreed or strongly agreed that *all* secondary level pupils should have to study Irish language and culture, compared to only 13 per cent of Protestants. At the disagree/strongly disagree end of the scale were 26 per cent of Catholics and 71 per cent of Protestants. Overall, Catholics were significantly more sympathetic to Irish than Protestants, a not unexpected finding.

The issue of signage – this time in relation to the provision of Irish-language signs in public places and buildings – also featured in data used by Dunn, Morgan and Dawson (2001) in a report on the demand for services in the language in Northern Ireland. Of those who believed that signage in Irish should never be provided in any circumstances, 87 per cent were Protestants, 7 per cent were Catholics and 6 per cent neither. Of those who believed it should always be provided as a matter of right and equality, 18 per cent were Protestants, 76 per cent were Catholics and 7 per cent neither.

A question on attitudes towards government advertising in Irish showed equally divided views. Of those who believed it should never be provided, 85 per cent were Protestants, 7 per cent were Catholics and 8 per cent neither. Of those who believed it should always be provided, 19 per cent were Protestants, 68 per cent were Catholics and 13 per cent neither.

The qualitative element of this research involved interviews and focus groups with a wide range of interests, including officials, civil servants, members of quangos, voluntary organisations and individuals.

The researchers note that most of those 'opposed in one way or another to the language came from the Protestant/unionist tradition'. Some participants saw Irish as 'dead' and unsophisticated, while others looked upon it as a political matter, the language being used as a pawn (ibid:41):

> Many were afraid that, if they lowered their guard, Irish would be forced upon them, and through the schools upon their children, and they were very opposed to and frightened of this. [...] A considerable proportion of those opposed to Irish in the schools were completely and uncompromisingly opposed: for them English was the natural and *de facto* language of the people, and they wondered how anyone would wish to be taught through any other language.

In a more general piece of research, Co-operation Ireland asked how respondents felt about certain 'cultural/historical' topics, among them the Irish language. Table 1 (below) is quite revealing, not because it shows that 87 per cent of Protestants were not interested in knowing more about Irish (high Protestant percentages on this and related matters are probably to be expected by now) but because it seems to suggest that 42 per cent of Catholics shared that view. Figures for the Republic of Ireland are an interesting addition to the equation but are not broken down by religion.

Table 1		Very interested	Interested	Not interested	Don't know
The Irish	NI (All)	9	21	67	3
Language	NI Protestant	3	7	87	3
	NI Catholic	18	37	42	3
	Republic of Ireland	15	34	52	0

Source: Research and Evaluation Services, 2001. Public Attitudes to North/South Relations. Unpublished research for Co-operation Ireland

Intriguingly, another question in the Co-operation Ireland survey revealed that 71 per cent of Protestants were not interested in learning about Ulster-Scots either.

Qualitative research on behalf of the language promotion body Foras na Gaeilge examined strategies for the promotion of the Irish language on an all-Ireland basis, but produced some interesting findings in relation to Northern Ireland. Focus groups conducted by MORI for Foras showed that no respondent 'could name someone from Northern Ireland associated with the language that was not a politician'. As one participant told the researchers (2006:27):

> ... there's no celebrity in entertainment or sport ... the most famous speaker is Gerry Adams.

The study showed that the language remains a political symbol, but young people in particular wanted its promotion to be 'apolitical and *now*' (ibid). It noted that they had a desire to learn the language 'without the historical and political baggage that previously discouraged them from learning' (ibid).

The 2001 census

This is how 'Knowledge of Irish' is defined in the 2001 census: 'A person has knowledge of Irish if they can do one or more of the following: Understand spoken Irish, Speak Irish, Read Irish, Write Irish' (NISRA,[20] 2005b). However, NISRA recognised the problem of ascertaining religious affiliation in Northern Ireland and introduced a new variable, Community Background, based on religion and religion brought up in, for the 2001 census. It noted that since 1971 a sizeable proportion of the population had declined to answer the stock Religion question. In addition, the 1991 census included a 'None' category and together with the 'Not Stated' responses these accounted for 11 per cent of the population.

McAllister (2005:7) has explored the phenomenon of increasing secularisation and believes that if current trends continue 'secularists will represent the second or third largest group in Northern Ireland society by the time of the next Census'. The Community Background variable has the disadvantage of lumping together 'Protestant and Other Christian (including Christian related)' into one category, but does broadly label more respondents than the Religion variable. On the other hand, Religion allows us to be more specific, as it includes named categories for the main Protestant Churches: Presbyterian, Church of Ireland and Methodist.

Figures for knowledge of Irish by all Protestant subgroups would be useful but the request for an appropriate tabulation was refused 'for reasons of confidentiality and disclosure control'.

Analysis by community background

The 2001 census records that, based on a table population of 1,617,957 (all persons aged three and over), 167,490 (10 per cent) have some knowledge of Irish. Table CAS375, Knowledge of Irish by Community Background, shows that Protestant and Other Christian (including Christian related) represent 6.5 per cent, or 10,987. This figure can be further broken down, as per Table S375 (persons aged three and over). Gender analysis reveals that 6,136 Protestant and Other Christian (including Christian related) females have knowledge of Irish, compared with 4,851 males. Analysis of age group by knowledge of Irish is shown in Figure 1.[21]

The 'clumping together' of those with knowledge of Irish in the age brackets 25–39 and 40–59 might indicate that many Protestants 'discover' the language later in life. Given that Irish is not studied in most Protestant schools, the adult learning phenomenon explored by McCoy (see later in this chapter) could account for this 'bulge'. Similarly, the fact that more in the 3–11 age group 'know' Irish than in the 12–15 age group might be a demographic blip but could be related to the growth in integrated education – or even the fact that these persons are the children of those in the 25–39 and 40–59 'bulge'.

Analysis by religion

Community Background does not allow comparisons with the 1991

Figure 1: Protestant Knowledge of Irish by Age Group (Community Background)

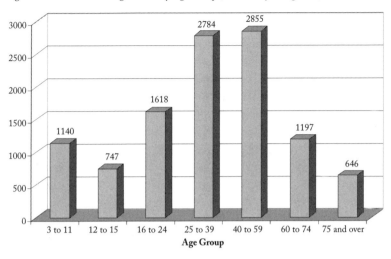

census. The Religion variable does. Summarising the 1991 census, 142,003 people in Northern Ireland, some 9.45 per cent of the total population, claimed some knowledge of Irish. Catholics made up 89.17 per cent of those – 126,626 – while 9,831 either stated they had no religious affiliation or did not state any religious affiliation. Of those from identifiable Protestant denominations, 5,546 claimed knowledge of the language.

In Figure 2 the categories 'Catholic', 'Other Religions' and 'Not Stated'[22] are omitted. We can make concrete conclusions about the three main Protestant denominations but must remember that the Other (Protestant) category is open to a modicum of ambiguity.

As Figure 2 shows, the number of Protestants with knowledge of Irish has grown significantly (at a 'micro' level) between 1991 and 2001: Presbyterian by 124 per cent, Church of Ireland by 56 per cent and Methodist by 114 per cent. The 'Other (Protestant)' category has shown a slight fall, more than compensated for by the increase seen in the other groups.

Further investigation of the Religion and Knowledge of Irish cross-tabulation (S375A) reinforces the theory that Protestants

Figure 2: Protestant Knowledge of Irish, 1991-v-2001 (Religion)

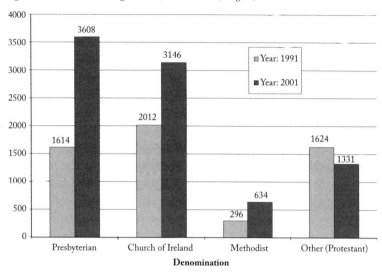

appear to learn Irish later in life. Figure 3 (based on NISRA's table S375A) examines Age by Religion and we note that the 'bulge' mirrors that seen in the Community Background variable. There is consistency in the four 'Protestant' curves. The corresponding curve for Catholic Knowledge of Irish by Age (not shown because of the scale differential) reveals a very steep incline through categories 3 to 11, 12 to 15 and 16 to 24, almost certainly reflecting the growth of the Irish-medium education movement.

The 2001 census is the most recent full dataset on the strength of Irish in Northern Ireland and provides other interesting data. For the purposes of this study, the relatively small number of Protestants with knowledge of Irish means that further analyses will produce output of marginal statistical relevance, but the 'headline' figures show that Protestant interest in Irish is growing, albeit at a 'micro' level.

Summarising data from both the census and the Life and Times survey, DCAL (2007:7) came to the rather obvious conclusion that 'those speaking and possessing some knowledge of Irish are more likely to be Roman Catholic, nationalist and young'.

Figure 3: Protestant Knowledge of Irish by Age, 2001 (Religion)

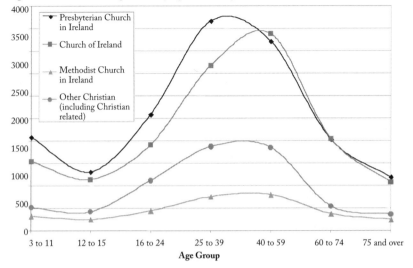

THE PRICE OF FEAR

'Turning' Protestants

The verb 'to turn' is often used in Northern Ireland to imply disloyalty and treachery. When used in the context that 'X has "turned"', it can mean that 'X' has either given up his/her Protestantism to become a Catholic, or vice versa, perhaps because he/she is going to marry 'one of the other sort'. Such use of the verb is never positive and it is also employed in this 'loaded' way with regard to Irish.

An often-expressed unionist fear about Irish is that it might be used as a tool to 'turn' northern Protestants into nationalists (McGimpsey, 1994:9). Some Catholics felt that 'cultured nationalism' could make Protestants see the error of their ways. In Northern Ireland today there does seem to be a Protestant search for an identity, perhaps evolving through the Ulster-Scots issue. Nevertheless, Irish-speaking Catholic motivations for attracting Protestants to the language do include a belief that unionists can be converted to their cause, assuming that the 'Irish speaker' label will become 'a master identity which subsumes all others' (McCoy, 2006:167).

Some Protestant learners are defiantly nationalist in outlook and one of McCoy's informants believed the language 'encourages you to think in a more sort of Irish way'; another reckoned that Irish was 'the thin edge of the wedge' in persuading unionists to make the transition, believing that people who learn Irish have a leaning towards nationalism (ibid). O'Reilly uses discourse analysis in her important study of the language in Northern Ireland and encounters an Irish-speaking Protestant from a working-class background who has turned his back on loyalist culture (1998:96/97). 'Iain' praises Sinn Féin, berates the Royal Ulster Constabulary (forerunner to the Police Service of Northern Ireland) and, says O'Reilly, clearly identifies himself as a Protestant who has rejected 'unionist' culture in favour of 'Irish' culture. He says:

I made the choice to go forward through the Irish culture and the Irish identity. It's a big step to take, because I can never live in east Belfast again. I've made my bed and have to live in it. […] to me it's not just learning Irish, it's becoming part of the culture.

This is a real-life manifestation of unionists' fear that Irish can 'turn' speakers into republicans or nationalists. McCoy (2006:168), however, says there is no evidence to support the theory, while another of O'Reilly's informants – 'Proinsias' – states that those in Sinn Féin who think that learning Irish will make them better republicans are as wrong as those who think that learning Irish will 'make you less of a unionist' (O'Reilly, 1998:91). Of course, statistically, there will always be small numbers of Protestants with nationalist views and Catholics with unionist views.

Everything is entangled with the constitutional position of Northern Ireland as part of the United Kingdom and to identify with Irish as a unionist, therefore, is to be 'subversive' – unionists themselves are 'profoundly aware' of this fact, and it in turn is a barrier to greater unionist involvement, even though its existence is denied by most language activists (Mac Póilin, 2000:92). Mac Póilin excoriates the hypocrisy of those who 'talk of inclusiveness while maintaining the conditions where inclusiveness is impossible' (ibid).

Losing out on culture

This fear of 'turning', though, extends beyond the realm of language and even Protestant writers can be perceived as group deviants because of hostility to artistic expression, according to Longley (1992:15), who contends that literature – because of its historic role in 'nationalistic eloquence about its political demands' – has become 'assimilated into nationalism' by default. This 'logic' was taken to an appalling extreme when the Protestant playwright Gary Mitchell was expelled from his home in 2005 by loyalist paramilitaries who may have interpreted his examination of the Protestant psyche as a sell-out. For the paramilitaries in his working-class community, culture was something only for 'Taigs and faggots' – a bizarre interpretation of artistic expression (Chrisafis, 2005).

However, there appear to be similarities between the case of the Protestant Irish speaker and his/her fellows in the literary world, nationalists extending a double-edged 'welcome' (Longley, 1992:14):

Sometimes Protestant writers are cited rather in the welcoming, yet patronising, spirit of nationalist rhetoric listing the Protestant patriots who saw the light.

Longley argues (1995:27) that those Protestants who do feel 'shut out' by emphasis on Irish need to look at the totality of language and realise that they could learn more about themselves through the English language in Northern Ireland. Culture and diversity, of course, can be positive forces in the community but, partly because of the educational system, most young Protestants remain largely unaware of Irish literature and history, never mind the language. Consequently, Irish is not a factor in enriching their sense of cultural identity. It is certainly not part of the working-class loyalist cultural mix that includes flute bands, bonfires and the seemingly ubiquitous Glasgow Rangers FC shirt.

But the promotion of better understanding through a thorough grounding in the composite heritage that everyone in Northern Ireland is a part of (if not party to) so far remains hostage to political circumstances. Pritchard (2004:21) believes that the education system has led to an 'integrationist consciousness' – of Northern Ireland with Great Britain – which means that 'the identity of unionists ... has been constructed somewhat narrowly in a way that alienates them from their roots and their historical heritage'. She says:

> Protestant schoolchildren in the past learned little about Irish language and folklore, and this contributed to a narrow basis for the construction of their identity, thereby making them vulnerable to feelings of anomie and a 'frontier mentality'. Having become alienated from Irish 'cultural capital', they cling all the more passionately to what they can call 'theirs'. (ibid)

Thomson (2000:50) perhaps takes an over-pessimistic view when he asserts that it cannot be assumed that 'a little education will make it all right':

> ... most educated Protestants are not interested in Gaelic culture and Gaelic language. In fact their culture is largely western and modern; they are part of a much bigger culture than either Ulster Protestantism or Gaelic Irish culture ... What matters is that the Irish language is perceived to belong to one side of a divided community.

But he might have a point. In working-class areas in particular, mistrust is common on both sides and young people are often afraid to travel outside their localities or associate with people of other religions. After visiting some of Northern Ireland's 'hardest' estates, international delegates at a 2000 conference felt that 'tribalism and territorialism seemed to be not only embraced but indulged and celebrated' (Smyth and Goldie, 2001:11). Important cross-community work appeared to be 'sporadic' and one delegate made the telling remark that there are 'very few neutral places where [local residents] feel safe'. Surprise was expressed that religion is used so widely as an identifier, although generally people maintained that they were not very religious.

My own research provides little evidence of meaningful informal cross-community contact among the pupils surveyed, and most contact seems to have been initiated through formal programmes. Others also note that many such contacts come about as a result of inter-school projects. Devine and Schubotz (2004:4) conclude that 16-year-olds in Northern Ireland see both religious and national identity as important and although many respondents 'do not say that they are favourable about the other religious community, very few feel overtly negative'. The importance of respondents' families in informing their children's views was noted.

There is, therefore, a lack of engagement with Irish and other parts of 'Irish culture', but the opportunities even to engage with the 'other side' are limited. Building trust between young people is obviously important in a segregated society. Ewart, Schubotz et al. (2004) explored teenagers' views of sectarianism in Northern Ireland. The research remit included religious and national identities, attitude formation, sport and politics. Territorial identifiers, such as flags, murals and kerb-painting, were seen as intimidating by most.

On this point, the visibility of loyalist paramilitaries in Protestant areas has declined. In communities where symbolism is important, steps are being taken to remove paramilitary flags. Warmongering murals of gunmen in balaclavas and eulogies to their 'glorious dead' are being replaced with images that reflect the heritage of the areas. Footballers – including George Best – and paintings of the iconic Belfast-built *Titanic* have taken over as the 'language of the wall' in many areas.

In July 2006, the Northern Ireland Office promised £3.3m to expedite this transition through the 'Re-Imaging Communities Programme', which would give people the opportunity to reclaim public spaces. Even some linked to loyalist paramilitaries saw this as positive. Removing paramilitary murals could ease tensions, particularly in interface areas, and create an atmosphere where the shadow of the gunman is not so all-pervasive.

The research of Ewart, Schubotz et al. (2004:9) allowed young people to come up with their own ideas to improve community relations. Overall, it presented a positive picture but interestingly, from a language standpoint, the Ulster-Scots heritage was an item some Catholics liked about the 'other' culture, whereas none of the Protestant participants mentioned this as part of their heritage at all. Asked what they 'liked', 'found acceptable' or 'disliked' about the 'other' culture, none of those identifying themselves as Protestants mentioned Irish, suggesting that minority languages are not on their radar.

PROTESTANT LEARNERS OF IRISH

Gordon McCoy has carried out important research into 'ordinary' Protestants who do learn Irish. They include a small constituency who favour Irish unity and others who want to learn for cultural reasons, rejecting nationalism but drawing on elements of Britishness and Irishness. McCoy says some middle-class unionists who promote Irish do so in the belief that if working-class learners learn it they will adopt middle-class liberal views, a perceived benefit in their eyes.

McCoy draws a distinction between *Protestant* learners of Irish with nationalist views and *unionist* learners (this distinction has rarely been made), but again rejects the notion that unionists can be converted to nationalism through Irish – most of the nationalist learners he encountered in his research had 'rejected unionism *before* they learned Irish' (1997b:134). Unionist learners felt that they could draw upon both elements of Britishness and Irishness, the language allowing them 'to express an Irish identity which they feel is harmonious with their allegiance to Britain' (ibid:137).

Some do seem to rationalise their interest in Irish by using historical evidence. McCoy found that unionist learners had difficulty with extra-mural aspects of the Irish-language scene, such as republican songs and discussions about the GAA (Gaelic Athletic Associaton, responsible for 'indigenous' Irish sports such as Gaelic football and hurling); others dislike the frequent assumption that they must be Catholic because they learn Irish. These factors appeared to make unionist speakers feel marginalised when attending classes, even in comparatively neutral areas. Avoidance of contentious issues, primarily politics, was a useful strategy for some Protestants. At the time of McCoy's research Protestants were afraid to venture into nationalist areas to learn Irish for a variety of reasons.

An organisation that has helped Northern Ireland Protestants become acquainted with Irish is, ironically, located in the Republic. A primary aim of Oideas Gael in County Donegal is to bring together people of all cultural, religious and political backgrounds through the medium of the Irish language. It seems to have provided a neutral environment, transformed the nature of the traditional summer Gaeltacht Irish-language colleges and provided a cultural oasis for Protestant learners. The weakness in this strategy, however, is that the Oideas Gael experience is essentially a 'holiday' phenomenon, involving a week of intensive learning; once that is over, learners return home with few opportunities to use the language socially.

McCoy also discovered that social class was a significant factor: middle-class learners could afford to be more open about learning Irish in their own community than working-class counterparts who often took risks in doing so. His study included middle-class mini-groups in affluent north Down and working-class learners in the Protestant Glencairn estate in west Belfast. Middle-class learners, he concludes, are relatively insulated from sectarian strife, and have the advantage of greater mobility. Additionally, it can be harder for working-class learners to disassociate Irish from Catholic/nationalist speakers and the language (1997b:166):

Like other members of their class, working-class learners often perceive these Irish speakers to be their adversaries; therefore they experience feelings of ambivalence arising from their desire to learn the 'enemy's' language.

DEPOLITICISATION[23] – WHOSE INITIATIVE?

Hume (1990:19/20) sums up the views of many Protestants when he says that politicisation of the language had meant an inevitable aversion to it because it is seen as a 'weapon': Protestants could not find any value in Irish until it was divorced from all political connotations and 'made inoffensive to them'. Protestants, he felt, were not overly concerned about the future of the language but might become 'interested spectators on the sidelines' if it were no longer seen as a 'weighted dice' they associated with 'subversion'.

McGimpsey, meanwhile, draws on the nineteenth-century Protestant-led revival to argue for greater unionist involvement today. The onus, he believes, is on nationalists to depoliticise the language: altering unionist perceptions could lead to a popular demand for the chance to learn it, but making it compulsory in Protestant schools would be counterproductive. The context in which the language appears – on street signs in republican areas, for example – leaves unionists feeling threatened. He claims (1994:15–16):

> A neutral stance from the language in all but linguistic and cultural issues is essential to increase its credibility … But I fear that there is not the will amongst a large number of the Irish movement within Northern Ireland to help. Many unionists have watched from a distance the efforts of Irish language activists to resurrect the language. […] there is a willingness to look at the language issue anew. Whether we are permitted so to do rests with those already in the field.

While unionist politicians demand that Irish be depoliticised as a precursor to greater involvement in the language, there is a belief that Protestants, despite their past contribution to the language's fortunes, cannot realistically be expected to come to terms with Irish now unless it exists in a non-threatening environment. Irish's association with 'the freedom struggle', even if that 'struggle' is no longer a military one, remains a significant deterrent.

However, unionists hoping for a swift separation of Irish and politics may be over-optimistic, for the past thirty or more years have strengthened links between the two. It cannot even be taken as read that all Irish speakers are willing to 'share' the language with their unionist neighbours. For many republicans, to use Irish is to make a statement about their national and cultural identity.

In 1997, the then President of the Gaelic League, Belfast man Gearóid Ó Caireálláin, described attempts to make Irish attractive to the Protestant community in Northern Ireland as a 'disease' that was 'contagious' and 'widespread' ('Irish for Protestants seen as a "disease"', *Irish Times*, 10/12/1997). Ó Caireálláin also 'disparaged the Protestant contribution to the language in the North' and said special educational measures to promote Irish among Protestants were unnecessary and 'boring'. Following criticism and calls for his resignation as League President, Ó Caireálláin said that his 'tongue-in-cheek' comments had been taken out of context and that 'the way to make the Irish language appeal to Protestants is to make the Irish language more appealing full-stop' ('Resign as Gaelic League president says SDLP', *Irish News*, 11/12/1997).

In a Scots Gaelic television programme on the language revival in Belfast several years later, Ó Caireálláin stated that by speaking and using Irish, people 'are celebrating their nationalism, their Irishness and the Gaelic heritage' (BBC Scotland, *Eorpa*, 19/11/2002). In this interview, he was probably not addressing an external unionist audience; nevertheless, celebrations of 'nationalism' and 'Irishness' are not key selling points for most Protestants interested in the language and may deter those who might like to find out more.

O'Reilly sees dangers for nationalists and republicans in 'depoliticising' the language as this would 'have consequences for the way Irish identity is imagined in relation to it, and for the use of Irish as a political tool' (1998:177). Perhaps, she adds, everything which contributed to the association of Irish with a Catholic/nationalist cultural package will continue to have consequences for Protestants interested in a language that has moved from the eccentric margins to become an important symbol of Irish identity. This means that nationalists will be reluctant to surrender what they have achieved culturally and 'neuter' Irish to satisfy unionist demands. If culture is a process of inclusion and exclusion, it is Catholics, for so long given second-class status by unionist politicians in the old Stormont government, who now exercise power and control regarding Irish.

Other people from nationalist/republican backgrounds are more understanding. Even a former republican prisoner interviewed by O'Reilly (1998:82) felt that Irish was for everyone, Catholic or Protestant, and had to be separated from politics. And Bríd Rodgers, when taken to task by a caller on a radio programme (mentioned earlier) who said that the only Irish Protestants usually hear is '*Tiocfaidh Ár Lá*' and that many Irish speakers use the language to proclaim 'I am a Catholic/nationalist and I speak Gaelic', replied:

> I agree entirely. It should never have been made into a political weapon. I regret the fact that it has been made into a political weapon because it's a beautiful thing, it's a lovely language. It can give us a lot – all of us – a lot. (BBC Northern Ireland, *Talkback*, 7/9/2004)

Many Irish speakers and scholars also see the need for a fresh approach. Ó Buachalla, for example, says it is incumbent on those who profess to promote Irish 'to ensure that it be presented at all times in an apolitical and secular context' by jettisoning old and untenable arguments (1994:43). The Cultural Traditions Group (CTG, 1995:24) saw the necessity to take Irish out of politics in the early 1990s because of the association with republicanism and even suggested that it might be offered in Protestant schools on a voluntary basis (an important theme later in this book).

Pritchard (2004:25) believes that unionists themselves *might* be able to depoliticise Irish by laying claim to it and possibly transforming it into 'a benign element'. She warns, however, that the movement among many Protestants is to 'assert a distinctive identity by developing Ulster-Scots'. Goldenberg (2002:49) feels that 'it will take some time, if ever' before politics and language can be separated. Despite increased cross-community initiatives since the peace process, Irish has not yet become a focus of reconciliation efforts. Part of the problem, claims Gallagher (2001:38), is that in the absence of a 'political endgame' cultural themes and icons will continue to be used 'as part of essentialist political struggles'.

The peace process has been helpful but 'politicisation of the language remains a difficulty for many interested in speaking Irish in the North, particularly within the workplace' (MORI, 2006:14, 15). However, if Mac Póilin (2002) is correct in his more optimistic assessment that Irish is less political than it was ten years ago and more widely accepted in society, there is hope for the future and opportunities for sharing the language may already exist.

Creating 'neutral' spaces

As mentioned above, Protestants often have difficulty accessing classes in areas where they will not feel threatened. There have been classes in a few neutral venues, such as the Linen Hall Library in Belfast. Sadly, the options are not many.

For decades Cumann Chluain Ard in west Belfast has literally kept politics out of the language. It has consistently maintained a strict policy of barring two things – English, as in the language, and politics. This non-sectarian approach meant that even during the 1950s and 1960s Protestants could still find an outlet for their 'Gaelic' dimension without ever having to address tricky matters of state. Whatever the personal views of members, there was no 'national question' in Cumann Chluain Ard, an organisation that prided itself on maintaining a neutral space.

Sadly, the intervention of the Troubles removed yet another choice for Irish-speaking Protestants (Craig, 2007:52):

This club enriched the lives of a good many people, not all of them Catholic. […] By the 1970s, with the Troubles raging, very few Protestants, however liberal-minded, would have dared to set foot in west Belfast.[24]

Nonetheless, Cumann Chluain Ard remains as a non-sectarian, non-political sanctuary for Irish speakers of all backgrounds and faiths, even if it might be some time yet before Protestants and unionists feel comfortable crossing into 'republican' west Belfast in any numbers.

A diploma/degree course at the University of Ulster's Belfast campus has attracted Protestants. Queen's University runs adult education classes in Irish, which have aroused Protestant interest:[25] some Protestants have gone on to achieve degrees at the university, among them the Reverend Bill Boyd, who is also involved in another 'neutral space' initiative, namely the monthly Presbyterian service in Irish at Fitzroy Presbyterian Church in Belfast. The reality is, however, that opportunities for Protestants to learn Irish are still rather limited.

Outside Belfast, there are few towns where Protestants could access classes without having to cross a divide that still runs deep in the mindset of many in Northern Ireland. Even those who reach a reasonable standard of Irish in neutral classes but wish to become fluent find that they must either venture into nationalist areas or go to the Gaeltacht. For those without the wherewithal, these are not easy options and – again – working-class Protestants must take the biggest leap into the unknown, be it cultural or financial.

A more formal initiative is the Ultach Trust, founded in 1989 with a core objective of encouraging cross-community involvement in Irish. Its board includes members from both traditions and its creation marked the first Government involvement in the promotion of Irish in Northern Ireland. However the Trust came in for criticism from republicans who saw it as an organ of the government and were suspicious of its efforts to accommodate unionists. Mac Póilin, who works for the Trust and is from 'Catholic west Belfast', records (2000:93) that some in the Irish-language movement had labelled him as a Stormont (i.e. government) 'spy' and even a 'unionist'. McCoy, however, has hard evidence that Ultach's critics do not come exclusively from the 'green' side of the house (2006:174).

The Trust seeks to identify obstacles to Protestant and unionist engagement with the language and to raise awareness within the Catholic and nationalist community to the difficulties experienced by learners from other traditions. This has meant trying to stimulate interest in Irish across the political divide and provide opportunities to learn and use the language in areas and among communities not normally associated with it. Ultach's original remit has changed since Foras na Gaeilge became the main language promotion and funding organisation in Ireland as a whole, but it still reaches out to try and make the language less controversial and contentious.

Ultach was also closely involved with the establishment of the Columba Initiative (Iomairt Cholm Cille, now simply Colmcille), founded in 1998 with the aim of bringing together speakers of Irish and Scots Gaelic. Its activities include community exchanges, cultural events and language courses. One of its stated aims is to develop strategies and projects in which the Gaelic language in Ireland and Scotland can draw together people from diverse backgrounds, within and between each country and region.

Colmcille, however, does not have the same potential for introducing Northern Ireland Protestants to Irish as Ultach. After all, a knowledge of 'Catholic' Irish is necessary to understand the mainly Protestant speakers of Scots Gaelic – Colmcille sponsors Scottish Gaelic courses for speakers of Irish Gaelic. Set in this context, the notion of 'cross-community' becomes more difficult to define. However, while doing little cross-community work, Colmcille sponsored a tour of *An Leabhar Mór* (The Great Book of Gaelic), a celebration of modern Irish and Scots Gaelic poetry and art, in both parts of Ireland between 2006 and 2009. The tour went to venues in a number of 'Protestant' towns and areas.

The Good Friday Agreement

The Good Friday/Belfast Agreement of 1998 set an entirely new language agenda for Northern Ireland. Politicians from most of the major parties (the DUP excused themselves from the process) drew up a political roadmap and language was part of the plan. The government set out its commitment to the promotion of linguistic diversity, promising to:

> recognise the importance of respect, understanding and tolerance in relation to linguistic diversity, including in Northern Ireland, the Irish language, Ulster-Scots and the languages of the various ethnic minority communities, all of which are part of the cultural wealth of the island of Ireland. (GFA, 1998:19)

This led to the creation of a North–South Language Implement-ation Body responsible for implementing the Agreement commit-ments through two agencies, Foras na Gaeilge for Irish and Tha Boord o Ulstèr-Scotch for Ulster-Scots. While Foras na Gaeilge has not laid out an agenda for the specific promotion of the Irish language among Protestants, it and its Ulster-Scots counterpart have helped move issues of minority languages from the realms of embittered 'them and us' arguments into a marginally less combative sphere.

ULSTER-SCOTS AND LANGUAGE 'COMPETITION'

Searching for a 'Protestant' heritage

Even before the Ulster-Scots debate came to prominence, there were those who argued that Ulster Protestants were becoming more interested in their culture (Hume, 1990:19). The 'search' for a Protestant/unionist identity has been perplexing and Tannahill (1995:13) suggests that Protestants have been brainwashed – and have brainwashed themselves – into believing that they are without any valued identity or culture, culture being seen as a 'Catholic activity'. However, Hayes (1995:9) casts doubt on the 'well-hawked stereotype' that the unionist is insecure because of a crisis of cultural identity, while the Catholic is secure in his identity as Irishman and Catholic.

According to Hudson (2004:32) one of the contrasts between 'language' and 'dialect' is *prestige* and this takes us into difficult territory as regards Ulster-Scots. Scholars such as Milroy (1987:78, 195) readily refer to it as 'rural' dialect and many – unionists included – deride it. Others describe it as a regional variety of the Scots language which maintains a strong presence in areas settled by Scottish Planters in the seventeenth century. Edmund (2002) charts the Ulster-Scots revival from the 1990s onwards and acknowledges the 'dialect-v-language' debate, but dismisses it as largely irrelevant to the Ulster-Scots population. Much energy has been expended on arguments about whether or not Ulster-Scots is a dialect of Scots or a distinct language.

Officially, it is recognised by government as a variant of Scots but the relatively small distance on the dialect continuum between Ulster-Scots and English – the same holds true for Scots and English – means that some do not see it as a distinct form of language. Even James Fenton, the Ulster-Scots poet and lexicographer who has provided much inspiration for the 'movement' with his book *The Hamely Tongue*, recognises this:

If you look upon it as a sliding scale, with dialect at one end and language at the other, Ulster-Scots is far closer to language than dialect. It all depends on how you define language. If you're in a country context where they're talking about the crops or about the weather, it's very close to a language, but if you're talking about last night's football or a political debate, it moves back down the spectrum towards a dialect. (quoted in Malcolm, 1999)

Perhaps the word 'tongue' is a useful compromise. Fenton also touches upon the so-called 'cultural cringe' factor, whereby Ulster-Scots speakers code-switch, using standard English in formal situations but reverting to a more localised way of speaking when the situation again becomes informal (ibid).

Fenton has a sharp understanding of language issues and prefers not to get drawn into debates beyond his remit. Avery (2003) offers a considered academic evaluation of Ulster-Scots and its development as a linguistic variant of Scots, while Coulter (2004) uses journalese to excoriate it as 'carefully hyped-up and carefully spin-doctored country chit-chat'. He dismisses Ulster-Scots as a cultural bulwark against a confident nationalism assured of its high status:

Protestants' British identity is being slowly but surely undermined by an increasingly pluralist and multi-racial England with the Protestant Throne seemingly determined to distance itself from the defence of the Reformed Faith.

Nevertheless, Ulster-Scots (or Ullans, as it is sometimes known) has made significant progress since the recognition gained in the 1998

Belfast/Good Friday Agreement. A grammar has been produced, as have dictionaries, such as Fenton's folksy *The Hamely Tongue* (2000). The letterheads and websites of some government departments include translations of their titles in Ulster-Scots and Irish, as well as English (e.g. the Department of Education Northern Ireland) and job advertisements have appeared in newspapers in Ulster-Scots.

A few examples of the 'leid', to illustrate the difference between it and standard English, might be useful for those who have not encountered Ulster-Scots. They are taken from Liam Logan's regular column 'A Word of Ulster Scots' in *The Ulster Scot*[26] and are representative of Ulster-Scots in a normal colloquial context.

(1) *A had me doots but A pit thim a tae yin side.* I was dubious but I overcame my qualms.

(2) *[A] tuk a sprachle at daein a A had tae dae.* [I] made an attempt to do what had to be done.

Robinson, prefacing his grammar, notes the particular difficulties of speakers to express it in written form (1997:1). Spelling is an area where there are still competing varieties. However, it might be argued that Ulster-Scots is being fast-tracked to a sort-of standardisation. Its proponents' claims that these moves are to iron out dialectal differences echo the standardisation of Irish in the 1940s/50s to reconcile differences between its dialects.

The Life and Times Survey (ARK, 1999) asked participants if they could speak Ulster-Scots: only 2 per cent of Protestants and 1 per cent of Catholics answered Yes, but 7 per cent and 4 per cent respectively claimed to personally know someone who could. There was a reasonable degree of ignorance about Ulster-Scots, for 10 per cent of Catholics and 12 per cent of Protestants had never heard of it or did not know what it was. Unsurprisingly, everyone was aware of Irish, but at the time Ulster-Scots had a much lower profile than it now enjoys. Asked to consider the statement 'Ulster-Scots is a vital part of Northern Ireland's heritage', only 16 per cent of Protestants agreed,[27] compared to 14 per cent of Catholics (disagree figures were 56 per cent for Protestants and 58 per cent for Catholics).

Other statistics from that survey showed a dismissive view among both religious denominations: more than 50 per cent of both categorised it as a dialect and more Protestants than Catholics thought translating official papers into it is a waste of money. When asked if *all* secondary level pupils should have to learn it, fewer Protestants (12 per cent) than Catholics (28 per cent) agreed. The figures – at that time – were hardly a glowing Protestant endorsement of Ulster-Scots as 'their' language. Another survey, cited by Edmund (2002:176), might underline fast-changing views: it revealed that 31% of Protestants and 10% of Catholics saw Ulster-Scots *identity* as very/fairly important; 23% of Protestants and 19% of Catholics saw Ulster-Scots *language* and *culture* as very/fairly important.

The old Stormont was hostile to Irish but Dolan (2002:152) rightly asks what the unionist government did for Ulster-Scots during its fifty-five-year rule. He notes a distinct lack of 'will' in regard to the 'language' until recently and wonders to what extent there is 'genuine interest' in it. Like other scholars, he mentions an incident when signs in Ulster-Scots in a Protestant area were torn down because locals thought they were in Irish (cited Görlach, 2000:15). McCoy (2006:157) believes that current unionist interest in Ulster-Scots is partly a response to the association of the Irish language and political identity, adding that it 'also represents the abandonment of modernism by some unionists for an alternative self-minoritizing approach', 'minority status' having become associated with positive benefits.

Avery and Gilbert's Ulster-Scots curriculum development project, under the auspices of Stranmillis University College, aims to provide 'first encounters with Ulster-Scots language, history and culture for pupils in primary and secondary schools' (2006). They say that the 'overlooked' Ulster-Scots tradition is finding 'substantial interest' throughout Northern Ireland. Teaching materials have been trialled in both Protestant and Catholic schools in all Northern Ireland counties and east County Donegal, where the Ulster-Scots Agency has an office. Other academic initiatives are also under way.

'Dialect-v-language' arguments are losing their intensity as Ulster-Scots becomes an accepted part of the Northern Ireland language scene, even if many issues hinge mainly around the expression of cultural identity. Kirk and Ó Baoill warn of 'entrenched polarities' between the 'Irish-speaking community' and 'the Ulster-Scots-speaking community' (2000:10): their observation that we all have an obligation to recognise, respect and understand our linguistic diversity is often overlooked in Northern Ireland. Indeed, it appears that English itself has become the forgotten language, almost ignored and championed by no one in the rivalry between Irish and Ulster-Scots.

CONCLUSIONS

The loyalist prisoners' engagement with Irish was probably rather artificial and transient but other Protestants' experiences have been more natural and there is a range of reasons why a minority of Protestants learn the language. As McCoy showed, learning Irish is an easy extension of political idealism into a cultural domain for Protestant nationalists, but Protestant unionists have to use a variety of mechanisms and discourses to reconcile their political beliefs with the language and its speech community. For some, that trade-off is too high a price to pay but others persist and find a niche. There are signs that the Irish language debate has lost some of its sting in the past decade. Even so, unionist politicians have still found time to attack the language, most notably in the Stormont Assembly where an attempt to ban Irish reignited old hostilities in late 2007. Similarly, arguments over whether Northern Ireland should have an Irish language act brought the issue back into the public consciousness in a highly negative way.

On a more positive note, increased recognition for Ulster-Scots has perhaps helped remove some of the heat, creating a less poisonous atmosphere. Republican insults that Ulster-Scots is a 'made-up language for Orangemen' have almost disappeared and there are fewer attacks on its authenticity as a language.

Whether Protestants and unionists decide to 'reclaim' Irish from republicans or simply accept it as a neglected part of a shared heritage that was around them all along in place names, surnames and even the way English is spoken in Northern Ireland, the conditions for re-engagement will probably only slowly improve. While the IRA has put its arms 'beyond use', it might still be fanciful to believe that republicans will 'decommission' Irish. The challenge now is to create the circumstances for a new, broader Protestant and unionist rapprochement with the language that is not dependent on a spurious act of cultural generosity by republicans. It seems more likely that if change is to occur, it will be effected through the education system.

3

SHARED HERITAGE, DIVIDED HORIZONS

INTRODUCTION

This chapter examines the Enrichment Programme in Gaelic Studies (EPGS) for schools operated in Northern Ireland by Gael-Linn. The scheme gives pupils in what are regarded as 'Protestant' schools the opportunity to engage with Irish at an introductory level. Firstly, though, I discuss the education system in Northern Ireland, as a basic understanding of how it functions (and why it is segregated) is essential in order to satisfactorily define the labels 'Protestant schools' and 'Catholic schools'.

The background and history of Gael-Linn, a voluntary organisation devoted to the promotion of the Irish language on an all-Ireland basis, will be explored, as will the evolution of the enrichment course. Examination of its components will place particular emphasis on the language course which is at its centre and Gael-Linn's own evaluation processes will be considered. This comprehensive analysis of the programme and its aims will, I hope, establish why it offers a highly effective way of gaining an insight into the attitudes of young Protestants.

THE EDUCATION SYSTEM IN NORTHERN IRELAND

Education, as seen earlier, was a highly controversial matter for unionist politicians shortly after Northern Ireland's inception and the current system – although changed – remains part of that legacy, with a structure that is for the most part segregated. However, many new measures in response to duplication of provision and falling pupil numbers mean that the whole issue is being revisited. If fully implemented, proposed policy changes will have a significant impact on how schooling is delivered.

The Department of Education (DENI) is responsible for the central administration of education and related services in Northern Ireland. The structure is, by its own admission, 'complex', with ten statutory bodies and a number of voluntary organisations involved in the provision of education. At the centre of the system are five education and library boards (ELBs), delivering on statutory responsibilities. The boards – the local education authorities – provide all the finance for the schools under their management and equip, maintain and meet other running costs of maintained schools. ELB expenditure is funded at 100 per cent by the Department.

DENI (2005a) points out that the education system in Northern Ireland has a number of distinctive features:

> Secondary education retains largely a selective system with pupils going to grammar schools or secondary schools according to academic ability. There is also a very large voluntary school sector consisting of voluntary grammar schools (under either Catholic or nondenominational management) and Catholic maintained schools.

In effect, the system is segregated, and, while the terms may be unpalatable to some, schools can broadly be categorised as 'Protestant' or 'Catholic'. Education in Northern Ireland has rightly been described as 'a highly contested and complicated area with deeply held convictions based on religious, linguistic, ideological or other views' (DCAL, 2007:7). Lee (1989:137) notes that a segregated education system can exist in other societies 'without reaping the harvest of hatred that has distinguished Northern Ireland' but goes on to suggest that attitudes in the home play no small part in spreading the 'virus' of intolerance.

Historically, the tradition of education along denominational lines is long-established in Northern Ireland and the issue of 'religious instruction' was at the centre of debate in the 1920s when Lord Londonderry, the Stormont Education Minister, attempted to reform the system into one which would create schools where children of different faiths might study and play together, with denominational religious instruction allowed only outside hours of compulsory attendance (Bardon, 1992:502). This would have brought integrated education to Northern Ireland perhaps sixty years before the first tentative steps in that direction were taken.

Londonderry's proposals faced intense hostility from the Catholic and Protestant churches, both sides mobilising to attack the Education Bill of 1923 because they wanted to maintain control over 'their' schools. In 1925, after Londonderry had stated that his Education Act would not be changed, pressure grew to such an extent that Prime Minister James Craig capitulated: an amending bill was rushed through Parliament. This allowed clergy to advise on teaching appointments and education authorities could take a candidate's religion into account. Teachers were compelled to give 'simple Bible instruction' as part of their contractual duties.

Londonderry subsequently resigned but both the Catholic bishops and the Protestant churches continued their agitation. The outcome was the 1930 Education Act, which effectively permitted two different systems, the 'Catholic' one, partly funded from local and government sources, and the fully funded one attended almost exclusively by Protestants.

Put simply, the three main Protestant churches – Church of Ireland, Presbyterian and Methodist – transferred their schools to the ownership of the state, receiving key roles in the management of the education system in return. The Catholic Church retained ownership in its schools; these were not fully financed by the state at the time but today, after changes in the system of management arrangements, Catholic-maintained schools can enjoy the same level of funding as state (i.e. 'controlled' or 'Protestant') schools.

The labels 'Protestant' or 'Catholic' schools do require some qualification in that it is not necessarily the case that a 'Protestant' school will have 100 per cent Protestant attendance. A minority of Catholic families do send their children to 'Protestant' schools and in some heavily mixed areas the proportion can be relatively high, particularly in grammar schools. Nonetheless, the vast majority of pupils in such schools will be from a Protestant background and I can feel safe in using the terms as a convenient shorthand.

As Kernohan (1995) puts it:

In Northern Ireland, as elsewhere in the United Kingdom, the law guarantees that every school is open to all pupils regardless of religious denomination. Some schools have both Protestant and Catholic pupils, but most Catholic pupils attend Catholic schools and most Protestant children attend State (controlled) schools. Segregated housing has been an important determinant of patterns of school attendance in many areas.

In a way, Londonderry's vision of 'schools where children of different faiths might study and play together' began to be realised in the 1980s when the first 'integrated' school – Lagan College – was opened. The basic concept behind integrated schooling is that students of all faiths and none study in an environment free of sectarianism. Such schools struggled at first, reliant on donations and fund-raising, but in 1990 the Department became obliged to 'encourage and facilitate' integrated education, with 100 per cent funding.

The Northern Ireland Council for Integrated Education (NICIE) describes integrated education as the bringing together in one school of pupils, staff and governors from Protestant, Catholic, other faiths and none. 'It is about cultivating the individual's self-respect and therefore respect for other people and other cultures. Integrated Education means bringing children up to live as adults in a pluralist society, recognising what they hold in common as well as what separates them, and accepting both' (NICIE, 2005).

By 2005 the integrated sector in Northern Ireland comprised 19 second-level colleges and 38 primary schools and the organisation claims that in September 2004 over 670 applicants for places in integrated schools had to be turned away due to lack of places. The growth has been significant, with some state schools 'transforming' to integrated status, and NICIE points to opinion polls which 'show widespread support for the concept of integrated education'. It does, however, concede that growth in the sector has not been without opposition.

Another growing sector is Irish-medium education (IME), in which pupils study the standard curriculum through the Irish language. The movement began in west Belfast in the 1970s and, as with the integrated sector, faced significant funding difficulties at first, with wrangling over official recognition. Comhairle na Gaelscolaíochta (the Council for Irish-medium Education) was set up by the Department of Education in 2000 to promote, facilitate and encourage Irish-medium schools in Northern Ireland. It regulates the planning of new Irish-medium schools and coordinates the activities of all those involved in the sector (Comhairle, 2005). Iontaobhas na Gaelscolaíochta is a trust fund set up by Comhairle na Gaelscolaíochta and the Department of Education to assist new schools that have still to meet the eligibility requirement for mainstream funding.

In the school year 2006/07, 4,072 children were receiving Irish-medium education: 44 nurseries with 855 pupils; 23 primary schools with 2,542 pupils; and two secondary schools and a post-primary unit with 610 pupils (Ultach, 2008). Irish-medium 'streams' also operate in some Catholic schools, a development that 'worries' Fitzduff (2000:80) as it 'may ghettoize the language still further'. Irish-medium education is looked upon with suspicion by Protestants and unionists, who believe it to be an extension of republicanism and frown upon the allocation of state money to the sector. Despite the avowedly non-denominational ethos of some Irish-medium schools (*Gaelscoileanna*), most Protestants are sceptical: the fact that they tend to be located in nationalist areas reinforces this negative view.

A Protestant Irish speaker in Belfast felt that because most pupils in those schools were from a different background, 'it would be hard for my children to go into those surroundings' (BBC Scotland, *Eorpa*, 19/11/2002). Tantalisingly, there was the vaguest hint of engagement with Irish-medium education in provisional figures which suggested that two out of 3,150 IME pupils were Protestants in the 2006/07 school year (DCAL, 2007:8). The political inclinations of the parents are unknown.

Peover (2002:129) recognises the difficulties for those who either do not come from the Catholic community or do not want their children educated in a school with the Catholic ethos and feels it is important to develop a strategy that 'keeps options open rather than closes them down' so that all can enjoy access to the language.

CURRICULUM ISSUES

Four 'Key Stages' cover the twelve years of compulsory schooling in Northern Ireland and for many years most pupils have transferred from primary to post-primary schooling at the age of eleven. A significant change in the education system was announced in 2004 when, after a review, the decision was taken to end the transfer tests, better known as the 11-Plus. Post-primary schools would be required to 'admit all pupils whose parents have expressed a preference for their child to attend the school, provided the school has sufficient places' (CCEA,[28] 2005b). If sufficient places were not available, schools would select pupils according to their admission criteria.

However, grammar (selective) schools have for decades used results of the transfer tests, which cover English, mathematics, and science and technology, to decide which pupils to admit, giving preference to those with the highest grades. The controversial system is vilified by some, yet prized by others and most unionist politicians saw the decision to end the selection process as politically motivated, particularly as Sinn Féin's Martin McGuinness announced a provisional date for its end in one of his final acts as Education Minister before the power-sharing Stormont Assembly was suspended in October 2002.

Many unionists regarded it as an act of malice and grammar schools were bitterly opposed to proposals to end selection. They argued for the retention of some form of academic selection and discussed joining forces to establish a test of their own. Critics of selection, however, claimed that it branded those who did not pass as 'failures' at eleven years old and instead favoured new arrangements based on parental choice, informed by pupil profile and better information about options.

Whatever their ultimate shape, any changes would inevitably have a massive impact on the grammar school system in the Province (and post-primary education in general) but – despite years of wrangling – the issue was still unresolved in 2009. The Sinn Féin Education Minister Caitriona Ruane confirmed that academic selection would cease, much to the chagrin of unionists (her support for Irish-medium education also provoked much bitterness).

Meanwhile another relatively recent change in the examination and curriculum structure had already exerted a significant influence in relation to Gael-Linn's EPGS. The AS (Advanced Subsidiary) qualification was introduced in 2000. Taken by students after GCSE, it is equivalent to the first year of study of a traditional A Level. Most students are required to take four subjects in the first year of post-16 study, as opposed to the three generally taken under the old system. As a stand-alone qualification, AS reduces the numbers who drop out after one year of study with nothing to show for their efforts and places emphasis on feedback and support from teachers.

The second year element of A Level study is known as A2: its modules do not make up a qualification in their own right but when taken together with the AS units comprise a full A Level. Teachers complain, however, that the extra workload placed on them and students by the system has killed off elective 'extras' such as Gael-Linn's course.

A new factor is the so-called 'Entitlement Framework', which guarantees access to a wider range of options. Schools are expected to offer pupils access to a minimum of twenty-four courses at Key Stage 4 (14–16 years) and twenty-seven at post-16: at least one-third of these courses should be academic and at least one-third vocational. The aim is greater parity of esteem between both routes. DENI says that schools will work in collaboration with each other and with FE (Further Education) colleges to provide pupils with access to the full range of courses required by the framework:

All school types, including grammar schools, have a role in future arrangements as long as they provide pupils with access to the Curriculum Entitlement Framework. There will be an opportunity for schools to develop as Specialist Schools, which will be centres of excellence and expertise in particular areas of the curriculum. (DENI, 2006a)

Intriguingly, the Department adds: 'New arrangements will be determined locally to take account of local needs, wishes and circumstances.' It says these collaborations 'will be flexible and may change over time' but schools will 'retain their autonomy'. Just what this will mean on the ground remains to be seen, but it offers some very interesting possibilities.

BACKGROUND TO GAEL-LINN

In many ways, Gael-Linn, as an organisation seeking to promote Irish on an all-Ireland basis, is happily unencumbered by the political baggage of the Gaelic League (Conradh na Gaeilge). The League, by deliberately linking Irish with the 'national' question at its acrimonious 1915 Ard Fheis (see Chapter One), damaged the language in the eyes of many Protestants who still regarded Gaelic as part of their heritage.

A non-governmental organisation established in 1953, Gael-Linn endeavours to promote the language in different ways, including music, song, sport, debating and courses. Inspired by the success of the football pools in the UK, a group of graduates and undergraduates realised that a similar scheme based on Gaelic games scores could be the catalyst for fund-raising that would 'pressurise the Dublin Government to take a more pro-active role in promoting the Irish language and associated culture' (Gael-Linn, 2005b):

The idea of marketing an Irish Pools project, not for profit but for the benefit of the language and the communities of the Gaeltacht, appealed to the idealism of many young Irish men and women, who soon became enthusiastic promoters of the new idea.

In some ways, Gael-Linn was born out of the frustration many felt with the Dublin government's attempts to restore Irish as the major language of the Republic. The vague notion that giving Irish a central place in the school curriculum would restore it as the national language had proven unfulfillable. In reality, 'the people still speaking Irish were in the main the poorest in the land, and there remained a strong connection in the popular mind between poverty and the language' (Gael-Linn, 2005b). In *An Béal Bocht* (1942) the sublime Flann O'Brien had already both incisively and, perhaps, cruelly, mocked the concept of naive Dublin outsiders, setting off to the Gaeltacht with their 'book' Irish and a prescription for the salvation of the native tongue.

Scholarly intervention led to Gael-Linn's formation. An Comhchaidreamh, a confederation of the Irish Societies of universities in Ireland (including Queen's University Belfast) which established the Irish-language monthly Comhar in 1942, looked askance at the Dublin government's Comhdháil Náisiúnta na Gaeilge, a body formed in 1943 to spearhead the language revival: '... many of the younger supporters of the language believed it little better than the moribund Gaelic League' (Gael-Linn, 2005b). Despite overtures to the government, little progress was made and, after rejection of proposals for state-funded films in Irish, An Comhchaidreamh, hoping to shame the government into supporting the project, decided they would try to make the films themselves: in March 1953 Dónall Ó Móráin, who would become the new body's director, recommended the formation of Gael-Linn, and the (Gaelic) football pools, which were to become the financial heartbeat of the organisation, were launched.

Nonetheless, there were tensions between Gael-Linn (*Linn* is the Irish word for pool) and the Gaelic Athletic Association (GAA). The Association, on whose results the pools would be based, viewed the project with suspicion, wondering how it might benefit from this curious initiative. Breandán Ó hEithir, later to become a celebrated journalist, commentator and a scriptwriter for some of Gael-Linn's ground-breaking movies, records (1991:152):

He [a confidant close to GAA thinking] informed me that Croke Park [headquarters of the Association], which in those days really meant Paddy O'Keefe, the General Secretary of the GAA, was not all that happy about Gael-Linn ... I replied innocently that I found all that very strange for did not the world and his wife know that Paddy O'Keefe's side-kick, Seán Ó Síocháin, was one of the trustees of Gael-Linn ... Many dedicated Gaels, he [the informant] said, wondered how the GAA was going to benefit by all this.

Surely, said I, the GAA is delighted to see the Language (you said it with a capital letter in rarefied English-speaking company) benefit in this way and wouldn't the games be played anyway? That indeed was the case but the GAA had its own priorities and would have to keep them uppermost in its thoughts at all times.

Later, according to Ó hEithir, the tensions were evident as 'a series of niggling rows, bureaucratic forms of tripping and jersey-pulling' which resembled some form of 'unarmed civil war'. The GAA, he concludes, 'resented this Johnny-come-lately'.

Nevertheless, by the end of the 1950s, Gael-Linn already had an office in Armagh city to coordinate activities in the North. At grassroots level, 'timirí' acted as local organisers and ticket sellers travelled from door to door with the weekly pools forms. The organisation was particularly active in the North and Ó Baoighill (2004:6) claims that it provided one-third of the organisation's total income during the 1950s and 1960s. As an all-Ireland body, of course, Gael-Linn's 'North' included all nine Ulster counties. While we can say that Gael-Linn did not bear the self-imposed political burdens of Conradh na Gaeilge, some leading republican figures were involved in the organisation.

One of the first trustees was the author Máirtín Ó Cadhain from Connemara. He wrote the landmark Irish novel *Cré na Cille* and other important works in the language. Ó Cadhain had been heavily involved in the republican movement. Becoming an IRA recruiting officer and a member of the Army Council, he was imprisoned in the Curragh by the Irish government for most the Second World War. Ó Cadhain, who later became Professor of Irish at Trinity College

Dublin, was a fiery standard-bearer for the cause of native speakers and 'it was no surprise that he heavily influenced Gael-Linn's policies with regard to the Gaeltacht' (Ó Baoighill, 2004a:7). Art Mac Eachaidh, another republican who became involved with Gael-Linn, was a prominent Irish-language activist. He had been responsible for a small annual drama festival in Dungannon but when, in the late 1950s, Gael-Linn gave each province £70 to organise a festival, Mac Eachaidh was unable to play a part in the prestigious 'féile' planned for his home-town as he 'was in prison because of his republican view' (ibid:9).

However, Gael-Linn's ethos was not republican and the involvement of such figures cannot be interpreted as anything other than incidental. Máirtín Ó Cadhain, for example, on later occasions lambasted Gael-Linn over the inability of one of its scholarship students 'domiciled for six months in the heart of a Connemara Gaeltacht' to give evidence to a court in Irish, accused its experts of being unable to use the language in discussions with government officials and castigated one of its industrial projects with the words: 'Even a little shanty of a seaweed factory cannot be conducted in Irish' (Ó Cadhain, 1965). Taking into account Ó Cadhain's inclination to fire off vitriolic letters in all directions in his later years, his description of Gael-Linn/government scholarship holders as 'an infestation' is nonetheless a fierce attack on an organisation he had previously been so closely involved with.

Pádraig Ó Baoighill, in his personal reflections on the group's golden jubilee year, suggests a movement which had the best interests of Irish at heart, free from the political agenda that had cast a dark shadow over Conradh na Gaeilge (2004b:12/13):

This inter-university organisation [An Comhchaidreamh], which embodied all shades of political and religious opinion, had a unified bond of interest to preserve and extend the use of Irish, similar to the *original objectives* [my emphasis] of the Gaelic League at the end of the nineteenth century. As a person who was involved in the early years and in its organisation nationwide up until the nineties, I am proud that the original objectives of the founders fifty years ago are being continued and will develop in the years to come.

Initiatives included promotion of the language among native speakers, film-making, musical recordings, general cultural activities and socio-economic projects designed to develop Gaeltacht areas. Instead of the academic emphasis of nineteenth-century revivalists, Gael-Linn's remit was heavily biased towards preservation and advancement of the language in the Gaeltacht. However, it used contemporary media to take the message further afield: in a period when cinema was still king, Gael-Linn's short documentary films in Irish featured in picture-houses the length and breadth of Ireland. *Amharc Éireann*, a weekly newsreel of events in Ireland with commentary in Irish, was a prelude to the seminal movies of the 1960s. *Mise Éire*, based on actual newsreel footage with a music score by the illustrious composer Seán Ó Riada, covered the 'struggle' for Irish independence from the 1890s to 1917. Several big-screen successes followed, including one Oscar nomination.

Founded on a strict principle of non-profit making, the organisation funded Gaeltacht industries, including a fish and vegetable processing plant in the Galway Gaeltacht – buying boats from 'Protestant' Kilkeel[29] in Northern Ireland – and even purchased the rights to a 135-acre estate at Teelin in south Donegal. Add in a seaweed processing factory, a bee-keeping scheme, a furniture company, holiday properties, a metalworking enterprise and a foray into the restaurant business and we get some idea of Gael-Linn's diversity. In Northern Ireland, a majority shareholding was purchased in County Antrim's Glens of Antrim Tweed Co. Ltd. Significantly, the Glens had been one of the last strongholds of Irish in Northern Ireland. Women from all parts of Ireland produced knitted goods for another Gael-Linn initiative, Inisfree Handknits.

During the 1960s, Gael-Linn applied for the licence to run the first national television channel in the Republic but the government's decision to establish Teilifís Éireann forced a rethink on strategy. In the 1970s, Gael-Linn placed more emphasis on promoting the language beyond the Gaeltacht areas and among the general population, with summer courses in Irish, debates and drama. In 1975, it worked with Linguaphone (the market leader in home language-learning) to produce an Irish course for beginners. Classes for adults have been a consistent part of Gael-Linn's efforts to promote the language since its inception. An annual course for adults in Donegal's Gaoth Dobhair area attracts many learners of all levels from the Province, in both the nine-county and six-county sense.

The 1970s and 1980s saw an increased emphasis on youth activities, such as Slógadh, local events which culminated in a national final involving singing, storytelling and the visual arts. Significant artists such as Clannad, the Hothouse Flowers and Altan first came to prominence through the scheme. The 1980s, though, represented a period of retrenchment as the Irish economy fell into recession. When the RTÉ authority decided to axe sponsored programmes on Raidió Éireann in 1980, Gael-Linn's weekly radio show (which had for decades brought Irish into the homes of Ireland, as well as announcing the eagerly awaited pools results) ended.

Gael-Linn's remit includes some specific activities for Northern Ireland and 1992 saw the introduction of table quizzes. *Tráth na gCeist* – for secondary and grammar-school students in Northern Ireland – involves at least 3,000 teenagers every year. A similar series for adults, in conjunction with BBC Radio Ulster, *Freagair*, was also launched. New technology also brought opportunities and CD-ROM material enhanced the body's ability to make the language accessible to all. As well as a wealth of cultural activities for young people – including the popular scholarships whereby students spend part of the summer in the Gaeltacht, living with local families and attending colleges such as Machaire Rabhartaigh and Bun an Inbhir in County Donegal – Gael-Linn continues to provide a huge music catalogue and a comprehensive cultural programme.

More recently, an innovative language course called *Gaeilge agus Fáilte*, developed in conjunction with Institiúid Teangeolaíochta Éireann and aimed at adult learners, was widely acclaimed and used to teach beginners at Queen's University in Belfast. Debating and public speaking competitions such as *Abair* promote the language specifically among school pupils in Northern Ireland. Most of the youth events are directed at those with facility in Irish (i.e. Catholic children), so Gael-Linn entered entirely new territory when it developed the enrichment programme for students in predominantly Protestant schools.

INCEPTION AND EARLY UPTAKE OF THE COURSE

The Gael-Linn enrichment programme in Gaelic Studies, *Aspects of a Shared Heritage*, was conceived in the mid-1990s as a way to dispel some of the many misconceptions among young Protestants about the Irish language. Even as early as 1986, in a document submitted to the Irish Joint-Chairman of the Anglo-Irish Intergovernmental Conference on the status of Irish in the Northern Ireland education system, Gael-Linn expressed the view that 'a course in Irish studies would be desirable in the state schools' (Gael-Linn, 1988). This submission focused primarily on Irish's place and development in Catholic schools but it is interesting to note that it saw benefit in the provision of 'a course giving a general view of Ireland's history, geography and cultural heritage' (ibid) in Protestant schools.

Many years later, that opportunity arose. In the 1990s, following dialogue between Gael-Linn and the Central Community Relations Unit (CCRU),[30] there was a consensus that an enrichment course operating in state schools could help make the language appear more appealing to unionists and Protestants. According to Ó Ciaráin (2004):

It was believed that unionists and Protestants felt alienated from the language and associated it with the IRA, 'Tiocfaidh Ár Lá' and so on. We did a little market research ... and we put this scheme together.

The scheme was piloted in the Western Education and Library Board and the North Eastern Education and Library Board areas during the 1995/96 academic year. Following positive feedback, it was decided to make it more widely available. At that stage, finance was provided by a European Union funding initiative. Financing came later from the CCRU and, subsequently, from the Department of Education Northern Ireland. Thirty per cent of the costs were covered by Gael-Linn itself.

The decision to run the enrichment course in Northern Ireland

enjoyed wholehearted support from the Dublin leadership. States Ó
Ciaráin:

> The Gael-Linn mission statement speaks about carrying out work
> like this to make the language and heritage available to all. This is
> one example of acting on that mission statement to the full and
> everyone in Gael-Linn was positive about it. Even people known
> for their republican outlook saw that it was good work and well
> overdue.

Following the successful pilot,[31] letters were sent to the schools in
conjunction with the education boards' language advisers and every
State school in Northern Ireland was offered the programme. It was
also offered to integrated schools and – later – made available to adults
over a three-year period in Armagh, Ballymena and Ballymoney. In
the grammar schools the course was aimed at the Sixth Form[32] as part
of a wide-ranging options programme which offered a diverse
selection of non-compulsory subjects such as Japanese, self-defence,
sign language and cooking.

In the 1995/96 academic year ten schools participated and the
scheme's success appears to be reflected in increasing numbers over
the following three years. Twelve took part in 1996/97, eighteen in
1997/98 and nineteen the following year. Many of the schools quickly
became regular 'consumers', hosting the course each year. A list (Table
1) of the schools, their type, location and the number of pupils
involved in the 1998/99 academic year gives some idea of the scheme's
coverage and penetration at its zenith.

It will be noted that figures for most of the integrated schools in
the table are significantly higher than those for the grammar schools.
This is because the integrated colleges which took up the enrichment
programme built it into the curriculum for full classes and year
groups, rather than providing it as an optional module. The age profile
of course-takers in the integrated schools was generally younger.

In terms of the grammar sector, participating schools included
girls-only, boys-only and co-educational. The table shows an uptake
in every county of Northern Ireland. Other state schools also took part

Table 1 – Course Participation in Academic Year 1998/99

School name	Type of school	School location	Pupils involved
Armagh Royal	Grammar	Co. Armagh	12
Ballyclare High	Grammar	Co. Antrim	35
Bangor Grammar	Grammar	Co. Down	33
Bangor High (girls)	Secondary	Co. Down	21
Belfast Royal Academy	Grammar	Belfast city	Not recorded
Brownlow College	Integrated	Co. Armagh	17
Carrickfergus Grammar	Grammar	Co. Antrim	26
Coleraine Girls' High	Grammar	Co. Londonderry	16
Dalriada High School	Grammar	Co. Antrim	18
Drumragh College	Integrated	Co. Tyrone	63
Dungannon Royal	Grammar	Co. Tyrone	23
Foyle/Londonderry College	Grammar	Co. Londonderry	39
Friends School	Grammar	Co. Antrim	17
Portora	Grammar	Co. Fermanagh	23
Rainey Endowed	Grammar	Co. Londonderry	18
Slemish	Integrated	Co. Antrim	111
Strangford College	Integrated	Co. Down	67
Sullivan Upper	Grammar	Co. Down	23
Ulidia	Integrated	Co. Down	91

in the programme, but are not listed above as they were not involved during the 1998/99 academic year. Geographically, the spread is interesting, as it demonstrates that Gael-Linn was able to run the course in solidly Protestant/unionist areas, such as Bangor, Ballyclare and Carrickfergus, as well as areas where Protestants/unionists would not be in the majority, such as Magherafelt and Londonderry.

Only modest penetration was achieved in Belfast and, although several city schools did take part at various times, they were the exception rather than the rule. Outside the city, the principal in a leading Ballymena grammar school expressed interest in running the course but, after 'floating' it with the pupils, found that none were prepared to enrol. Nor did the scheme 'take off' in places with very small Protestant populations, such as south Armagh.[33] Similarly, Kilkeel, mentioned above, was not involved. This may be reflective of a 'siege mentality' in such areas. Social attitudes in specific areas may also have been a factor.

Ó Ciaráin identifies a 'broad-minded ethos' as one common factor in all of the schools which did take part and praises the individual teachers who 'took the course and ran with it'. He points out that while some of the teachers were themselves interested in Irish, all extended the hand of friendship:

> In the years that I've been involved with the scheme, I have always had a very strong welcome from the teachers of every school. In many ways we were treated like ambassadors for the Irish language and the cause of anti-sectarianism. At first you felt you were involved in something ground-breaking. In my own case, who would have thought that a Crossmaglen man would be helping students close to Harryville Church in Ballymena increase their knowledge of matters relating to the Irish language and Irish culture.[34]

Reaction from pupils was 'almost always positive'. While one student, for example, told the Gael-Linn lecturer that 'we could keep our clapped-out culture', negative feedback was minimal, according to Ó Ciaráin.

The introduction of the new examination system in 2000, however, impacted heavily on uptake of the enrichment course. The AS Level structure has been blamed for increasing the pressure on teachers and pupils, thus reducing – if not altogether extinguishing – the opportunity to offer elective modules such as Gael-Linn's EPGS. As will be seen later, all of the school teachers interviewed for this research stress that the advent of the AS Level meant a downturn in extra-curricular activities.

In the academic year following the introduction of the AS Level the number of schools taking part fell to twelve and subsequently became 'a trickle', with only a handful now involved. Despite this, the scheme continues to operate and Gael-Linn offers it to long-standing 'clients' but does not actively go out to seek new schools. While the scheme is just 'ticking over', however, four schools participated in the full enrichment course during the year 2004/05, and another, with a younger age group, ran the language element.

STRUCTURE OF THE COURSE

In developing the enrichment programme, Gael-Linn specifically targeted those students who would not normally have an opportunity to study aspects of their Gaelic heritage. This essentially translates to Protestant pupils, although a few Catholic students attending some of the schools researched also took up the course. The aim was to encourage and facilitate young (predominantly Protestant) people to discover and reclaim a common Gaelic heritage of which most would be unaware. Mac an Fhailigh immediately identifies the problem of cultural exclusivism (1997:1):

The cultural and linguistic heritage of Northern Ireland is a combination of many different influences. In modern times the Gaelic heritage that is common to all has come to be regarded as the sole preserve of one section of the community, when in effect it has impacted on all of us through place names, surnames, music and even in the ways we speak English.

In setting out to help 'disperse some of the myths surrounding the Irish language and culture', Gael-Linn drew on a wide range of sources and subjects. At the core of the programme was an introduction to the language itself, but this was carefully placed into a broader cultural/heritage context, where Irish was used as a backdrop to facilitate a greater understanding of its influence on – and in – contemporary Northern Ireland. While the programme has undergone some modification since its introduction, the overall structure is broadly unchanged.

A comprehensive and professionally produced resource pack accompanies the course – the package is entitled *Aspects of a Shared Heritage*. It includes well-written essays by academics and experts in each topic and a double cassette to assist the students with pronunciation. In recent years the resource pack has not always been available but Gael-Linn is planning to update and republish it. In the meantime, learning materials are provided in the form of handouts by individual lecturers.

The following is a summary of the course, which lasts from eight to ten weeks, depending on whatever suits the schools:

Irish language lessons

The course on spoken Irish is for complete beginners, bringing pupils up to a very basic conversational standard by using common phrases and idioms as building blocks. The course begins with essential greetings such as *Maidin mhaith*/Good morning, *Slán go fóill*/Cheerio and *Go raibh maith agat*/Thank you. Students quickly learn how to ask simple questions, such as someone's name, say where they come from and express likes or dislikes in the present tense.

As with every language course, the weather features prominently and the wide range of adjectives introduced at this stage provides useful 'bricks' for more sustained conversations. Numbers up to 100 are taught and students learn how to tell the time, as well as being able to describe their daily routine. Given the brevity of the course, scope is limited but it does provide a very useful 'taster' to pupils. As most students unfamiliar with Irish find pronunciation something of a challenge, care is taken to overcome early difficulties through the use of simple phonetics, as demonstrated by the following examples in the resource pack (Mac Nia, 1997:54):

Maidin mhaith	(ma'jeen woy)	Good morning
Oíche mhaith	(ee-hah woy)	Good night
Tá fáilte romhat	(tah fwall-cha row-it)	You're welcome
Tá mé go maith	(tah may gaw moy)	I'm well/fine

The course uses Ulster Irish (i.e. that spoken in the Donegal Gaeltacht) and this is seen in the appearance of particular words and expressions which, if not necessarily exclusive to, would generally be associated with the dialect. The choice of Ulster Irish for young

Protestant learners is a logical one given that pupils from Northern Ireland (some of whom would go on holiday in Donegal) are more likely to come into contact with Ulster Irish[35] than other dialects.

Learning and pronunciation are reinforced by simple conversations between students and the lecturers in an atmosphere that is friendly and relaxed. In the resource pack, for example, the enquiry '*Cén dóigh?*' is translated as 'What about ya?' and the response, '*Dóigh mhaith*', as 'Dead on': both are colloquialisms specific to Northern Ireland and would be seen as highly informal, with currency among young people.

Given the obvious effort made to promote Irish as fun, grammar, with its associated complexities, has a peripheral role and only essential points are explained as required. At this level of learning, detailed explanation of gender issues or initial mutations might be off-putting but, because they are a central tenet of Irish, students can at least be made aware of the reasons for major structural changes not encountered in English. Curious students might reasonably seek reasons for associated pronunciation changes.

The whole tenor of the language course is neutral and it contains nothing to colour pupils' perceptions of Irish, in contrast to many traditional textbooks that use Catholic, nationalist and even republican stereotypes. This tendency to produce material for learners in what Protestants would perceive as a 'biased' manner may often have been unconscious on the part of the authors, but some do seem to have been working to a clear agenda (see, e.g. Mac Póilin, 1999:110). There has been a general shift from texts that tended to lock Irish into a rigid Catholic/nationalist framework. Many such works were written by priests and drew freely on Church traditions and imagery, as shown by the following example in *The New Irish Grammar* (Christian Brothers, 1995):

Ba é an t-easpag féin a bheannaigh an scoil/It was the bishop himself who blessed the school. (p.86)

Most of these texts use 'Irish' names like Máire and Séamas. This in itself is not a criticism as Protestants in County Donegal's

Gaeltacht areas often have such names, but in the more charged political atmosphere of Northern Ireland they could be interpreted as labels. Traditional texts also dwell excessively on nationalist pursuits such as Gaelic football and hurling,[36] with no mention of 'foreign' games like soccer or rugby, with which young Protestants could more readily identify. Teaching materials like these would do little to dispel negative Protestant perceptions of the language.

Even a more secular modern vocabulary for GCSE pupils (Ó hEaráin, 1996:71) mentions 'the Six Counties', a republican description of Northern Ireland which enrages unionists, and, in attempting to show Irish in use in everyday life, includes a photograph of a wall mural depicting an IRA volunteer giving a clenched fist salute, the Maze prison in the background and the slogan '*Chifidh muid éirí na Gealaí*', which means 'We shall see the rising of the moon' (ibid:19). Another illustration commemorates the opening of a leisure centre in west Belfast by Sinn Féin leader Gerry Adams. Such imagery would be unlikely to 'sell' the Irish language to Protestants of any age.

Aspects of a Shared Heritage deliberately avoids anything which might impart a 'Catholic' flavour to the language course. The only personal name used is the neutral 'John', never translated as the Irish equivalent 'Seán' (the name itself is not uncommon among Northern Ireland Protestants, but the spelling 'Shaun' is often used), while the list of sports in the pastimes section includes rugby but not hurling, a pursuit perceived as nationalist. In effect, the language course provides a solid foundation and a neutral backdrop to the other components.

Place names

A session on the place names of Northern Ireland, with particular reference to those within the school catchment area, capitalises on the curiosity most people have about their native place. They provide an easy and non-contentious 'living link' to Irish through English. As Ó Mainnín (1997:4) points out:

The majority of place names which are familiar to us are of Irish origin and survived the decline of the Irish language because they were an integral part of the administrative system by which the country was governed. [...] place names which originated in the Irish language were ... adopted into English and assumed an anglicised dress.

Students see Irish used in a context they can readily understand, especially when it relates to the areas in which they themselves live. ('Dromore', for example, can be broken down to the Irish elements *droim* (meaning ridge) and *mór* (meaning big), giving 'large ridge'. Similarly, 'Ballymoney' can be explained as *baile* (meaning townland) and *monaidh* (meaning moor), giving 'town/land of the moor or bog'.) The session not only shows how Irish/Gaelic place names can be identified and translated, but looks at other influences on the toponymy by later settlers: Vikings, Anglo-Normans and post-Plantation English and Scots.

Surnames

A workshop on the most common surnames of Northern Ireland includes a study of the family names of each student, again providing a non-contentious point of contact with Gaelic. Many pupils with 'English' names are surprised to discover that their family surnames can disguise a Gaelic origin. (The surname 'Wright', for instance, is sometimes an anglicisation of the Irish *Mac an tSaoir*, meaning 'son of the craftsman' [cf. *wright*, as in *wheelwright* or *shipwright*].) Even those whose names are not derived from Gaelic will, of course, have friends and neighbours with 'Irish' connections. As with place names, the curiosity factor provides access to the language in a 'harmless' way.

In the *Aspects of a Shared Heritage* resource pack, Mac Póilin (1997:20) stresses that the study of Gaelic surnames in English, while satisfying, 'is extremely complex'. An exploration of the anglicisation of Irish and Scots Gaelic names during this session illustrates the complexities in an approachable way, but also subtly reinforces the point that – historically at least – the language is not the property of one side or the other in Northern Ireland.

Hiberno-English

This class provides an overview of the influence of the Gaelic languages on the Ulster dialect of English. The process whereby languages which come into contact with and exert an influence on each other is explored in detail and, as with most elements of the course, again places Irish in a non-contentious context. As Hughes (1997:36) says, 'When people, for whatever social or political reasons, stop speaking one language and take up another, they more often than not carry across certain words (lexical items) and phrases from their own native language into the incoming language – not to mention certain phonetic features and elements of word order (or "syntax") etc.'

A particularly strong influence on Hiberno-English is the underlying verbal aspect of Gaelic. The session is illustrated with many examples that students will recognise in their own everyday speech. The expression 'He let on he never heard me', for example, equates to the standard English 'He pretended he didn't hear me' and comes from the Irish 'Lig sé air nár chuala sé mé'.

The Ulster Protestant Gaelic tradition

This class examines the history of the Irish language in Ulster, with reference to the work done by and the influence of members of the Protestant tradition in the previous two centuries (see Chapter One).

The Irish language past and present

This element provides a short history of the Irish language and offers a statement of its present position. Tracing the origins of the language, it places Irish in a broader Celtic setting (especially with regard to Scots Gaelic). It then goes on to examine the decline of Irish as the anglicisation of Ireland in the seventeenth and eighteenth centuries became firmly established. Even so, Ireland still had an estimated four million speakers of the language in the early part of the nineteenth century (Ó Máirtín, 1997:14). The class also looks at the position of Irish in Northern Ireland after Partition, when 'official policies and

SHARED HERITAGE, DIVIDED HORIZONS | 105

attitudes were extremely hostile to the language, with the result that Irish received no official recognition', despite the existence of Irish-speaking areas in Northern Ireland.[37]

In the session, students are also made aware of the present Irish-language revival on both sides of the border. It is stressed that people from all walks of life and from all political backgrounds 'seem genuinely interested in wanting to know about and to learn the language' (ibid:18). A brief look at the expanding Irish-language media sector, involving broadcasters Raidió na Gaeltachta, BBC Radio Ulster and TG4, and the print sector, which includes the weekly newspaper *Foinse*, indicates Irish is not the 'dead' language many perceive it to be.

The Irish language – a Protestant perspective

In this strand an Irish speaker looks at the language from a Protestant perspective, providing students with an opportunity to see that it is possible to remain true to one's unionist beliefs while embracing Irish as a valuable part of a broader heritage. Helping to dispel the notion that only Catholics and republicans speak Gaelic, the talk demonstrates that Irish is a living, versatile language which can be used and abused by those with a political agenda in just the same way that English can. On a number of occasions in the past I took this strand, but I must make it absolutely clear that my lecture was delivered to none of the participants in this research.

In my talks I showed that the republican slogan '*Tiocfaidh ár lá*' ('Our day will come') can easily be countered with '*Ní thiocfaidh bhur lá*' ('Your day will not come!'). Similarly, students learned that '*Dia leis an Bhanríon*' means 'God Save The Queen', a definitive unionist expression of loyalty. I related my own experience as a unionist, living in a strongly loyalist area, who speaks the language. I explored the various reactions – both positive and negative – that flowed from this when friends, family and others realised I use Irish. The aim is to show that Irish belongs to everyone in Northern Ireland. Unlike the class on the Ulster Protestant Gaelic tradition, which is history-centred, this session looks at Irish in a truly contemporary light. I must stress, however, that my delivery method was unique to me – other lecturers who take this strand may make their points in a less personal and direct way.

Our joint musical heritage

An examination of songs and tunes which are common to both 'green' and 'orange' traditions dispels the notion that each 'side' in Northern Ireland has its own music. This session shows that singers and musicians can take a tune from any source and make it work within their own context. In effect 'a tune can cross religious and political divides' (Mullen, 1997:33). During the class the lecturer makes good use of recordings which prove that many tunes which people think of as exclusive to one tradition are often shared by both. One example given is 'Rosc Catha na Mumhan' (Munster's Battle Cry), a stirring 'rebel' ballad, and its 'loyal' alter-ego, 'The Bold Orange Heroes of Comber'. The tune is the same, yet the sentiment entirely different.

The tapes included with the resource pack feature some of the songs discussed during the class, showing that music, like the language itself, is a 'well' from which both sides draw pleasure and inspiration. Students learn, for example, that 'The Sash',[38] a parade-pleasing favourite of loyalist marching bands, shares the same tune as 'Irish Molly-O', which the County Down singer and broadcaster Tommy Sands unearthed in a book published in Philadelphia in 1830:

The Sash
It is old but it is beautiful
And its colours they are fine.
It was worn at Derry, Aughrim,
Enniskillen and the Boyne.
My father wore it as a youth
In the bygone days of yore,
And it's on the Twelfth I love to wear
The Sash my father wore.

Irish Molly-O
She is young and she is beautiful
And her likes I've never known.
She's the lily of old Ireland
And the primrose of Tyrone.
She's the lily of old Ireland
And no matter where I go,
My heart will always hunger for
My Irish Molly-O.

Céilí dancing

This element is only provided if the school is co-educational and has appropriate facilities free during the enrichment course period. On those occasions when it has been held it proved very popular, according to Gael-Linn. As it is not possible to hold the céilí in every school, however, it was not included in my research.

EPGS EVALUATION AND EVOLUTION

Since the introduction of the Enrichment Programme in Gaelic Studies, Gael-Linn has monitored its progress. Over the years, modifications have been made, some as a result of feedback from pupils and others as a result of natural evolution or, occasionally, financial issues. This has seen changes in the way the course is delivered, most notably with regard to the language component. The first stage of evaluation was a natural follow-up to the pilot scheme offered to Sixth Form students in the 1995/96 academic year, when a total of 275 pupils in ten schools took part.

Gael-Linn's own research, following discussions with students who had taken the course, indicated the need for some changes. A lecture on 'Links Between Gaelic Ulster and Gaelic Scotland' was, pupils felt, already covered in 'The Ulster Protestant Gaelic Tradition'; accordingly, these two lectures were amalgamated. Students also wanted to learn more about the state of the Irish language, so the session on the history and present position of Gaelic was introduced, as was the lecture on learning Irish from a Protestant perspective. A large number of students also wanted to have more time devoted to learning Irish itself and Gael-Linn amended the course as far as possible to accommodate this.

A more comprehensive post-pilot evaluation, on which future funding of the EPGS under an EU scheme would depend, was carried out by the Central Community Relations Unit's research branch (CCRU, n.d.). Two focus groups were held, both in the Northern Education and Library Board area. Each group had eight participants (one with six females and two males, the other all female) and key issues were addressed; students were invited to rate the material/lectures, outline their expectations of the course and discuss their feelings about stereotypical images of Protestants and the Irish language. Results indicated that participants had found the course 'useful and interesting', with the language component especially well received, 'particularly as it resulted in more interaction between the participants and the lecturers'. However:

The lack of interaction at other stages of the programme was viewed negatively by all participants. The singing part of the programme was also well received, however overall the consensus was that more time should be spent on language and less on the more cultural aspects of the course. (CCRU:2)

Similarly:

One of the groups stated that they had felt patronised by the lecturer who had talked to them about the role that Protestants had played in encouraging use of the language. Generally the feeling was that this point had been over-emphasised and that the lecturer's assumption that they need to be persuaded to learn the language was unfounded.[39]

The findings from the focus groups were essentially positive and all students said they would be happy to recommend the course to fellow pupils. The music element was described as being 'particularly enjoyable' and the majority 'commented that they would have liked to learn a lot more about the Irish language' (CCRU:4).

Gael-Linn itself continues to monitor the course, with pupils completing simple evaluation forms at the end of the programme to rate the individual components. While the course still has the same objectives as it had in the initial phase, there have been changes. For many years the language element was provided towards the end of each lecture, with time set aside for learning Irish. Today, however, the language classes and the specific lectures are discrete components. This, says Ó Ciaráin (2005), is how the course evolved, in that 'it seemed more effective to send one lecturer/teacher rather than a lecturer and Irish teacher'. He concedes that it has shortcomings with regard to teaching Irish but points out that Gael-Linn in Northern Ireland now only has two full-time staff, where there once were three.

The organisation, while regretting that the AS system has reduced the number of schools able to take part, does not doubt that the scheme has been highly successful in achieving its aims. Following changes in elective module funding, Gael-Linn itself now finances the course in its entirety. The organisation receives core funding from Foras na Gaeilge, and the EPGS is an important part of its programme of work.

As the only group actively involved in this sort of scheme to promote Irish among young Protestants in Northern Ireland's schools, Gael-Linn has found that its remit sometimes goes beyond just language:

> At the very least, the knee-jerk responses of street politics will have been lessened significantly. At one stage, some of the people who went into the schools were fielding broad questions about the Roman Catholic religion and the GAA because there was a genuine lack of understanding about such matters – because of a lack of exposure to anything seen to be from 'the other side of the house'. It is, of course, a two-way understanding. (Ó Ciaráin, 2004)

The EPGS has been 'money well spent' because Gael-Linn was 'asking respected people in the various subject areas to deliver quality, reliable information which was well received'. Ó Ciaráin says that some of the students who took the course may well now be in positions of influence in the civil service and 'are bound to be more open-minded to matters relating to the Irish language and Irish culture'. Equally, he feels that, because everyone on this island lives close to Gaelic in some way – through place names, surnames, Hiberno-English, music and so on – there should be more curriculum space devoted to exploring this heritage:

> A programme such as ours should be part of school studies. We were doing something that the Government should itself have been promoting as an optional part of the curriculum and working to develop resource and learning materials. I would be optimistic that young Protestants can enjoy the Irish language in future. Children were telling us that they wished they had had the opportunity to find out more about the Irish language much earlier in their education.

CONCLUSIONS

The Irish language does not feature on the regular curriculum in Protestant schools in Northern Ireland. While it is available in some integrated schools, most Protestant students do not come into contact with the language in a classroom context. Some non-integrated Protestant schools do sporadically provide enrichment classes of their own in Irish but the number is small. The Gael-Linn course, therefore, broke new ground by making Gaelic studies more widely available, with a programme that offers a brief yet diverse introduction to the language and heritage.

It might be fair criticism to say that at least one contentious area of the current Irish revival is overlooked, namely the predilection of some *Gaeilgeoirí* to blame the language's decline on the 'Brits' or the Stormont government. Then again, such a short course could not possibly be expected to do any more than scratch the proverbial surface and the politics of language is undoubtedly a study in itself.

Unfortunately, changes to the examination structure have been to the detriment of the programme, greatly reducing the number of schools able to set aside time for elective modules. What remains clear is that Gael-Linn has been very careful to develop an enrichment programme that is totally neutral, allowing young Protestants to see that Irish and its associated heritage transcend Northern Ireland's political and tribal boundaries. Consequently, it provides an excellent foundation for an exploration of the views of young Northern Ireland Protestants towards the Irish language.

4

BACKGROUND TO THE SCHOOLS

INTRODUCTION

This chapter examines the Gael-Linn enrichment programme primarily from the perspective of the teachers who facilitate the programme in their schools. Interviews with the teachers are summarised by theme, but points of particular importance are quoted directly. Interview depth varies from subject to subject and, as might be expected, all respondents did not address each topic with the same level of detail. Nonetheless, the interviews provide a 'snapshot' of each college and establish how the EPGS is offered, operated and perceived.

While the chapter is largely based on these semi-structured interviews, additional material has been drawn from prospectuses and official websites to provide a brief factfile, outlining the general demographic and academic reach. 'Transfer' means results achieved in the 11-Plus test, where grade A is the highest. The 'B' category is sub-graded into B1 and B2. Some grammar schools would regard grades C and D as being poor and consequently refuse to accept pupils with such a 'low' grade.

SCHOOL FACTFILES

School A

This school is an all-ability co-educational voluntary grammar, with around 670 pupils and a roughly equal gender breakdown – at the time of research, girls were slightly in the majority. Located in County Armagh, it serves an area that was heavily affected by the Troubles. It was originally a boys-only school but became co-educational during the 1980s. The school is sited in a large town, but pupils come from a wide geographic area that includes many smaller towns and villages. Some of its students are Protestants from the Republic of Ireland.

School A also has a complement of overseas students, including pupils from Africa, England and Hong Kong. It is in a highly mixed region in terms of religion and some of its predominantly Protestant enrolment would live in outlying areas where they and their families would be in the minority. Academically, the school can genuinely be described as 'all-ability', with around a third of its annual intake achieving A at Transfer. Pupils are accepted down to Grade D at Transfer.

School B

This school is an all-ability co-educational grammar, with around 1,200 pupils and a gender breakdown close to 50:50 – at the time research was conducted girls were slightly in the majority. Located in mid County Antrim, it serves what has increasingly become a 'dormitory' town for Belfast and has seen pupil numbers grow dramatically since the 1970s. While the school is sited in a small market town, pupils come from a wide geographic area, including the outskirts of Belfast and various smaller towns and villages in its more immediate rural hinterland. Enrolment reflects its location in a predominantly unionist part of County Antrim – the vast majority of pupils are Protestant. School B has a very high academic profile, taking only A grades from the Transfer procedure in most years, but sometimes accepting B1s.

School C

This school is a boys-only voluntary grammar, with approximately 900 pupils. Located in an area of County Down generally unaffected by the Troubles, pupil numbers have grown considerably in recent years, despite the constraints of a relatively small site: extension and modernisation programmes have been a constant feature of the school's development. While sited in a large town, it has become attractive to many families from outside the area. In addition to accommodating pupils from surrounding towns and villages, a significant number of students are the children of parents who have moved to the area from Belfast in recent years. Enrolment mirrors the school's location in a predominantly unionist area. School C has a reasonably high academic profile. Applicants achieving lower than B2 at Transfer are normally only admitted on regrading to B2 or higher or as a result of requests for consideration on the grounds of special circumstances.

School D

This school is a co-educational voluntary grammar, with around 850 pupils. The gender breakdown is 50:50, although at the time of research approximately 60 per cent of the Sixth Form were girls. Located in northern County Antrim, it has a prestigious reputation. The school is sited in a medium-size market town, serving a largely rural area. Pupils, however, come from much farther afield and the catchment area includes other towns of equal size, as well as many villages. The general area is mainly Protestant but nonetheless comparatively 'mixed' in terms of religion. Consequently, the school population would reflect that. School D has a reasonably high academic profile, accepting down to Grade B2 at the Transfer Test.

School E

School E is a co-educational voluntary grammar school, with close to 1,000 pupils and a gender breakdown of 50:50. Located in the southern part of County Antrim, it has continued to develop in recent years, with ongoing improvement and upgrading work. Regarded as a 'prestige' grammar school, it has a distinctive interdenominational ethos which sets it apart from the other colleges surveyed. A place at the school is highly sought after, as shown by the wide geographical spread of applications. While the school is sited in a strongly unionist town, it prides itself on its ethos and prefers not to speculate on the religious affiliations of its pupils. The general perception, though, is of a 'Protestant' school but the percentage of Catholic pupils is quite high, despite its location. School E has a very high academic profile, generally accepting only Grade As at Transfer. In recent years the only exceptions have been special circumstances/provisions or appeal upgrades.

All of the schools are broadly similar in profile, generally middle/upper-middle class and serving a major town with a large hinterland. School A is slightly different in that it caters for a greater range of academic abilities. Many of its pupils are from areas well outside its natural catchment area because parents who want a grammar-school education for children who have performed badly (or 'failed') in the 11-Plus know that they can 'get in' with lower Transfer grades that would be unacceptable to colleges in, and close to, Belfast.

While all of the schools are located in the eastern half of Northern Ireland, the research covers a wide geographic area that stretches from north to south and covers three counties. Prior to the advent of AS Level, the geographic spread was all-county and Northern-Ireland-wide. Figure 1 below gives details of the religious breakdown in the schools surveyed.

	Protestant	Catholic	Other Christian	Non Christian	None known	Total pupils
Figure 1: Religious breakdown of pupils at specified schools 2004/05						
School B	1,092	14	92	0	24	1,222
School E	644	116	#	*	160	970
School D	724	42	#	*	66	847
School A	586	22	#	*	49	666
School C	741	30	#	*	98	886

Source: NI school census

Note: * relates to less than 5 pupils. # means figure has been suppressed under rules of disclosure.

TEACHER INTERVIEWS IN SUMMARY

Four of the five teachers interviewed in this section were male. Only two were language teachers but the others were involved in coordinating the Gael-Linn course in their capacity as Heads of Year 13/14 (Sixth Form), responsible for the running of enrichment programmes. All were asked the same questions, based on a loose framework which allowed for follow-up probing where necessary. On the rare occasion when it was obvious that an interviewee was uncomfortable with a particular question, it was thought best to move on without further enquiry.

Teacher attitudes to Irish

By means of gentle questioning, it was possible to establish that two of the teachers were from a Protestant background, one from a Catholic background and one from a mixed background. The fifth teacher chose not to specify his religious background.

Of the five teachers interviewed, three had knowledge of – or, at least, some acquaintance with – the Irish language. One interviewee, a Protestant, explained that his mother, having been raised in a border area, had learned Irish at school but the language played no part whatsoever in his upbringing, other than that she (his mother) 'was aware of one or two words and phrases'. He added that some friends and relatives in the Republic could speak Irish but that it was not something he regarded as important:

> I think it is interesting to be aware of the culture of the land we live in but I have no strong feelings either way. I'm not a linguist, so I wouldn't see it as any different from French or German. I wouldn't particularly want to learn the language because, as I said, I'm not a linguist.

Another interviewee, from a mixed-religion background, said he had studied the language for just one year at a school in Belfast but was 'neutral' on the issue. There was no Irish-speaking tradition in his family and, consequently, no 'encouragement or reinforcement' in the home. Conversely, 'there was no negativity towards it either'. While he understood the importance of Gaelic as used in the Gaeltacht areas (which he had visited during his brief flirtation with the language), he had no personal desire to learn (or re-learn) Irish and was scathing of 'wasteful' spending on the language in what he saw as a political context:

It has its place and I'm glad to see that the Irish-medium schools are flourishing and that you have Gaeltachts and Irish-speaking areas. Above and beyond that, I'm not sure there should be much more given to it. I do feel a lot of money is wasted in the Assembly on translating documents. There were some figures recently where the money spent on advertising jobs came to hundreds of thousands of pounds and they had a minimum number of applicants. That doesn't seem to me to be a fair way to spend money.

A third subject – a language teacher – said he had learned Irish at school but not to a high standard. He refused to elaborate on his current facility in Gaelic when pressed. The remaining two interviewees, while happy that the Gael-Linn course was running in their schools, expressed neither strong interest in the language nor any personal desire to learn it.

An attempt was made to establish the importance of the teachers themselves in facilitating Gael-Linn and to what extent their personal commitment to the course ensured its continuation. Of the four teachers questioned (the fifth was involved for the first time), three believed that the EPGS would probably continue even if they were no longer facilitating it. They acknowledged that a change of personnel in any school could lead to changes but felt that the commitment of senior staff to the programme would help guarantee its place in the options programme.

One, however, felt that his role went beyond that of mere facilitator and did not think 'Gael-Linn could just come in and take a course'. This subject took a more 'hands-on' approach than the other interviewees, believing that it was important that a teacher – specifically a language teacher – was present in classes that were, essentially, language-orientated. He was of the opinion that his skills as a language teacher with some Irish meant that he was able to provide reinforcement and augmentation for pupils. Were he not involved, he said, the school would have to find another language teacher with some knowledge of Irish if it were to be able to continue running the course.

Provision and uptake of the Gael-Linn EPGS

All but one of the schools are long-term 'customers' of the Gael-Linn programme and have been operating the course since the late 1990s. The only school not to offer it regularly did participate on a one-off basis around five years previously and only reintroduced it during the year when this research was conducted. It is generally offered by schools under the banner of 'Options' or 'Key Skills' as part of a range of elective non-compulsory subjects for Sixth Form students that last between eight and ten weeks. The schools' options programmes can include Photography, Japanese, Media Studies, Italian, First Aid, Sign Language and the ECDL (European Computer Driving Licence, a Europe-wide standard for computer literacy).

Pupil uptake of the Gael-Linn EPGS varies from school to school and from year to year: one college which normally has an uptake of around sixteen had less than half that figure in the year of research, but enjoyed strong participation the following year. The programme is brought to pupils' attention in different ways: in several of the schools, it is simply listed as one of the options, while in others teachers make a 'sales pitch' to stimulate interest. One teacher said he tries 'to sell it at the start of the year and encourage them as much as possible', adding: 'I don't have any problems at all.'

In another school, a student from the previous year's course will talk it through with potential participants, encouraging them through his or her own experience of the EPGS. This school differs from the others in that the Gael-Linn programme is the only surviving 'extra': pressure on timetabling caused by the introduction of the AS Level has meant that it can only be offered over lunchtime. Nevertheless, it still attracts a healthy audience and the teacher concerned believes it is to the pupils' credit that so many are prepared to surrender their free time to attend:

We would like to have timetabled it in: we think the school sees it as something valuable. It does mean a sacrifice on their part: they have to bring their lunch with them. The fact that it's their free time and they're having to make a sacrifice shows a certain degree of commitment. If it was done during another class and they were getting time off to do it you could understand. But this is totally their free time and they are making the sacrifice.

All teachers interviewed were highly critical of the AS Level structure, which has severely restricted the time for options. And even when elective modules remain available, pupils cannot necessarily avail of them. One interviewee pointed out that students who are already struggling with timetabled subjects sometimes have to jettison any 'extras', while another said that the amount of pressure meant that 'something had to give' and struggling pupils might have to be taken out of extra-curricular activities to allow them to concentrate on exam priorities:

> Unfortunately, the examination system seems to dictate the educational process. I'm not very happy with it, but it's the system we have. Something that doesn't have a certificate or a particular qualification won't count – even if it's the most interesting lesson in the world – unless it's on the exam. So I think the numbers have gone down because of that.

Another teacher pointed out that the EPGS had originally been offered in all three terms and ran successfully on that basis until the AS Level was introduced. Now, he noted, it is only viable for one term each year and 'appears to be declining in popularity'. Nonetheless, this school is 'very keen to keep it'. Similarly, another interviewee explained that the course had to be run in the first term in his school because pupils could not afford to take on any extra work after Christmas:

> The pressure of exams means that anything that's not essential tends to drift off and this would be one of those. We had in the past tried to offer two terms to cater for those who couldn't make it in the first term but, despite our good intentions, come the end of Christmas they realised they couldn't do it after all – not because of the content but because of all the pressures there. It

extends to sports too. After Christmas, rugby-wise, the Firsts and Seconds would continue, but the Thirds' and Fourths' season would end.

Despite the pressure caused by AS, the Gael-Linn programme has survived in these schools, even if the numbers are smaller and the courses run less frequently – but it must be borne in mind that around twenty colleges in every part of Northern Ireland ran the EPGS in the year prior to the examination's introduction.

Reactions to the course

All teachers reported that the course had been a success, reflected in the continuing participation of a healthy number of students, although some qualified its relevance in different ways. One teacher saw it as 'slotting in to the whole concept of living in a multicultural society'. Another felt that pupils today are highly conscious of the importance of a good Curriculum Vitae and realised that having some – albeit limited – acquaintance with the Irish language might be useful when applying for jobs. He continued:

> A lot of kids would see it as something they could put on their CV, something to broaden their outlook on life and to broaden their appeal. The kids today are very focused on what's in it for them. There has to be a point in it – UCAS points, how's it going to help me get to university? And they can see value in Gaelic Studies as something they can put on their CV, something to talk about.

All teachers said that their schools were very comfortable with running the course and would continue to do so as long as the demand was there. One was quite specific on the issue of numbers, however, saying that she would want a minimum of 14 or 15 and would not want to bring in Gael-Linn lecturers for a handful of pupils.

Despite all schools being 'comfortable' with the course, several teachers were keenly aware of the broader political context outside the school gates and made sure that pupils knew what was involved before they signed up to the course. One stressed that he explained to them that the language was examined from 'a fairly broad perspective'. Another said he 'wanted to make sure people knew what they were letting themselves in for and what the course consisted of'.

Although clearly mindful of the areas in which their schools are located, and of associated political sensitivities, none reported any negative reaction to the course. It's not unusual for a few pupils to start the course and leave after the first week – but this was seen as something that happens with most courses. One interviewee conceded that opposition to the programme among some pupils probably did exist but did not have an impact upon its effective operation:

> There has not been any open resistance. I thought there might have been, given the nature of our country, but it hasn't been the case. There would be a few who definitely wouldn't be involved themselves but there's never any pressure on their peers: there's never any antagonism that way. They have their own personal views. They don't want to do it; that's up to them. Fine.

The school referred to in the above quotation is in a deeply divided area where sectarian tensions run high. A number of pupils lost parents during the Troubles but events outside the gates have rarely intruded and the school interacts well with its Catholic counterparts in the area. The small Catholic minority at the school is well integrated. Even so, the interviewee was surprised – 'given the potential for tension and trouble' – that the Gael-Linn course has never encountered opposition. 'Despite a bit of reluctance, word of mouth sells it,' he said.

Another interviewee said that a few pupils would always say 'No, that's not for me: I want nothing to do with it', once the nature of the course was explained to them but were happy to leave it at that. All of the schools, bar one,[40] list the EPGS in their prospectuses, meaning that parents are aware that it is on offer to their children. No attempt is made to 'conceal' the course. One teacher said he understood the potential for negative reaction and consequently advised pupils to go home and discuss it with their parents before they started the course, thus 'defusing any problems in advance'. However, none of the teachers interviewed were aware of any hostile reaction or complaints from parents or local politicians.

Despite some personal criticisms (see below), four of the five teachers believed that the course enjoys a positive reaction from students, who, they said, find it 'interesting and informative', 'relevant', 'very positive' and 'non-threatening'; the other teacher, having only reintroduced the course after a long gap, said that the options programme would be reviewed and pupils' opinions surveyed at the end of the school year. She was, however, encouraged by the number who chose the Gaelic Studies option and felt that it would probably run again if sufficient numbers expressed interest. All were of the opinion that the course was a valuable part of the curriculum in their schools.

When asked if they thought an equivalent course in Ulster-Scots, including language, piping and Scottish Country/Highland Dancing, for example, would be equally well received, two of the five were highly sceptical. One described Ulster-Scots as 'nonsense' and a 'vocabulary-driven dialect' which would be a waste of time to learn. Pupils' time, the teacher said, would be badly misspent on something that was 'like part of the PC movement'. The other teacher who shared this view refused to even discuss the potential of Ulster-Scots as either an alternative or companion to the Gael-Linn course.

On the other hand, one school had actively considered the possibility of introducing Ulster-Scots:

> Just to redress the balance. We talked about this before, perhaps finding a grouping that could maybe offer something, but I haven't done anything about that yet. Such a course might be useful, but no group has approached us.

Another teacher also thought that such a course might be useful, but seemed to look at the issue primarily as one of providing a counterbalance to Gael-Linn's EPGS. He said:

> In many ways, I think their [the pupils'] attitude to that would be

similar. That might make it easier to sell [the Gael-Linn course] in some respects. If such a course were available, I think we would consider running it too. I think you'd want something that combines both, rather than two separate courses.

The final interviewee on this topic thought that it might be useful to have some representation from the 'other' culture but doubted that pupils would see the 'value' in Ulster-Scots when compared to Irish, a language that was both 'used' and 'recognised'. He believed that Irish gives his students 'an extra dimension' but thought it unlikely that Ulster-Scots would give them 'anything extra'.

Problems and criticisms

All of the teachers who had at some stage sat in on lectures were generally happy with the way the course operates (one deliberately did not sit in as she 'did not want to put pupils off', while another made a point of listening to every speaker and 'found it hard not to become involved').

However, two of the five teachers identified problems with the course and believed Gael-Linn should take steps to improve the delivery in the classroom. One teacher felt that Gael-Linn, in an attempt to make the course as appealing to as many pupils as possible, deliberately played down the amount of language content in the EPGS:[41]

Sometimes I think people assume there will be negativity there and they tend to play down the amount of language content in the course. I would take the opposite view – that it's better for them to know and be clear about what you are offering and then people can decide whether it's for them or not.

This interviewee voiced another concern:

Sometimes a reservation I would have would be with the quality of people delivering the course. You're not always sure whether they have the [classroom] experience and whether they can cope with that. I've witnessed one or two [lectures] which I thought weren't particularly good: not so much in terms of the content, more in terms of the way they were delivered.

He continued by saying that a lack of quality in delivery impacted on the pupils' attitudes to the content and suggested that Gael-Linn take a closer look at how its lecturers operate in the classroom: if lecturers failed to hold attention and, for example, pupils started chatting among themselves, even those who did find the subject interesting would feel frustrated and get less from it. Generally, though, he was very satisfied with the standard of lecturers.

Another teacher's criticism centred on bad timekeeping on the part of the guest lecturers, whom he described as 'notoriously poor' in that regard:

They don't realise that a school [period] ends at a certain time when a bell goes and the most fascinating topics are not interesting after the bell has gone. And some don't realise the pupils are about to go for their fifteen-minute break and it would take something absolutely exceptional to be more interesting. And the number of times you hear 'Oh, and another thing', or 'Here's another interesting word', but it's no longer interesting after the bell.

This interviewee conceded that his criticism may have been harsh as the speakers have to give lectures in a number of schools, with different period lengths, and may find it difficult to adapt. He felt that just a little more cognisance of the timetable in a particular school on the part of the guest lecturers would overcome the problem.

However, while lecturers have a duty to the school, the school has a reciprocal responsibility. One guest speaker interviewed said that he normally had no difficulty in the classroom but felt that seating arrangements could sometimes be a problem. He gave the example of a classroom set out in discussion-group format (from a previous class), which meant that pupils were arranged in small insular groups more suited to intensive face-to-face discussion than class-wide learning. He said:

> It's very difficult to connect with discrete groups, particularly if the tables are arranged so that pupils are facing each other, rather than the lecturer. As a guest in the school did I have the right to ask the students to change the seating to suit my lecture? Sometimes I feel it would be useful if a teacher was in the room for a few minutes at the start to make sure everything is set up satisfactorily.

CONCLUSIONS

Teachers in the schools surveyed seem happy with the EPGS and view it as an important options choice. Indeed, the fact that students in one school are prepared to give up their free time to take the course is a firm indication of its appeal. This school has continued to make the course available at a time when all other optional modules have disappeared, demonstrating a dual commitment from staff and pupils. Equally, in a period when the strictures of AS Level have killed off options programmes, it is to the credit of the other schools that they have ring-fenced valuable timetable space for a subject that might be viewed with suspicion in Protestant schools.

The non-political nature of the Gael-Linn course must be a factor in the equation and some of the teachers interviewed seemed almost surprised that Irish could be taught in a 'non-threatening' way. It was apparent that some adopted a more 'hands-on' approach to the course than others but all were aware of the content and the methods.

The criticisms were few: that guest speakers over-run their time is a charge that could probably be levelled at many visitors unused to speaking in schools. However, the view expressed by one subject – that classroom delivery was not always up to standard – might be something that Gael-Linn could usefully examine. From the opposite perspective, schools have to make sure that the class geography and facilities are correctly geared towards lecturers' needs.

In conclusion, there is a high satisfaction level among the teachers who facilitate Gael-Linn. Despite the fact that they acknowledge that some pupils might not be happy to participate in the EPGS themselves, open opposition to the course is negligible and the commitment of the schools to the programme is not in doubt.

5
LETTING THE YOUNG
PEOPLE SPEAK

INTRODUCTION

School 'backgrounders' and interviews with the teachers who facilitate Gael-Linn provide a basic introduction to the scheme and how it is perceived. More important, though, are the views of the 'consumers' – the pupils – and this chapter is a summary of focus group sessions held in four of the schools (one school was not able to facilitate a focus group).[42] Six pupils participated in each group, three who had done the Gael-Linn course and three who had not. Focus groups generate a tremendous amount of material and it is necessary to break this down into manageable units. Therefore, the transcripts were examined closely to identify recurring themes.

A semi-structured approach was employed, allowing a certain degree of consistency across the groups, but pupils were encouraged to 'lead' the dialogue as far as possible. Issues were not necessarily addressed in the same order each time, but pupils had the opportunity to introduce new themes and ideas not covered by the questionnaire. This meant that the groups produced interesting and sometimes unexpected information but also yielded irrelevant asides and cul-de-sacs: material that is deemed to be too far off-topic will not be reported but, as with the teacher interviews, important points and exchanges between pupils will be quoted directly.

Towards the end of the chapter, in an attempt to evaluate the course and summarise the views of all research participants, material from the focus groups is augmented by additional qualitative information provided by several open-ended questions included in the questionnaire.

'THINK IRISH, THINK ...'

After the introductions and an explanation of the research project, members of each group were asked to state what word or phrase came to mind when they thought of 'Irish'. The item, while light-hearted and an extension of the ice-breaking process, revealed a wide range of perceptions and associations, some decidedly negative. Responses included:

The south of Ireland	*Catholics*
Munster	*TG4*
Tiocfaidh Ár Lá	*POP 4 (an Irish pop show)*
Pointless	*Old-fashioned*
Road signs	*Republican*
Politicians	*Dead language*
Green	*Union*
Ireland	*Politics*

This simple exercise gave a foretaste of some of the main themes which were to recur during the focus groups.

PERCEPTIONS OF IRISH

When asked to explore their opinions on Irish, the focus group participants used two primary discourses, politics and culture.

Irish as 'politics'

Politics and the language was a theme which came speedily to the fore in the focus groups. The issue was on the interview schedule but in some cases pupils raised it right at the beginning (as seen in the 'ice-breakers' above), indicating its importance to them as something that helped shape their opinions of Irish.[43] There was almost total agreement with the perception that the language is too closely associated with republicanism and this, they felt, discouraged Protestants and unionists from developing any interest in it.

There was little difference between course-takers and non-takers on this issue. One respondent summed up the views of many when he said he felt it would be automatically assumed that an Irish speaker would be Catholic and nationalist/republican. The terms 'Catholic', 'nationalist' and 'republican' were a constant refrain and seemingly interchangeable (in the same way, perhaps, that 'Protestant', 'unionist' and 'loyalist' are used):

> … whenever you ask me about Irish, I just think 'Catholic'. That's the one word that triggers in my mind.

> I would probably think 'Catholicism' or something like that.

> … it sort of comes across as sort of like Irish nationalism …

> Oh aye, it's a republican thing.

Sinn Féin was castigated by respondents for 'hijacking' the language. Party leader Gerry Adams, who occasionally speaks Irish in television interviews, came under fire for using it in his speeches. As mentioned earlier, MORI found that for some he is 'the most famous speaker' of Irish in Northern Ireland (2006:4). Continual references to him by participants seem to confirm his perceived status as the highest-profile *Gaeilgeoir* in Northern Ireland, but his competence in the language was questioned by pupils who were doubtful about his fluency:

> Like, sometimes he just sounds really awful, sort of struggling with it. I think a lot of people even in Sinn Féin probably don't speak that much either.

Even setting Adams' 'halting delivery' (McCoy, 2006:151) aside, another pupil saw the equation in simple terms:

> You see, like, Gerry Adams on television doing speeches entirely in Irish. You think, 'Oh, the Irish language' – you connect it with Sinn Féin and maybe with the IRA.

However, the 'instant assumption' that Catholics would understand Adams when he spoke in Irish was wrong, according to a participant who rightly pointed out that being a Catholic did not automatically mean that one either empathised with or understood the language.

Sinn Féin as a whole was accused of using Irish as a political tool to 'play on the idea of Irish culture and try to stir up more nationalist feeling'. Some pupils thought that republicans used the language in a 'provocative' way and were culturally 'showing off', sometimes to the extent of being 'elitist'. One believed that Catholic speakers had an 'I can speak Irish and you can't. Look at me!' attitude.

Several respondents in different groups were sceptical about Sinn Féin's use of Irish in election and promotional material and doubted its value even to the party's own supporters.

A lot of people, like, just sort of at a very basic [Sinn Féin] party level probably look at the leaflets with the Irish on it and just think 'What's going on?'

Even when you see the election posters for them, it says '*Vótáil*', which is 'Vote' in Irish. They just use it for that. You don't need to put '*Vótáil*' up, because it wouldn't make any difference. It's just stuck on there because it's a Sinn Féin thing and it's Irish.

There was nonetheless an alternative 'take' on the politics issue, one respondent suggesting that the perceived linkage between Sinn Féin and Irish was being deliberately 'pushed' by the unionist parties, making it an unattractive proposition for Protestants. Another respondent accused the DUP in general and the then party leader Ian Paisley in particular of 'creating this illusion of fear'. While the general consensus was that the language had been 'hijacked' by republicans, several pupils used an alternative discourse in suggesting that Protestants and unionists may have 'surrendered' it. The following extract sums up this train of thought:

GARETH: It [Irish] should be both for Protestants and Catholics but I think, like, the Irish language, Catholics have ...

JOHN: ... hijacked it!

GARETH: Hijacked it!

SUSAN: Do you not think, maybe, they haven't hijacked it, it's just that we've ...

GARETH: Surrendered!

KAREN: Yeah, we've ...

The debate became very animated and noisy at this stage and, unfortunately, with several pupils talking at once, was impossible to transcribe accurately. The hijacked thesis was also rejected elsewhere:

I think it's unfair how the language has been, like, not hijacked, but all the politics have gone into the language. Like the way you automatically assume that Protestants don't know Irish.

In a different group exchange, a participant leapt to the defence of Adams, although 'Victoria' found herself very much in the minority:

VICTORIA: He has every right to speak it [Irish]. It's his language. He can speak it if he wants to.

SAMANTHA: Yeah, he can, but he doesn't have to force it on other people.

VICTORIA: He's not forcing it on other people just because he's speaking his native language.

SAMANTHA: All the jobs which are advertised in Irish ... it costs a lot of extra money to the taxpayer to have to translate everything into Irish when most people speak English.[44]

VICTORIA: That's their problem then. They should be learning the language of their country.

The language was regarded by many as being 'just for the Catholic side of the community', although another point cogently argued by one participant was that associations made between religion and language can be disingenuous. France, he said, was a 'Catholic country', yet learning French in no way meant that one would be perceived as Catholic.

Even though the 'Catholic language' discourse was often used, it was Sinn Féin and broader republican engagement with the language that was viewed as the most negative and 'off-putting' factor, because it seemed to be part of a wider unpleasant agenda that respondents could not identify with:

As soon as you say Irish, I think, sort of, Sinn Féin, with their rhetoric of 'everyone should be speaking Irish' to try and influence towards, like, as if we're united: like, the one island and everything.

While virtually all respondents thought that Irish was too politicised, most believed it was a pity that it had been brought into the political arena in the first place:

I don't think that the Irish language should have anything to do with how people feel about politics. It shouldn't matter what language people speak. They shouldn't be pigeonholed into a specific way of thinking just because of the language they speak.

I think, because it is politicised, then we see it as something that brings the divide between Protestants and Catholics and, right, so we've no interest in it.

Irish as 'culture'

Students often saw Irish not as an item in its own right, but as part of a broader culture, with negative and positive connotations. A majority of respondents in one group, for example, defined this culture as 'Catholic' and 'nationalist'. For them, 'Irish culture' was tied to republican ideals and several expressed the view that it was an integral part of life 'down South' (i.e. in the Republic) but did not have the same meaning in Northern Ireland.

One respondent felt that the language was not central to 'Irish' culture and believed it could be easily bypassed:

> You don't have to learn a language to get into the culture. You can read some Yeats, you can read some Heaney – sort of, you can get the Irish culture that way. You don't have to do it through the language.

McMinn (1992:52) observes that third-level Protestant students often come to university with little knowledge of Irish literature, language or culture and some respondents felt that they had been deprived of a substantial grounding in this 'Irish dimension', history in particular having been the subject of a passing glance rather than a 'real focus':

> Irish culture's more about the history. In the school here we did a wee bit about the history, like the Rebellion, but there was no sort of culture side to it.

In one focus group participants spent a great deal of time debating the stance of the Gaelic Athletic Association (GAA) on the playing of other sports at its prestigious Croke Park headquarters in Dublin. At the time this group was held, the GAA was embroiled in controversy over its ban on 'foreign sports', primarily rugby and soccer, but a few weeks later (in April 2005) gave permission for the national teams to use the stadium. Another GAA ban on members of the security forces in Northern Ireland from taking part in its games (the controversial Rule 21) had been lifted in 2001 after a special congress in Dublin, but remained a talking point for students:

> WILLIAM: Actually, I quite like the Irish culture ... but you see

when it comes to sport ... My da was in the police and he wouldn't be allowed to join it by the rules.[45] I mean, that's complete discrimination. So I have absolutely no respect for Gaelic football or hurling.

TREVOR: It does, like, give it an identity. If I saw either of those sports, you know, I would think of Irish. You would just think Ireland and Irishness if you saw those sports.

This group discussed the matter at length and several participants accused the GAA of inviting people to look at and admire 'their culture' from the outside while not allowing them 'in' or to get too close. 'Trevor' described the GAA as 'insular' and guilty of 'bigotry'. Most Protestants have always been wary of the organisation and in its early years it drew in those of whom they would naturally have been suspicious (Ó hUallacháin, 1994:57; Pritchard, 2004:5). In Northern Ireland, sport often provides an arena for the playing out of complex identity issues, combining perceptions of ethnicity, religious affiliation and culture that go beyond mere games (Barnier, 2003). Cosgrove (2003:62), for example, proffers a delightful account of Catholic reluctance to publicise any personal love of leather and willow: cricket, after all, was a game 'for the cold-blooded race that tried – and tried in vain – to impose their petty will on the civilised world!'

Sport, however, had fewer negative connotations in other groups. In one, a young Protestant said he had made some friends in the Republic through rugby, while another – from a mixed religious background – said that he had played Gaelic football and hurling. Some of the other male respondents voiced a certain curiosity about Gaelic sports and expressed disappointment that they had never had the opportunity to play football and hurling.

Pupils in a different group viewed the annual St Patrick's Day celebrations as a divisive expression of 'Irish culture', saying that Protestants were not welcome at the parade in Belfast. Even though one pupil said that she personally celebrated St Patrick's Day, her counterparts in the group drew parallels between the 'hijacking' of the Irish language and perceived 'Catholic' appropriation of 17 March.[46]

For some years, the St Patrick's Day celebrations were seen by Protestants as a triumphal 'Greenfest' for nationalists and republicans, particularly in Belfast, where the carnival was for a long time organised by 'an exclusively nationalist/republican organisation', with the result 'that many people felt unwelcome or excluded' (Long, 2006). Some pupils were convinced that the 'carnival' had an inbuilt anti-unionist/Protestant chill-factor:

I see it [Irish] like St Patrick's Day, for Protestants aren't really welcomed in Belfast [on 17 March].

I think if you'd gone into Belfast [during the parade] with the Union Jack, it wouldn't have lasted too long.

Another interviewee's view of the celebrations in his town was neutral and he hinted at a 'pick-and-mix' approach to culture by saying that he 'enjoyed the flutes and that there' but could not tolerate Irish dancing (presumably on aesthetic grounds). St Patrick's Day was a good example of how some respondents interpreted Irish as one part of a broader nationalist cultural agenda that was anathema to them. Invited to summarise his feelings on Irish, a respondent replied: 'Catholics! Probably just Irish culture: the tricolour, the language.' During this discussion on St Patrick's Day, the Twelfth of July, a Protestant/unionist celebration with which many Catholics would have difficulties, was not mentioned.

Attitudes towards 'Irish culture', however, were not unrelentingly negative and many participants saw certain aspects in a kinder light without making an explicit link between it and Sinn Féin as they had with the Irish language on its own. A number of female respondents had learned Irish dancing as children and even though all had since stopped attending classes, they seemed to look upon it with fondness. This is not necessarily a surprise, as Irish dancing has long been popular with both communities and is a staple of annual traditional festivals in many parts of Northern Ireland. Indeed, the activity seems to be gaining in popularity with young Protestants, some classes even being held in Orange halls (*Sunday Times*, 'Irish dancing reels in Protestant fans', 16/3/2008, p.11).

Similarly, some spoke of Irish music in positive terms, though the tendency was to mention instantly recognisable 'Irish' pop bands such as U2 and Westlife rather than traditional music. The definitively 'Irish' drink Guinness also got an occasional light-hearted mention. These are possibly best seen as contemporary Irish 'brands', owing less to Gaelic heritage and more to the power of advertising. Nonetheless, several respondents said that they occasionally tuned in to the Irish-language television channel TG4 to watch pop music programmes and rugby matches.[47]

Some students adopted a positive attitude to Irish as culture and felt that it could help to make them more attuned to the world around them. One thought that knowledge of Irish could help to 'bring back' a culture which was 'dying out completely' (discussed below as a separate theme). Another said:

> I think it's [Irish] a positive thing, because you don't just learn the words and the language, you learn the culture and where it originated from and there's a tradition and everything to do with it. I think that's a good thing.

IRISH IN A WIDER CONTEXT

When asked to consider Irish as something with potential 'real-world' value, shorn of any political or cultural connotations, participants often rooted their responses in a contemporary and global context. In general, there was only limited perception of Irish as being a viable means of everyday communication, not surprising, perhaps, given that few, if any, of those who took part in the discussions would have had first-hand experience of Gaeltacht areas and the living language.

The European dimension/globalisation

Across all groups, many students placed Irish in a wider discourse of linguistic viability. For them, the language's value was more likely to be estimated not in terms of historical or cultural richness, but by where it was positioned in an unspoken league table of relevance. For some students, Irish did not feature as a 'useful language' which had any practical application:

> ... we're all moving into this European thing and it's probably better to learn French or German or Spanish or whatever.

> To me, Latin is far more important and, you know, Queen's [University] took away their Classics Department. Latin is important and we should be doing it. Like, it's basically the stem of every European language ...

This student, who was probably the most forceful voice in his group, had very definite opinions on language issues and thought that learning Irish (and Ulster-Scots) was 'insular'. His argument on the merits of studying Latin was perhaps at odds with the 'useful language' discourse, but he returned to the theme with his views on the 'core' European languages:

> You know, we don't get offered Spanish here. You get French and German but I don't get Spanish. It's like, one of the biggest languages in the world. So I'd prefer to learn that than some crappy Ulster-Scots or Irish that nobody barely even in our own island can understand.

Others shared this sentiment, one suggesting that people in Northern Ireland had a duty to become more 'cosmopolitan' by learning European languages:

> Obviously, we're moving towards the whole European thing, so we actually need to get more involved with their language[s]. You know, you hear about other countries over in Europe like, sort of feeling offended when an English person or someone from Ireland is coming over and expecting everyone there to speak their language.

Only one student mentioned the increasing importance of Eastern European languages, such as Polish and Lithuanian. He suggested that attention should be paid to them. That the point was little mentioned is no surprise, as the influx of migrant workers to Northern Ireland from the former Soviet Bloc was a new development at the time the groups were held. But it is now a very significant matter and will be examined in the final chapter.

Irish was not regarded as something likely to be of use in the job market, whereas facility in 'European languages' was considered an advantage by some. 'Would Irish help me get a job?' was a question posed by many participants. Most thought not. However, there were those who believed that all language learning was useful and that Irish had a value in this context, even if it was merely a matter of being polite:

> Say you had to deal with someone down South, it might be easier to talk to them through it.

A 'dead language'

The word-association exercise in the ice-breakers session gave an early hint of some of the themes which would be raised in the groups. Aside from the obvious political references, responses had included some very negative terms such as 'pointless', 'old-fashioned' and 'dead language'. The terminology reflected the views of many on the current position of Irish, as they saw it, but as they expanded on the theme it became clear that some still regarded Irish as being of value – although not as a means of communication in twenty-first-century Europe.

> I think that it's a worthwhile language that is dying out but it's a shame.

> I'd like to learn it, but I think it would be good if it was actually a proper language in Ireland as the predominant language.

LETTING THE YOUNG PEOPLE SPEAK | 139

I think Irish is useful to know but it's not really that important in, like, today's society. But it's a good thing to have just for interest, like.

The 'dead language' discourse was a common refrain during this segment and there was a view among some that Irish was a 'language of old people':

I don't have anything against people speaking Irish but, I think, probably the older generation ... I think they still speak it but I don't think there should be much point bringing it into our generation. Because will it actually carry on?

Another respondent concurred:

I don't have anything against people speaking it. Like, as part of their culture or whatever but I just don't see what the benefit in teaching children it is, because it is dying out and there is no point to it.

Disconnection from Irish was another feature of this strand and a female respondent made the point that a lack of family connections with Irish made it more or less irrelevant to her:

Maybe if my family spoke it, like my granny or granda or whatever. It's not part of what I've been brought up in, so to me it's not something I would want to learn.

Another respondent used a similar disconnection discourse, but also had other reasons for not wanting to learn Irish, citing culture and religion:

The only way I would learn it was if it was part of my culture, but it doesn't feel as if it is because it is mainly used by Catholic people, so I've no real urge to go out and learn it.

A common manifestation of this 'disconnection' theme was the perception among some respondents that while Irish had a certain resonance in the Republic of Ireland, it impacted little on life in Northern Ireland, apart from in political and religious ways. 'Down South' was something 'we're kind of separated from'. The 'South' overtly displayed its Irishness through place names, road signs and 'things like that'. This speaker added: 'But you don't really get much of it up here at all. I think when you go down South, there's a whole Irish culture really comes through.' While his rationale is sound, and all pupils learn Irish in school, the reality of an 'Irish Ireland' is quite different.[48]

Whatever the realities of the Republic's 'Irishness', however, another participant felt that the presence of the border meant that Northern Ireland republicans and nationalists were just as 'disconnected' from it as loyalists and unionists.

Those with negative opinions appeared to appreciate that Irish had a cultural value (even if it was part of a culture they did not understand or found distasteful) but did not equate this with real currency in today's world, again drawing upon European and global discourses. Irish, they felt, was not a 'universal language' and consequently irrelevant beyond the British Isles:

> ... outside of this island, no one cares really. Like, I'm sure there's plenty of people don't even realise that Ireland has a different language other than English. I think it's just completely pointless.

> I think if you calculated how many, like, the percentage of people, who speak it, it would be very low.

Other than through the course, few students had had any contact with Irish, although some had friends – Protestant and Catholic – who had learned the language in their schools 'down South'. One female student had been part of a cross-community programme in which young Protestants and young Catholics from all over Northern Ireland attended a series of workshops culminating in a fortnight in

America (see, e.g. McCafferty, 2001:100–102). She noted that some of the Catholic teenagers had occasionally spoken in Irish:

> But they didn't speak it in front of us to, like, speak to each other about us. Like, if they were asked to speak something, the Americans were quite impressed by it.

Irish had not featured formally in the group discussions and workshops associated with the exchange but this speaker, and others who had been on foreign holidays, found that merely being from 'Ireland' had a certain cachet when abroad (see Kramsch, 1998:69). They discovered that trying to explain the difference between 'Ireland' and 'Northern Ireland' was pointless and accepted that they were simply 'Irish', if only when away from home (McCoy, 2006:163). As one respondent put it:

> Especially when you're away on holiday, like, they don't say, 'Oh, you're Northern Irish'. They would just take it you're from Ireland and I wouldn't have any problem with that. I wouldn't have any strong view in correcting them, like saying, 'I'm from Northern Ireland'.

This mindset sits comfortably with Simone Zwickl's study of ethnic identities across the Northern Ireland/Republic border. She discovered that Protestants found it difficult to explain their nationality abroad and some did not object to being called Irish 'either because they considered the Irish to be more popular or because they could understand the mistake' (2002:86). Being British but having an Irish identity abroad may well just be a question of pragmatism.

Some participants had had little meaningful contact with Catholics at all, other than through school initiatives to bring young people from both sides together. Most agreed that these contacts had been positive and a few had kept in touch with those they had met through the programmes, but their 'core values' had not changed:

> You realise that, even though you have strong views, it doesn't mean that other people's views and other people's opinions don't

count. You end up understanding where they're coming from but, also for me, I think it made me believe a lot stronger in my background and, like, where I'd come from.

One point was clear, though – the Irish language was never discussed or raised by either side in these cross-community contacts.

PEERS AND PERCEPTIONS

Thus far, Irish has been considered in a variety of contexts: political, cultural and global. Equally important, of course, is how the students felt about Irish in their own communities and environments.

Family reactions and peer pressures

Most of those who had taken the Gael-Linn enrichment programme had not encountered any hostility from family or peers about learning Irish. A minority, however, had. One participant, for example, reported that some of his classmates had been less than favourable, while the reaction at home had been mixed:

> ... my mum didn't really care. My dad was brought up sort of really hard-line in an estate in Belfast. He's always been of the opinion ... he was a bit weird about that. I think he was quite pleased when he found out that it'd [the course] stopped.

The reactions encountered by this participant were the exception rather than the rule. Other interviewees said the response had ranged from 'indifferent' to 'interested', although one had been on the receiving end of 'the odd hint or slag'.[49] A respondent reported that her classmates thought the EPGS group were 'weird' – not because they were learning Irish, but because they were giving up their lunchtimes to do it. These responses were playful rather than threatening. She found that the reaction at home had been neutral:

I don't think they [my parents] were that bothered either way. Like, they didn't think it was a really good thing and they didn't think it was a really bad thing. They'd never a strong opinion either way.

For another attender, reaction in the home had been highly favourable:

Well, I minded to tell my da, and he actually thought it was a good thing, like learning about town names and stuff and where places originated from and where they got their names. He said it was a good thing.

Speculating on what the home reaction would have been had he done the course, a non-attender said his parents might wonder why he was learning Irish as he had never been 'brought up in a way that, you know, Irish is seen as okay'. He concluded that they would probably not have been 'hugely accepting of it'. Conversely, a fellow non-attender who had identified himself with strongly unionist beliefs throughout the group session said that his dad would be pleased 'because he hates narrow-mindedness'.

Although the majority of attenders had not met with hostility from friends or family members, there was a broad acknowledgement that peer pressure could determine whether one decided to learn Irish or not:

I would admit different people's opinions can affect, you know, whether you want to learn it or not. Yeah, some people want you opposed to it, even close friends or family. That can influence your decision whether to learn it or not.

This speaker was not alone: several felt that potentially negative reactions could discourage them from learning Irish and one implied that this was the reason he had not done the Gael-Linn course, although he had initially wanted to:

... it was the sort of pressure at the start. I think maybe your friends all being in bands[50] and stuff saying, 'Oh, you call yourself a Protestant and all, why're you going to go and do that there?' So there's that pressure sort of putting you off.

He thought it might have been easier to learn Irish outside school because his friends would not have known. In school, of course, peers would be aware of what subjects their friends were taking. Peer pressure, though, was not limited to what he called 'diehard Protestants' and he thought those with avowedly moderate views would 'probably still be opposed'.

A pupil in the same group said that peer pressure was unavoidable among teenagers, who had to be doing the 'in thing'. No one wanted to be 'rejected' or 'thought of as a freak' (see, e.g. Hudson, 2004:15). He had attended the course but shrugged off peer pressure by making light of the issue and, furthermore, believed that many of those who were 'slagging' him were envious that he had done the classes:

I tried to get boys and all to come to it, like, but they just slag you. You're saying to them, 'Why don't you come on and find out what it's like? How can you slag it off if you've never been?' You know there's ones interested in it, like.

Reservations, respect and role models

Many participants acknowledged that Protestant/unionist Irish speakers in Northern Ireland could find their politics and beliefs called into question and this was perhaps the more sinister side of the peer pressure equation. 'Labelling' was identified as a problem in Northern Ireland:

It's not what Church you're affiliated with. You're not Presbyterian, you're Protestant. Or maybe you're Catholic. If I went and spoke Gaelic here, people would probably look at me and think ... you know, the knee-jerk reaction would be that I was a Catholic.

A minority of interviewees admitted that they themselves would have reservations about an Irish speaker who claimed to be Protestant or unionist because they did not believe it was possible to be both. They stopped short of saying they would be suspicious, but conceded that they might have difficulty in understanding why someone from such a background would speak Irish, because 'you wouldn't know where they're coming from'.

> I don't mind, but I would just have to sit and think about why someone who came from a unionist background, [who] seemingly wanted to keep the Union, would want to go and learn something which to me is associated with Ireland and, you know, nationalism.

The above speaker, like others, had difficulty in the 'logic' of such a juxtaposition but admitted that his was a knee-jerk reaction, adding that 'you'll get over it'. He said he would actually like to see 'someone from our kind of unionist background' learning Irish. The issue for most of the other participants who had reservations was perhaps more to do with curiosity or interest than suspicion or doubt and all vigorously defended the right of Protestants to learn Irish. One interviewee even playfully suggested that Protestants should learn the language to understand what 'they' (i.e. republicans) were 'saying about them'.

Despite some reservations, the overwhelming response to this item was very positive and the majority of participants made it clear that a Protestant who took the time and trouble to learn Irish in the face of peer pressure and negative perceptions was to be admired rather than viewed with suspicion. Irish, despite differing estimations of its value and concerns about its 'politics', was 'just another language' when put into this context:

> I wouldn't mind if they were speaking Irish at all. It [the speaker's religion] wouldn't mean anything to me. I would be more interested in the fact they are speaking Irish because they've had time to learn it.

The next quote lauds Protestant learners of Irish as potential peacemakers, but it must be conceded that this participant's argument would cut little ice in working-class unionist/loyalist areas, where a 'bridge-building' motivation could be interpreted as a betrayal of community solidarity:

> People would probably think more highly of them because they're attempting to, like, get in touch with the Irish culture and, like, build bridges between Protestant and Catholic.

Nevertheless, there was a belief that those who defied convention and learned Irish were to be praised:

> I'd respect them more, like. A lot of people would give in to peer pressure, like, and they wouldn't say anything about it and they'd be afraid of people finding out. But, if they're open about it, give them the respect they deserve.

The quote above is interesting in that the interviewee refers to the power of peer pressure but also places emphasis on the need to 'be open about it' (learning Irish), possibly implying that there might be cause for suspicion in the case of someone who was discovered to have been learning Irish clandestinely. This conveniently introduces another theme – the absence of Protestant or unionist 'role models' who could help show that to speak Irish does not mean a surrender of core values and that one has the freedom to be 'open about it'. This question of just how 'open' one can be as a Protestant Irish speaker or learner led to some discussion. Students were asked to consider that in the past some prominent loyalists had learned Irish while in prison in Northern Ireland.

This came as a surprise to all of the pupils but none believed that such figures could serve as role models, despite their 'impeccable' loyalist credentials. Most participants who offered an opinion were highly dubious about their reasons for learning Irish:

> You, like, have to question their motives behind it because

obviously it wouldn't be to better themselves or learn about the Irish culture or anything. I don't know.

You'd have to wonder why they were learning it. Was it for political reasons or was it just for interest?

One respondent took an even more cynical view, perhaps based on a stereotypical belief that loyalists are 'stupid':

I mean, when you're locked up for twenty-three hours, what do you do? I mean, you don't know what else to do. And French and German would probably be a wee bit complicated for them boys.

There was an acknowledgement, nonetheless, that these people had sufficient 'symbolic capital' within their communities to be able to learn Irish with impunity and could 'do pretty much what they wanted'. Learning the language, therefore, would be easier for them because 'they've got the reputation and the power'. A participant felt that this gave them more freedom than most people in working-class unionist/loyalist communities enjoyed:

They could have played Gaelic [sport]. Nobody would have said anything because they would have been afraid of what would have happened to them. But someone just off the street – I think they would have been in a lot of trouble.

It should be added, however, that the former paramilitary figures mentioned above probably could not function as credible role models for those taking part in this research, as they belong to an entirely different generation. Furthermore, while paramilitaries remain a feature of the political landscape, the ending of the Troubles has led to a dilution of the claim that their sole purpose is defending Northern Ireland. The involvement of some elements in drug-dealing and petty criminality has further damaged claims to 'nobility' derived from historic association with the proud but bloody inheritance of the Somme, where young Protestant 'volunteers' gave their lives in the name of Ulster. Even when political representatives of loyalist paramilitary groups have stood for election, they have thus far failed to garner any significant Protestant support. But this is not to understate the crucial role that forward-thinking loyalists have played, and are playing, in both delivering the peace and helping bring former combatants to an understanding that politics and dialogue offer the best hope for their people in a post-conflict society.

THE 'SCOTTISH QUESTION'

The 'Scottish question' provoked some of the most vigorous debate of the focus group process. In truth, it was a two-part question, the first relating to Scots Gaelic, the second to Ulster-Scots. The Scottish Gaelic element was dealt with quickly, but the Ulster-Scots issue generated many lively exchanges as pupils considered whether it was a dialect or a language and, subsequently, its placement within a cultural/political context.

Scots Gaelic as an alternative to Irish

Asked to consider whether Scots Gaelic might be something to learn as an alternative – or even an adjunct – to Irish, all students acknowledged the strong historical links between Scotland and Northern Ireland. For most, though, those connections were not sufficient reason to prioritise Scots Gaelic at the expense of Irish. There was also a feeling that the connection with Scotland is no longer as significant as it once was:

> There's still a cultural link and we would see the Scottish influences, but I think it would be a lot more sort of withdrawn now. Like, Protestants over here think they have their own culture really.

> Scots Gaelic is Scottish culture, really. There's a lot of Scottish people over here – obviously there's quite close links with Scotland – but it's not Irish culture, really.

Given that Scots Gaelic is 'neutral' compared to Irish – crossing religious and political divisions in Scotland – it was thought that students might regard it as a 'safer' alternative. Only one agreed with this argument, believing that an interest in 'Scottish' might deflect the peer pressure which he thought would militate against displaying an interest in 'Irish'. Another said that as a Presbyterian he might be interested in Scots Gaelic because of his religion's historic ties with the language, but added that this alone was not sufficient reason to start learning.

Another respondent said she thought that anything involving the word 'Gaelic' would be controversial:

> I think over here it's just the whole culture thing. No matter what kind of Gaelic it is people are going to have a problem with it. I don't think it would work over here, with the situation as it is.

Even if it were true, it was argued, that Scots Gaelic is non-contentious, the situation in Northern Ireland was entirely different from that in Scotland because the politics of 'labelling' did not apply to the same extent. People in Scotland, one speaker surmised, would probably not make general assumptions about others on the basis of their religion, as they often did in Northern Ireland.[51]

While a few participants said they would be interested in learning Scottish Gaelic as well as Irish, most took a pragmatic approach, citing, for example, the probable lack of opportunities to have a conversation in the language.

No animosity was shown towards Scots Gaelic but it was not regarded as a practical alternative to Irish, which, among course-takers and non-takers alike, was seen as more accessible and more relevant:

> I think I'd rather learn Irish because Scots Gaelic is just a dialect of the Irish language. I'd rather learn the original. I feel that would be even more useful to me – more important.

> I would say I'd probably prefer to learn Irish because that's the country you live in ... so it's most relevant.

There's no problem with learning it, like. I wouldn't be opposed to anyone learning it, but I'd probably be more favoured towards the Irish Gaelic.

Ulster-Scots: cause for controversy

While discussion on the perceived political nature of Irish generated robust exposition of their opinions from participants, the Ulster-Scots strand excited equally intense debate, even though it was never meant to be an 'in-depth' theme. All but one student had heard of Ulster-Scots; some were aware of its existence but did not believe they had encountered it at first-hand. However, most were able to accurately locate some of the main areas associated with Ulster-Scots, including much of Northern Ireland's coastal rim and north Antrim. The question of whether Ulster-Scots is a dialect or language, however, generated no such harmony and one respondent described it as 'gibberish'. Another was even less generous:

I think it's an excuse for a language. [...] it's just shortened words said in a stupid accent by people who are too lazy to speak properly. There's no way anyone should learn that as a language, because it's so not.

Her view prompted a sharp exchange between her and several others in the group who stated defiantly that Ulster-Scots was a language. Another student asserted that it was in the process of shifting from dialect to language:

I think it's a language in its early stages, because languages always develop out of dialects in other languages. So, the more and more that it evolves and changes, the more it will become a language and it should be developed.

This speaker went on to say that she could speak Ulster-Scots and, when another girl repeated her claim that it was 'for people who can't be bothered to speak properly', she retorted: 'I was brought up with

Ulster-Scots and I talk properly when I want to. I can slip in and out of it quite easily.' While there was no reason to doubt her facility in code-switching, it is interesting that she used the term 'talk properly' during her defence. Is this evidence of the 'cultural cringe factor' that some advocates of Ulster-Scots employ in debates on Fenton's 'Hamely Tongue'?

Some felt that they had not been given enough information to come to a decision and for many students the dialect-v-language issue was not cut and dried; others pointed out that they could 'nearly understand' it. A student who leaned towards the dialect interpretation thought that it was a matter of opinion, while another said that 'people would speak Ulster-Scots without even knowing it'. He added that 'they've been brought up with it – the dialect'. An overall majority in the groups was of the view that Ulster-Scots is a dialect and claims by its proponents to the contrary were ridiculed:

I feel it is a forced language. You know, it's a form of a dialect; it's not really a language.

I think Ulster-Scots and that, I think it just looks like English in a Scottish accent. Like, it's a big farce – it'd take no effort to read.

The debate in all groups moved into a wider arena and it became apparent that views on 'dialect or language' were intertwined with politics and interpretations of culture. The 'dead language' discourse, already seen in relation to Irish, was also used to dismiss Ulster-Scots as outdated and irrelevant. A student who strongly opposed Irish, for example, was equally scathing of Ulster-Scots, describing both as dead. He accepted it as a language, however, claiming that his grandfather had been a speaker.

Another participant who used the dead language discourse introduced a key sub-theme in this strand when he said he felt that agitation on behalf of either Irish or Ulster-Scots was 'creating a further divide between Protestant and Catholic'. Earlier, we saw that many believed Irish had been associated with republicanism – to its detriment. Similarly, Ulster-Scots and unionist politics were seen to be linked in a deleterious way and the dangers in cross-contamination were apparent to many students:

> I think it's the cultural thing again. Like, Irish is kind of for Catholics and they're learning that … Ulster-Scots is more associated with Protestants, like. But if you're going to revive Irish and it's, like, a kind of dead language as it is, then they've got to revive Ulster-Scots as well.

> I think a lot of people don't see Ulster-Scots as a language. They just see it as a dialect but because they [republicans] make the big thing about Irish – you know, money into Irish – Prods sort of want to bring Ulster-Scots in because it's seen as equal rights.

> I think if Irish continues to be revived in a big way, people are going to feel threatened and then they are going to learn it [Ulster-Scots] … Like, it's going to be, 'If they have Irish, I'm going to learn this', just to counter it [Irish], rather than for positive reasons.

Equality was a major issue for many, even to the extent of learning Ulster-Scots to 'get even': one girl admitted that while she had no urge to learn it at the moment, she probably would do so 'if Irish became a big thing'. Large-scale Catholic involvement with Irish would, according to this rationale, legitimise Protestants learning Ulster-Scots, even if they had little interest in it. This is the classic 'win–lose' paradigm, where everything is seen as black or white, without any consideration of potential mutual benefit. The issue of funding was another aspect of this dichotomy, as shown by this exchange:[52]

> ROBIN: I don't think it should be given equal funding.

> ZOË: You can't give something that's a dialect equal status as a language. It just doesn't make sense.

> SAMANTHA: But it's equally part of our culture in this area and

you have to give everyone's culture equal attention. The majority of the people in this area would have some ancestors who came from Scotland in the Plantation.

Ultimately, it was difficult to separate Ulster-Scots from the political dimension, as had been true in the case of Irish. For the moment, though, the following comment is an interesting reflection on how languages (and dialects) are dragged into wider debates:

The only reason … Ulster-Scots is being pushed into our society is to try and equal out, 'cause the Catholic community are getting Irish. And that's so stupid, 'cause it's dividing our community yet again – that we don't need. Saying 'You can learn Ulster-Scots' and 'You can learn Irish' is so pathetic.

A MATTER OF CHOICE

While many of the above themes excited considerable debate about the value of Irish and its perceived location in a political milieu, all respondents were in agreement that everyone should have the right to learn the language. Some qualified this by declaring that learning Irish would be a waste of time or resources, but still believed that the right to learn was inviolable.

Irish as a school option

This was another intensely discussed sequence in all groups and it was noted that some of those who earlier appeared hostile towards the language had mellowed considerably. As the item was raised relatively late in the groups, it is possible that this had given them the opportunity to listen to the views of other pupils and slightly reposition their own attitudes. Their only caveat was that the language should never be 'forced' on anyone and that the decision to learn it should be taken voluntarily, but this was true of all participants.

Throughout, the positive discourses far outweighed the negative:

I don't really have an opinion on the language but it should be optional, the way different subjects ... the way we got to choose our A Levels. I think it could be an option from an earlier age.

I think if it was an option, like as an extra class or something, the way it was with that there [Gael-Linn] course, only a bigger thing ... Well it would help you not be bitter about it.

I don't think you can force people who view themselves as British to learn it, but everyone should definitely have the choice.

'Choice' was the keyword, with people here able to 'learn it if they want to'.

There was a substantial sub-debate on how the language should be offered. Some pupils were in favour of Irish being a full-scale subject on a par with French and German, whereas others felt it would be best provided as an enrichment programme in the style of Gael-Linn's EPGS. Also discussed was at what stage Irish should be made available to schoolchildren. Some saw advantages in introducing it at primary level:

The way people are growing up, maybe their parents are opposed to Catholics, Protestants and all. Like, it's a no-go, no mixing. But if you were learning the language from an early age you could have different viewpoints and then it's not 'you were brought up doing this here, so you have to do it'. You can still have that variety.

This argument found favour with a few pupils, as it would – they claimed – remove the 'stigma' from Irish at an early age, possibly meaning that it would not be an issue at all by the secondary school stage. The peer-pressure factor would be negated, they thought. The counter-argument, however, was that introducing Irish in primary school might mean that parents would make the decision for their children, thus removing the element of choice. Those parents who found it unpalatable that Irish was on the syllabus at a particular primary school level might, it was argued, decide to send their children elsewhere.

The optimal scenario was that Irish should be elective at all levels, with an acknowledgement that parents would most likely take the decision early in a child's time at school but that the student would exercise his or her right to choose at secondary level. Throughout the discussions, 'compulsory' as a word was treated with contempt. Most pupils contended that making Irish compulsory would create hostility on a variety of fronts. The political animosity such a decision might generate was taken as read, but there was even opposition from an academic standpoint. A student referred to Protestant friends, attending a school across the border, who disliked Irish, but not for any political or cultural reason:[53]

They're doing it for their Leaving Cert [the Republic's A Level equivalent] and they would look upon Irish as I would look on French. You know, I just couldn't wait to get it over. The thing about French is you have to do it here for the first five years. You know, it just made me despise it even more.

The general feeling was that those who did not like languages as a subject area would not willingly embrace Irish as a GCSE and would drop it at the earliest opportunity. On the other hand, those who were more language-friendly would, it was believed, appreciate the chance to choose an alternative, or complement, to French, German or Spanish.

There was – at first – apparently no dispute over the offering of Irish at secondary/grammar-school level. Even a degree of envy that it was available only in Catholic schools (integrated schools were not mentioned) was discernible:

I think it should be offered definitely. I mean, it's offered in the Catholic grammar schools and why shouldn't it be offered here? I think we should all get equal opportunities. Why is it associated with Catholics?

It has to be introduced into the Protestant schools as well, or else'll it never catch on. It has to be there as an option.

In one group, however, an additional variable was introduced by some pupils who thought that if Irish were to be offered, it would be essential to offer Ulster-Scots too. The argument was taken a stage further, when several pupils said that if Irish was to be introduced into Protestant schools, Ulster-Scots would have to be put on the syllabus in Catholic schools:

Adam said everyone around Ireland should have the opportunity to use Irish but everyone should have the opportunity to use Ulster-Scots as well. If they're going to be promoted at all, they should both be done equally.

While most pupils overall thought that Irish should be made available in Protestant schools, several members of this group adhered firmly to the 'dead language' discourse:

If I went home and said to my mum and dad, like, 'I might take up Ulster-Scots at GCSE. I might take up Irish at GCSE', they'd say: 'Do a proper subject. Do German! Do French!'

I don't see the point in learning either of them. I have no interest in learning it [Irish], as I've said. I probably wouldn't have any interest in learning Ulster-Scots either. […] I just think my time could be better spent.

I'm sure there's a lot of the Catholics who think, 'Why do we have to learn this?' because there's no real point.

Another pupil felt that it was important to offer Ulster-Scots as a counter-balance to Irish and declared that he 'would have something to say about it' if only Irish was put on the syllabus in his school: 'My personal belief is if you're going to give one as an option, give both of them.'

Not everyone agreed that Irish (or Ulster-Scots) had any place in the curriculum in their schools. Yes, young people had the right to learn Irish if they were interested in it and resources should be made available to facilitate them but there was no need 'to spend lots of money and bring it into schools'.

I don't have anything against people speaking it. Like, as part of their culture or whatever, but I just don't see what the benefit in teaching children it is, because it is dying out and there is no point to it.

The whole area of funding for language teaching was called into question by a participant who did not think that any language should receive special treatment, using the example of French: 'Like, it's just another language. If you want to learn it, you just go and learn it and that's it.'

The question of equal funding, which had drawn polarised responses in the questionnaire returns, saw division among the focus group participants, often depending on how pupils interpreted Ulster-Scots. Those who were broadly favourable towards Irish believed that it should receive more funding than Ulster-Scots, using the argument that if Ulster-Scots was only a dialect, it should not enjoy financial equality:

I don't see why a dialect should be given the same treatment as a language.

I think Irish should be given more funding but that's probably because, you know, Ulster-Scots would only be appreciated in an Ulster-Scots area. And that's not as big as the whole of Ireland.

This last speaker, in common with another who said that money spent on Ulster-Scots (or Irish) would be better spent on hospitals or education generally, nevertheless conceded the right of all to learn the language if they wished. The most commonly expressed negative views in this segment centred on the belief that throwing cash at Irish was a 'waste of money' because it was a 'dead language'. This extended beyond the educational sector, too, and a pupil lambasted government spending on the translation of official documents into Irish and Ulster-Scots on the grounds that they were 'dying languages which really haven't anything to do with parliament'.

In summary, all focus group respondents agreed that everyone had the right to learn Irish and only a few disagreed that school was the right place for this to happen. Even those who rejected curriculum-driven Irish conceded that learning it as a Protestant was something that could be done outside school in one's own time.

EVALUATING THE COURSE

Most of those pupils who had taken the Gael-Linn enrichment programme were fairly positive about the course. Asked if they would have taken a course in Irish had it been offered at an earlier stage, many agreed. Although 'mainstream' languages had earlier been identified by most as more useful than Irish, a recurring and positive theme in this segment was that it was 'closer to home' and 'only down the road' when compared to, say, French or German. This was seen as a reason why one might wish to learn Irish:

> I think it's a class language. It's really interesting. Like, French and German, I really like them, but [they're] really, like, far off, you know. I mean, why not learn something that's so close to home?

The 'closeness' of Irish was a particularly pertinent factor for the pupils in one group, as their school was fairly close to the border and most of them had friends and family in the Republic. The proximity factor did not apply in the other focus groups to the same degree but responses were still generally favourable.

On the language itself, one student who had thoroughly enjoyed the course, said she thought it was 'quite hard ... because of the silent hs and stuff'.[54] Pronunciation and spelling, for her, were the only difficulties. A colleague in the same group described Irish as 'cool':

It really all flowed together, which was class. It sounded interesting, like, listening to that and listening to other people who speak it. It was a lot different.

Course-takers had various reasons for enjoying the classes and while most felt that they would probably have few opportunities to use Irish in the future they believed that they had been enriched by what they had learned. No one thought that Irish would ever become something they could use on a day-to-day basis, but the benefits were clear and went beyond just language:

I think it's good as an experience but I don't really see myself using it a lot when I'm older. But it's good to have some sort of background information and, you know, history. Even to use in other countries as well, like England. You can say you've got that background.

I'd definitely like to learn more about it without taking a [another] course or something. I couldn't see myself being in a position to use it on a day-to-day basis, but I could maybe use it sometimes if I was down South. But I couldn't see me using it all the time.

If you wanted to learn it, it would be a good course. I mean, they do go through it all and give you wee sheets and things. It was a good course.

An attender who admitted that language was not really his 'cup of tea' had no objections to people learning Irish to further their knowledge. For him, 'the whole political stuff and all' was an additional problem but he said that his primary difficulty was simply that he 'couldn't really get into it':

I find it kind of difficult, not even so much to say, but I couldn't really picture myself speaking Irish. I just found it hard to get into and get, sort of, motivated. To get stuck into it, if you know what I mean.

Despite his views on Irish and lack of willingness to fully engage with the language, he praised the course as 'interesting and well-structured'. A majority of attenders appreciated the grounding in Irish provided by the enrichment programme:

> I liked the coursework and all and how it explains the meaning of place names and stuff like that. I found that quite interesting but I don't think I'd ever learn it as a language

> ... I'm not a very language-type orientated guy. But the likes of the history of it and the place names and stuff like that there ... it sort of gives you a background culture, to know where you're from and what you're about.

In the questionnaire, certain items scored more highly than others in terms of popularity with attenders, and the focus groups reflected this pattern. The elements on place names and surnames were mentioned frequently by students, whereas some other items rarely featured in the discussions. While these elements were being talked about in one group, for example, a female participant took pride in explaining that her name – Tara – was Irish and meant 'a hill in Ireland'.

One pupil believed that the study of place names and 'stuff like that' could play a valuable role in removing the 'significance' (political) of learning Irish and make it more neutral. Several of those who had not done the course made the same point: a non-taker thought that learning Irish could be de-politicised if set in the same harmless context as researching the family tree, something that involved heritage and culture with no political overtones.[55]

Even those course-takers who had their doubts about the usefulness of Irish – or its perceived political baggage – felt they had gained something from the programme. One student, for example, admitted that she had been 'in the dark' about Irish before the course:

> We didn't really know much about the whole Irish thing before – just, really, the political side. So I suppose it has kind of made me

less ignorant of the Irish language. Yeah, it was good to kind of know a bit about where it came from and all.

Another student who confessed that he had real problems with Irish nevertheless praised the course:

I think it's the sort of course that would be beneficial if you went into it sort of open-minded. But it's just the way I've been brought up. I've never had any interest in the Irish language. I think if you want to know about it, it would be quite a good course to do.

For some students, a drawback was that the classes took place only once a week and 'by the time you came back the next week you'd forgotten what you'd learned the last time'. That they were new to the language – 'learning from scratch', as one put it – made it more difficult. A further drawback for some was that the enrichment programme was held at a difficult time, as they were in the throes of AS Level study and could not give it the attention they might otherwise have been able to:

Because we're in our A Level stages, it is a bit, like, it's not really the right time. Because we're sort of beyond the GCSE and A Level levels of education, sort of, it'd be quite hard to try and actually get into the Irish. I mean, if we were coming into the first year and sort of, like, the option was there for us, it'd be more open to us.

There was a strong feeling that the course had broadened horizons without changing anyone's core beliefs. No one, attender or non-attender, felt threatened by the language and no one believed there was any reason why learning Irish should change political perspectives. Certainly, as the questionnaire results in the next chapter will show, political attitudes had not been changed. This point was summarised neatly by a student who said he had done the course simply to satisfy his curiosity and find out more about the language 'rather than [to] change my views on what the language was or what it meant to me'. As another participant said:

Saying we learn Irish is not saying we're from Ireland and we don't have our own views of loyalists and nationalists.

Having listened to their peers talk about the course, some non-attenders expressed disappointment that they had not done the programme and suggested that, were it to be available again, they would like to participate. For those in Upper Sixth,[56] of course, the chance would not return. And many of those who had done the course felt it was a pity they had not had the opportunity at an earlier stage.

OTHER QUALITATIVE SOURCES

In assessing the young people's overall attitudes, it is worth examining another element of the data collected during the fieldwork. Attenders' views of the course were dealt with by a number of closed questions in the questionnaire. However, another item on the questionnaire invited them to express their views on the programme in the penultimate – open-ended – question, which can best be considered as qualitative rather than quantitative data. As is to be expected with questionnaires, not everyone chose to proffer additional information but of the attenders who did, 85.7 per cent rated the course positively and 9.5 per cent negatively, with the remaining 4.8 per cent expressing their views in a way that was either a combination of the two or simply unclear.

As the focus groups provided a sample of participants who were able to rate the course at length, the comments of students about the course on the questionnaire are perhaps best regarded as an overall indicator of mainly positive opinions, without the depth of group responses. The advantage is that the views expressed owe nothing to focus group dynamics and can be considered as an honest reflection of the general mood. (Of course, the above percentages are perhaps a little biased in that only those who feel sufficiently motivated or interested in the subject will take the time to spell out their views in words rather than by merely ticking a box.)

Most expressed satisfaction that they had had the chance to learn a little Irish, some saying that this was because they had been given an opportunity to do something that they otherwise would not have had. What was again clear was that the elements on place names and surnames had been very well received:

It was a good course to attend. Most of the time is enjoyable. Learning how words and place names are linked, and some more about the history of the country in which we live, is a very good thing.

I now understand the history of the language and how it originated. I also enjoyed learning about where surnames come from, so have benefited from learning some of my own heritage.

It's good to find out name origins and overall to realise that even though Ireland is so small, it has so much culture and having its own language emphasises this.

Many felt that they had been given an introduction to more than just language and there were frequent references to having been given an insight into 'culture' and 'heritage'. This was something that they said they could not have encountered in any other way and they were therefore highly appreciative of the course. The culture theme was repeated often in the responses:

[I have a] better understanding of the Irish culture.

It helped me learn more about the Irish culture and how it has been incorporated into British culture in Northern Ireland.

It showed me how much my local area was connected to the Irish language and to the ancient Irish culture and how even though we live in an English-speaking country, Irish is everywhere. It helped me learn more about a culture that exists in my society but I have not been part of.

Quite a few respondents said they enjoyed the course because they had an interest in languages in general and the Gael-Linn programme had given them a chance to broaden horizons:

I feel like I've learned the basics of another language, as I have a particular interest in learning languages.

I didn't find the historical side of it terribly interesting, but I actually liked learning the language.

As I am interested in languages, I feel it [is] interesting to learn a bit of [the] Irish language and where the names of people and towns originated from.

Naturally, there were criticisms. Firstly, there were those from attenders who were hostile towards the language, although their comments have a rather 'pat' ring to them. Asked if they had benefited from the course, they said:

I haven't. More republican [in]doctrination.

[I] have seen that the Irish language is dying and will soon be extinct and is only used as a political tool to promote republican terrorism.

Secondly, there were constructive criticisms: a number of students complained that there had not been enough on place names and surnames; several complained that there had not been enough actual language tuition and a student who believed that it was too difficult to start learning a new language at 18 said Irish would 'be hard to master to any level unless taught intensively'. Another had clearly enjoyed the course but suggested greater use of phonetics to make the language element more approachable, 'as Irish is a funny language for pronunciation'. Judging by these comments, mostly favourable, the course had performed well with attenders. Even a pupil who admitted that he/she had not wanted to learn the language at first 'found it quite interesting', particularly the place names, surnames and history elements.

A number of attenders – despite appreciating the benefits of the course – did not think they would follow through their interest in Irish. Some, however, had been enthused and suggested that they would like to find out more, although most felt this would be best done through self-learning rather than formal courses, as will be demonstrated by questionnaire responses in the next chapter. A minority said they would like to take up Irish as a GCSE/A Level.

Final impressions

Attenders and non-attenders alike were given the opportunity to summarise their views on Irish and Ulster-Scots in a final open-ended question to round off the questionnaire. The last section of this chapter is a synopsis of the closing comments of the eighty-four pupils who responded to the invitation. As was anticipated, course-takers were much more positive about Irish than their non-attending peers.

All of the discourses put forward in the focus groups were also used in questionnaire responses and many firmly located Irish in a nationalist/republican environment, with negative references to Sinn Féin. The charge that Irish is a 'political tool' was predictably repeated, and the 'dead language' discourse was used in relation to both Ulster-Scots and Irish by many. To examine these in detail would be merely to cover old ground, but some responses from the questionnaire are worth mentioning.

Very few of those who offered comments on the language attacked Irish *per se*: the vast majority were conducted using the dead language discourse or the perceived link with republicanism/Sinn Féin. But the dead language argument was applied in equal measure to Ulster-Scots and another recurring discourse – that spending money on Irish is wasteful – was also used in relation to Ulster-Scots.

Occasionally, the blinkered outlook of the monoglot, which was not immediately obvious in the focus groups but may have been an undercurrent in the 'globalisation' discourse, appeared in the comments: several respondents used variations on the theme that 'English – not Irish – is the language of this country'. Some made it abundantly clear that they had no time for a language that was variously described as 'dead', 'outdated', 'undermined by English' and something that should be 'kept for the Republic'.

As in the focus groups, perceived politicisation was a key issue. One student accused some people of 'using Irish or Ulster-Scots to show how devoutly Protestant or Catholic you are', a variant on the 'labelling' theme. Other comments showed that the use – or misuse – of Irish is a source of irritation:

> Irish is associated with Sinn Féin/IRA and until this organisation ceases to exist, unionists will associate it [Irish] with terrorism and will have no interest in it whatsoever.

One respondent felt that Irish was used merely as a political tool 'to make unionists/loyalists appear in a bad light', while another was adamant that 'the Irish language has become a vessel to promote republican ideas'. Politicians were at fault, according to many questionnaire respondents. Sinn Féin in particular was excoriated, but parties of various hues came under fire for using language as a political weapon:

> I don't like to see it [Irish] being used as a political weapon, alienating people who choose not to speak it.

> I feel the use of Irish language, especially in the political fields, is insulting, especially in Ulster as most people do not understand it when Sinn Féin or SDLP members use it on TV.

Dangers inherent in 'reviving' either language were noted:

> I feel the re-interest in Irish and Ulster-Scots is just widening the divide between Protestants and Catholics in Northern Ireland.

> The Irish language, if made more publicly visible, would cause more sectarian violence, I believe, which I don't want to see.

A minority of respondents were of the view that making Irish acceptable to Protestants in general would be impossible to achieve and the best that could be hoped for would be 'a level of indifference, but not complete enthusiasm'. This, at least, is an improvement on downright hostility.

The link between language and those with 'hard-line views' was an off-putting factor but if the 'harmful' mixing of politics and Irish could be ended many students saw opportunities to actually improve the overall situation in Northern Ireland. There was a positive flipside to the revival debate in that rejuvenating Irish could have a wider impact with considerable benefits:

> By learning about the languages and the culture, people in this country will be more understanding and less prejudiced towards each other. The languages should be made available to both students and adults, especially in segregated areas.

Another student was a little more realistic about what could be achieved, but still saw the value of introducing Irish as an optional subject:

> [The] Irish language may not have much of an impact in reducing sectarianism or influencing political views but, just like Religious Studies being taught in schools, Irish and other languages should be introduced.

A pupil who believed that increasing awareness of Irish would help make people more aware of their backgrounds touched on a very important issue when he/she said it was important that any progress should be made with care. Others agreed that if Irish was to be promoted successfully as an option in Protestant schools – and this was a common view – a cautious approach was essential:

> The two languages should be available for all but promoting it [them] into a fragmented society is difficult and therefore careful

steps should be taken so that implementation does not cause offence.

There should be no emphasis on political affiliation with regard to who should learn Irish.

Some students, as seen already, believed that programmes such as the Gael-Linn package were the best way to introduce pupils in Protestant schools to Irish in a low-key manner that would not generate hostility. And even if it were on the syllabus in Protestant schools as an examination subject, the best approach would be 'not to brag about it, just have it available'.

A majority of pupils felt that they had benefited from a less polarised upbringing than their parents, many of whom would have been 'children of the Troubles'. This subject was not dealt with directly in the focus groups, but one student, who had not done the course, believed that there was cause for optimism about the future:

So, our generation and the next few, hopefully if everything goes well and everything's peaceful, then you could bring it [Irish] through a bit more in my eyes.

I think we need to concentrate more ... on the community thing, not worry about Irish, but actually trying to pull our two communities together and realise that we're just all human beings.

CONCLUSIONS

Overall, pupils' attitudes towards Irish in the focus groups were mixed, but the balance tipped definitely towards more positive than negative views. The groups provided the opportunity for an exchange of views that was occasionally forthright and it was to be noted that some of those who had appeared fiercely anti-Irish language at the beginning moderated later in the process.

There were major differences of opinion on many issues but the areas of agreement are extremely important in the context of this research and have potentially positive implications for the future. The acceptance by all that everyone has the right to learn Irish is highly significant, as is the acceptance by the vast majority of focus group participants that the language should have a place in Northern Ireland schools as an optional subject.

6
INSIGHTS FROM THE DATA

INTRODUCTION

In this chapter the data provided by the questionnaire administered in the five Northern Ireland grammar schools during the fieldwork phase provides another insight into the pupils' attitudes towards Irish. The key variables are presented in graphic form and the general trends apparent explored. As far as possible, the attitudes of course-takers are contrasted with those of pupils who did not take the enrichment programme. Inferential statistics were also used to examine links between variables: one practical example of this might be to find out whether or not religious affiliation affects respondents' attitudes towards the Irish language. However, only the key findings from this process are summarised. The chapter also includes a brief summary of data relating to Ulster-Scots.

THE QUESTIONNAIRE

The aim of the questionnaire[57] was to provide quantitative output, while qualitative material would come from the focus groups. A five-point scale (using scale points such as 'Strongly Agree', 'Agree', 'Don't Know', 'Disagree' and 'Strongly Disagree') was adopted for the majority of questions. Simply ticking the appropriate boxes was all that was required for most questions, while write-in items were kept to a minimum and held back until the end, ensuring that the most important quantitative information was given priority.

Guaranteeing the questionnaire's neutrality was essential, as was balancing 'negative' items with 'positive' ones, and an extensive pilot-testing process ensured that the finished instrument was fit for the purpose. The questionnaire ran to five pages for non-attenders and eight for attenders.

The inclusion of items on Ulster-Scots was not initially considered, but feedback from the piloting programme indicated that some respondents were uncomfortable with a questionnaire focused entirely on Irish. A few questions were introduced merely to make the questionnaire appear more general in nature, rather than Irish-language specific, and further piloting led to the inclusion of a more substantial sub-section. As I stressed at the outset, it was never the intention to fully investigate attitudes towards Ulster-Scots, although, as will be seen, some interesting data emerged.

INTRODUCING THE DATA

Data from the questionnaire are presented below as descriptive statistics, in the form of charts or tables (with observations where appropriate), to provide an overview of variables and detail pupils' responses to items on the questionnaire.

The overall sample included 131 pupils, 55 males (42 per cent) and 76 females (58 per cent). Of this total, 74 (56.5 per cent) had taken the Gael-Linn course, while 57 (43.5 per cent) had not. Figures by attendance are illustrated in Figure 1.

Figure 1: Gender by attendance

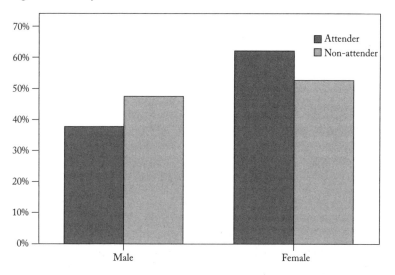

While more females than males took part in the survey, this difference is 'evened out' by statistical testing, allowing us to draw conclusions as to significance. The following charts summarise most variables covered by the questionnaire, although some sequences involving a primary and follow-up question (or questions) have been condensed. Other items on the questionnaire are omitted because they did not apply to all respondents. The question on the resource pack is an example, as not all pupils received one and any attempt at evaluation was considered pointless.

SECTION A DATA

Section A of the questionnaire was completed by all 131 respondents and consequently allows comparison between those who took the Gael-Linn course and those who did not. For convenience, clustered bar charts for each variable enable at-a-glance comparison. *Note that percentages are calculated within the 'Attend' variable: attenders across all categories will add up to 100 per cent and non-attenders will also total 100 per cent.*[58]

Key independent (causal) variables

Independent variables are those which may have an influence on attitudes towards the language. They include obvious factors such as gender, religion and politics and form the basis of the later statistical investigations.

Respondent religion (Figure 2 below) reveals the large number of Presbyterians who took part in the survey (a reflection of that denomination's position as the primary Protestant faith in Northern Ireland). However, a smaller proportion of Presbyterians (46 per cent) were attenders, while of the Church of Ireland complement 71 per cent participated. The 'Other Protestant denomination' category included members of the Baptist, Free Presbyterian and Elim churches, as well as smaller groups. Significantly, all categories except 'None' were better represented as participants in percentage terms than Presbyterians.

Figure 2: Respondent religion

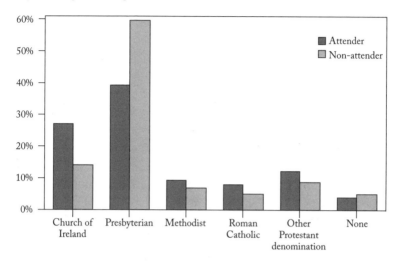

The number of other languages that a respondent speaks (or at least has a working knowledge of) might show whether or not a penchant for languages in general makes the respondent more likely to have taken the course. Figure 3 suggests not,[59] as a greater

Figure 3: Do you have any other languages?

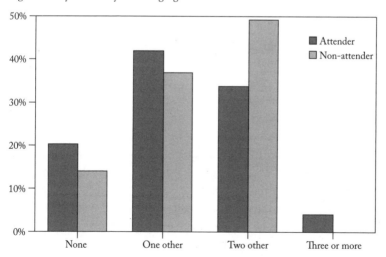

Figure 4: Have you encountered Irish in any form?

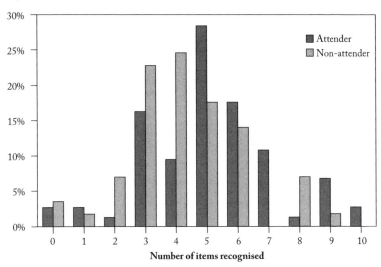

percentage of attenders have 'None' compared to their peers. Similarly, more of those with two languages are non-attenders. This, however, might have been down to perception of linguistic ability in that attenders set a higher standard of fluency/ability before claiming to 'know or speak' another language.

Figure 4 shows the number of ways in which respondents had encountered Irish. The highest potential score was twelve, although ten was the maximum achieved. Nevertheless, we see that attenders were in the ascendant from five items onwards (with the exception of eight items). The mode (i.e. most common response) for non-attenders was four items, but the attenders' mode was five items. The mean for non-attenders was 4.25, compared to 5.14 for attenders. Clearly, attenders are more conscious of Irish around them: this higher recognition level *could* be down to greater awareness of Irish as a result of having done the course but could also suggest that they were more conscious of Irish in the first place.

Of considerable interest is *how* the respondents had encountered Irish and the data for all questionnaire participants are shown in Table 1 below.

Table 1: How respondents (all) had encountered Irish

Contact point item on questionnaire	Total
On street/road signs	117
In place names	113
Through programmes on TV/radio	104
In Gaelic surnames	82
As used by politicians	52
In relation to music	34
In advertising/newspapers	33
In language classes	27
On official documents	21
In conversation	15
In other classes at school	13
In other ways	12

Interestingly, the two most-chosen items (street/road signs and place names) are closely related, possibly indicating a level of awareness in the respondents about the Irish language in terms of 'their' local environment. Gaelic surnames, the fourth most-chosen item, might also demonstrate awareness in a personal context. That 104 respondents had encountered Irish through TV/radio programmes shows the power of the electronic media and there was a reasonable score for Irish as used by politicians, which is most likely as a result of media coverage. Although revealing, the table does not indicate whether respondents viewed their contacts with the language positively or negatively.

The 'Other ways' category was an eclectic catch-all which included responses ranging from 'I was greeted at work in Irish' and 'On a trip to the all-Ireland championships'[60] to 'IRA/Sinn Féin propaganda' and 'republicans using it in an attempt to be smug'. The last two respondents, though, probably just used the question to proffer what sound like rehearsed stereotypical responses as they indicate no direct contact with the language.

The first point worth noting about the Politics variable (Figure 5) is the large number of respondents (53 per cent overall) who chose 'None'. This could be indicative of a general disinterest in politics

Figure 5: Which of the following best describes your political outlook?

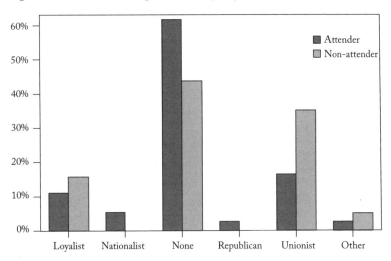

among the young, a malaise that affects both sides of the political spectrum. Equally, it could be a case of under-reporting, driven by a desire to avoid self-labelling. Whatever the reason, non-attenders were more likely to nominate themselves as loyalist, unionist or other. Loyalist respondents were split fairly evenly in terms of attendance (47.1 per cent-v-52.9 per cent), but only 37.5 per cent (v-62.5 per cent) of unionist respondents were attenders.

Although the numbers are small, all who described themselves as nationalist or republican did the course. 'Other' respondents included those who wrote in terms such as 'Socialist' and 'Independent', while several 'None' participants made it abundantly clear that they had no interest in political labelling whatsoever and added colourful 'glosses' to indicate their disillusionment with the state of Northern Ireland politics.

Attitudinal variables – general

A number of variables examines respondent attitudes towards Irish in general. Asked at different points in the questionnaire, they give us a broad flavour of pupils' feelings on the language.

Figure 6: What do you feel when you encounter Irish?

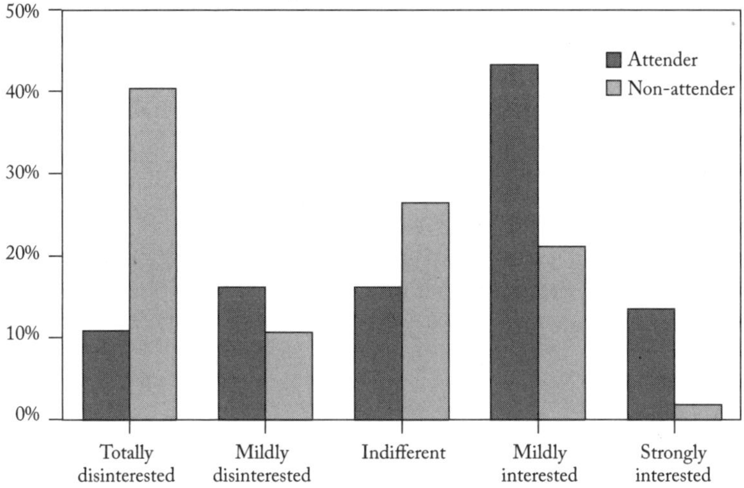

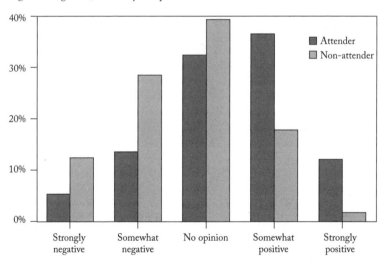

Figure 7: In general, what are your opinions of Irish?

Figures 6 and 7 essentially ask the same question in two different ways but the results, at first glance, seem to be quite contradictory: 40 per cent of non-attenders, for example, felt 'Totally disinterested' on encountering Irish in Figure 6, yet only 13 per cent had a 'Strongly negative' opinion of Irish in Figure 7. This may be due to the way the questions were phrased and the response options. However, when the data are collapsed, the combined category figures come close. For example, 77 per cent of non-attenders in Figure 6 fall into the Totally disinterested, Mildly disinterested or Indifferent categories, while 80 per cent in Figure 7 fall into Strongly negative, Somewhat negative or No opinion. Figures for both groups at the other end of the scale in both charts are stable in the Mildly interested/Strongly interested and Mildly positive/Strongly positive categories. Correlation testing on the variables confirmed a strong link between the two.

Figure 8: Who do you feel the Irish language is primarily for?

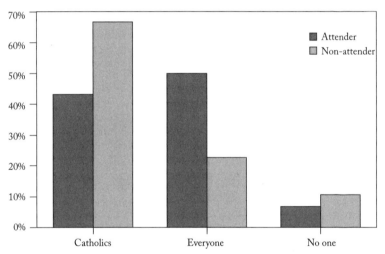

Figure 8 might be seen as a rather crude way of exploring attitudes towards Irish among the young people surveyed but appears to bear out the general Protestant perception of Irish as a 'Catholic' language. Attenders, once again, seem more open-minded on the issue than their counterparts but 43 per cent nevertheless perceive it as 'Catholic', although a greater percentage see Irish as being for 'Everyone'.

Several other variables provide a general insight into pupils'

Figure 9: Irish is a useful language and could help me get a better job

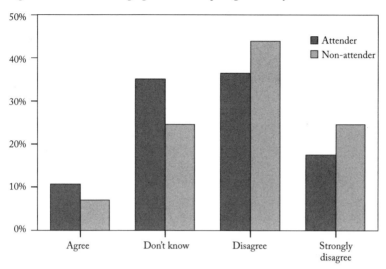

opinions from a different perspective – how useful, or otherwise, is the language?

No respondents strongly agreed that Irish was a useful language which could help lead to a better job (Figure 9) and even those who did the course were clearly doubtful about Irish's value in the employment market, as only 11 per cent agreed with the statement; indeed 36 per cent disagreed and 18 per cent strongly disagreed. Non-attenders' views were even more negative. However, when presented with the statement 'Irish is a dead language' (Figure 10), more than 50 per cent of attenders disagreed, reflecting the general trend of more sympathetic views from those who did the course. Therefore, while a majority of course-takers doubted the 'usefulness' of Irish, they were less likely to consider it a 'dead language'.

Figure 11 shows how important respondents considered Irish to be in cultural terms. Again, the now familiar general pattern is to be seen, in that attenders take a more positive but none the less measured view: precisely 50 per cent either disagreed or strongly disagreed with the 'my culture' statement, compared to 72 per cent of their counterparts.

Figure 10: Irish is a dead language

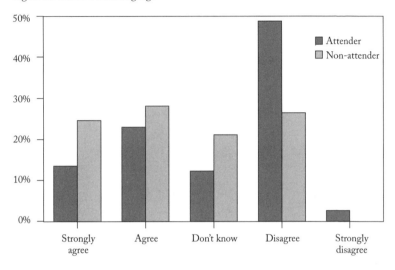

Figure 11: Irish is an important part of my culture

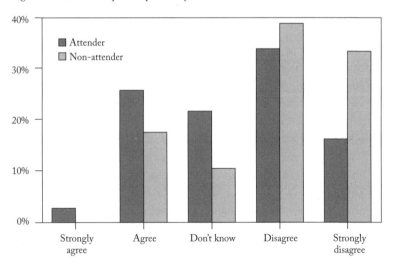

Attitudinal variables – education

This sub-section deals with a series of variables which go beyond general perceptions of Irish and seek respondents' opinions on more

Figure 12: Irish should be made available as an optional subject for every school pupil in Northern Ireland regardless of religion

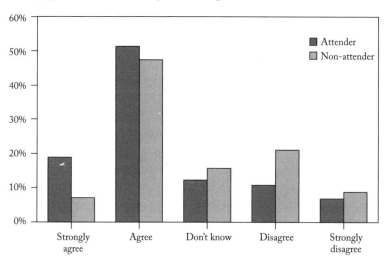

specific issues. The first sequence examines attitudes towards the availability of Irish.

Figure 12 shows a strong level of support for the statement that Irish should be an optional school subject for all pupils in Northern Ireland, course attenders registering over 70 per cent and non-attenders 54 per cent across the two 'Agree' categories. However, Figure 13 provides some rather unexpected results, given support for the statement in Figure 12. Presented with the statement that greater efforts should be made to make 'Protestants and unionists of all ages more aware of the Irish language', support falls away sharply and only a minority of both groups (46 per cent attenders, 21 per cent non-attenders) agree.

The question introduced several factors not in the previous item – age and religion/politics. It is clear that one, or more, of these changed the way that respondents think about the availability of Irish.

When the 'check' question – 'Everyone should have the chance to learn Irish' (Figure 14) – was asked later in the survey, responses were pleasingly similar to those on the 'optional subject' item, with combined agree levels of over 70 per cent for attenders and 56 per cent for non-attenders. The check question response indicates that

Figure 13: Greater efforts should be made to make Protestants and unionists of all ages more aware of the Irish language

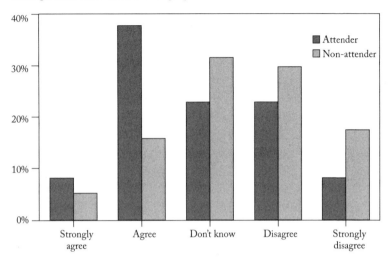

Figure 14: Everyone should have the chance to learn Irish

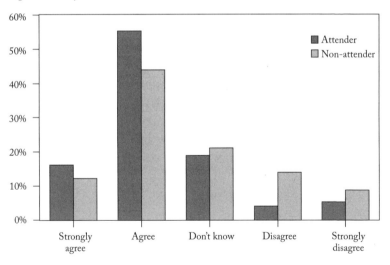

participants were thinking carefully about their answers but the way in which views changed when the statement became political/age-related is intriguing.

Figure 15: I wish I had had the chance to learn Irish at an earlier stage in my education

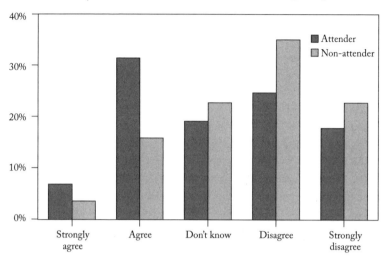

Two further variables scrutinise respondents' views on education and Irish but in a more direct and personal way. While a clear majority in both groups agreed that Irish should be made available as an optional subject for all pupils in Northern Ireland, respondents were less convinced that they personally should have had the opportunity to learn the language at an earlier stage (Figure 15). Attenders were reasonably evenly split between the Agree/Disagree categories, with a sizeable 'Don't know' component, while a majority of non-attenders (58 per cent) came strongly down on the Disagree side of the argument, albeit also with a significant 'Don't know' component. It should be noted, however, that while Figure 12 asks about the present/future, Figure 15 deals with the past.

Respondents across both groups were decidedly hostile to the idea of sending their children to an Irish-medium school (Figure 16). No one strongly agreed with the statement and the number of those who agreed was small. Indeed, over 71 per cent of attenders and almost 93 per cent of non-attenders Disagreed/Strongly disagreed. The common Protestant/unionist perception of such schools as being Catholic or republican in ethos is one explanation but an

Figure 16: If I was a parent I would be happy to send my children to an Irish-medium school

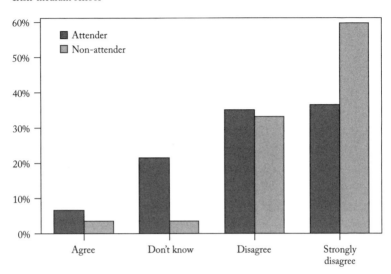

alternative interpretation is that pupils simply did not believe that an education delivered entirely in Irish would be useful.

Attitudinal variables – perceptions

Perceptions of Irish as 'nationalist, republican and Catholic' are addressed in several questions. Figure 17 deals with the vexed question of whether or not learning Irish could 'turn' Protestants, as discussed in Chapter Two.

Despite anecdotal evidence of suspicions about Irish-speaking Protestants from within their own communities, the questionnaire sample did not feel that learners would do a religious/political about-turn on exposure to the language. Figure 17 shows that an overwhelming majority of both groups (attenders 85 per cent and non-attenders 82 per cent) rejected the statement. Respondents also firmly rejected the statement that 'Irish is being forced on Protestants and unionists' (Figure 18), 72 per cent of attenders and 63 per cent of non-attenders disagreeing or strongly disagreeing.

However, another stereotyped view of Irish – that it is too closely

Figure 17: Do you feel that learning Irish would help turn Protestants and unionists into Catholics, nationalists and republicans?

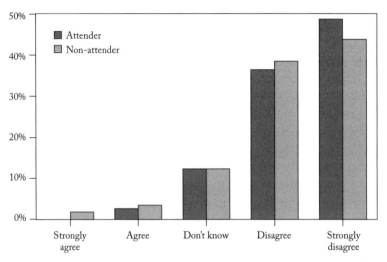

Figure 18: The Irish language is being forced on Protestants and unionists

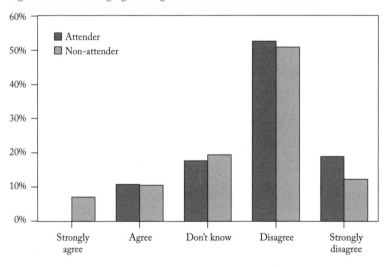

associated with republicans for Protestants and unionists to want to learn it – found strong support across the board. Figure 19 shows that 73 per cent of attenders and 80 per cent of non-attenders agreed with

Figure 19: Most Protestants and unionists would not want to learn Irish
because they feel it is too closely associated with republicans

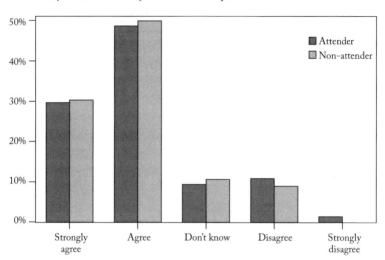

the statement. Indeed, attenders were only slightly more likely on this
occasion to take a less negative view, indicating that all have a problem
with perceived republican 'hijacking' of the language and its
implications for those wishing to learn Irish.

Summarising the three variables, it seems to be the case that
respondents did not feel any sense of a hidden agenda in terms of Irish
being forced upon Protestants/unionists. Nor did they believe that
core religious/political beliefs would be changed by dint of learning
Irish. What is clear, though, is that respondents have a problem with
the republican 'image' of Irish.

Attitudinal variables – miscellaneous

Three variables which do not sit comfortably in any of the above
sections complete the look at Section A data.

Asked if they felt they had been excluded from the Irish language
and culture (Figure 20), respondents were divided reasonably evenly.
Attenders were slightly more likely to say they had been excluded than
non-attenders but, on the other hand, were also more likely to say they

Figure 20: Do you feel that you have been excluded from the Irish language and culture?

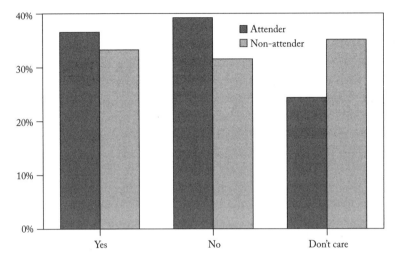

Figure 21: The government should not be spending taxpayers' money on the Irish language

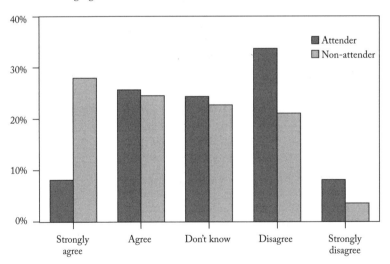

had not. Overall, 29 per cent of respondents said they didn't care, non-attenders being more likely to voice this opinion. Interpretation of this

Figure 22: The Irish language should be made more publicly visible

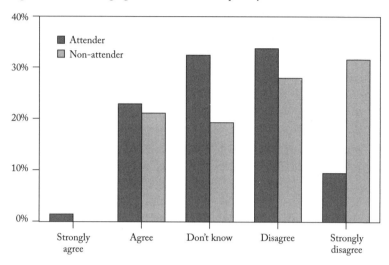

variable is difficult, however, because some respondents might be perfectly happy to have 'been excluded', while others may feel slighted, believing that they have been ignored or overlooked. The ambiguous nature of the question may explain this.

Government spending on the Irish language has frequently been a source of irritation for unionist politicians. Figure 21 shows that many respondents had a similar view. Non-attenders, at 53 per cent, were much more likely to oppose spending on Irish. While 34 per cent of attenders agreed with the statement, 42 per cent did not object. Finally, Figure 22 indicates only limited support for making Irish more publicly visible, the vast majority of both groups either disagreeing to some extent or ticking 'Don't know'.

SECTION B DATA

Section B was completed only by those who took the Gael-Linn course and, with no attender-v-non-attender comparisons to be made, can be summarised rather more concisely. The truncated sample included 74 respondents, 38 per cent male and 62 per cent female. At first glance, the contrast is quite marked and females seem more likely to have been attenders but this difference was not statistically significant.

Reasons for attending

Of particular interest are the reasons why respondents chose to attend the course and these data are presented in Table 2.

Table 2: Why respondents chose to do the course

Reason for attending	Per cent
I was curious	33.1%
I was interested in Irish	18.0%
I like learning languages	14.4%
I had nothing better to do	11.5%
Other reasons	11.5%
My friends were doing it	10.8%
There are Irish speakers in my family	0.7%

Curiosity was the most significant determining factor for many attenders by a large margin and a sizeable percentage indicated that they were 'interested in Irish'. An affinity for languages was the third most-chosen item and almost 11 per cent took the course because their friends were doing it.

The 'Other' category – not insubstantial – is rather interesting, a mixture of positive and negative reasons. Even though a large majority of respondents in Section A did not see Irish as being of value in the jobs marketplace (Figure 9), several specified the opportunity to enhance their CVs or to attain the Gael-Linn certificate at the end of the course as their 'other' reason in Table 2. Some cited 'culture' or 'wanting to learn my native language' as the catalyst, but several intimated that their choice had been determined by the logistics of the enrichment programme options in their schools. One female respondent felt she had been coerced into doing it by her teacher because she had previously learned Irish. Some pupils took a cynical view, one thinking 'it would be funny to laugh at the Irish language', and another wanting 'to understand why people wanted to revive a dead language'.

The family context

While only one respondent said they had done the course because there were Irish speakers in the family, more than 9 per cent of the attenders reported that they had relatives who spoke the language. Statistically, Catholics were more likely to have Irish-speaking relatives (50 per cent), but 15 per cent of Church of Ireland participants, 14 per cent of Presbyterians and 6 per cent of Other Protestants also had family links to Irish. These included parents, aunts/uncles, grandparents and cousins (one respondent ticked all boxes), but the questionnaire could not, of course, make assumptions about something as subjective as the fluency or facility of these relatives.

Respondents were asked how their families and friends reacted when they revealed that they were studying Irish and Figure 23 shows

Figure 23: How family and friends reacted

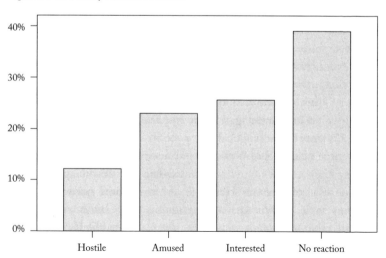

that 'No reaction' (39 per cent) was the most common response, while 26 per cent expressed interest. Almost 23 per cent reported that their families and friends were 'Amused' and only 12 per cent were 'Hostile'. Another question (not shown) asked pupils if they believed that it was easier for their generation to get to know Irish than it was for their parents' generation. Almost half the sample believed that it was indeed easier, although 19 per cent disagreed and there was a significant 'Don't know' component.

Taken together, the two variables offer an optimistic commentary on how Irish is perceived by the young people surveyed and their families. A generally benign in-the-home reaction and the popular view that it is easier to approach Irish now than it was a generation ago might offer hope that old stereotypes can be challenged.

It was not to be expected that many pupils would have the opportunity to use Irish outside school and, of the seven who said they did, only one mentioned 'in the home'. Other responses to the question 'If you do use it outside school, where?' produced little variety, mainly involving references to 'The South' and 'holidays in Ireland'. Indeed, when pupils were asked if they wished they had more opportunities to use Irish, there appeared to be only limited appetite for reinforcement outside school, as 40 per cent 'didn't care', 40 per cent said 'no' and only 20 per cent replied 'yes'.

Course elements

The Gael-Linn course introduces pupils to Irish in a variety of ways. The language component is at its core but, as demonstrated in Chapter Three, the aim is to place it in a wider context through specialist lectures on different facets of Irish, thus ensuring a more rounded perspective. Table 3, below, considers the popularity of most of the elements. Respondents were invited to choose the two items they most enjoyed but some pupils ticked more and, although a minor violation of questionnaire parameters, it seems sensible to include all.

Learning Irish was the most popular choice for students. The study of place names, too, was a popular choice, while the lecture on music and the two traditions also scored highly, as did Gaelic

Table 3: What attenders liked most about the course	
Items selected	*Per cent*
Learning Irish	23.1%
Place names	20.7%
Music and the two traditions	17.2%
Gaelic surnames in English	16.0%
The Protestant Gaelic tradition	9.5%
History of the Irish language	8.3%
Hiberno-English	3.6%
Other	1.8%

surnames in English. The relatively high percentages for place names and Gaelic surnames in English are consistent with the observation earlier in this chapter that high percentages of respondents listed these items as ways in which they had encountered Irish, possibly reflecting an awareness of the language in their local environments and in how it related to them personally.

The four most frequently chosen items in Table 3 have something else in common – they all place the Irish language in a contemporary context. Just as place names and surnames derived from Irish are all around people of all ages and religions in Northern Ireland, so is music easily accessible, either via radio/TV or in a live context. Percentages for these items contrast with lower scores for 'The Protestant Gaelic tradition', 'History of the Irish language' and 'Hiberno-English'. The comparative unpopularity of these items suggests that respondents had less interest in the historical perspective, while the most popular items can be broadly classified as 'living Irish'. This is a very significant point and not just in statistical terms.

On this occasion the 'Other' element was not especially informative, including music (already covered by the main categories) and sports, an item perhaps briefly mentioned in passing by Gael-Linn lecturers but not the subject of a lecture in its own right.

The political dimension

Attenders were asked if they felt their political views had changed as

Figure 24: Has learning Irish made you more sympathetic to nationalist or republican views?

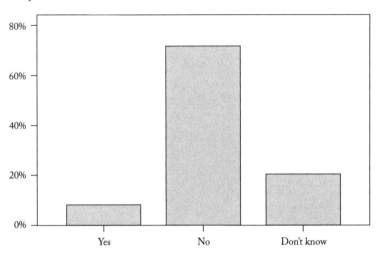

a result of learning Irish and the figures indicate a resounding 'No'. Offered the response options of 'A Little' and 'Not at All', more than 97 per cent chose the latter. A follow-up question dealt with the issue in a more specific way, asking if learning Irish had made attenders more sympathetic to nationalist or republican views (Figure 24).

The figures again support the view that the sample did not believe learning Irish would change their beliefs, 72 per cent saying they had not become more sympathetic towards nationalist/republican views. However, 20 per cent didn't know and 8 per cent agreed – but it should be noted that becoming 'more sympathetic' towards a particular view does not imply a move away from one's own beliefs.

Evaluating the course

A range of variables assesses the value of the course in providing pupils with the opportunity to learn Irish and to become acquainted with elements of the associated culture.

From Figure 25 it is clear that an overwhelming majority of respondents did not think they would have had the chance to learn

Figure 25: If you hadn't done the course, do you think you would ever have had the chance to learn Irish?

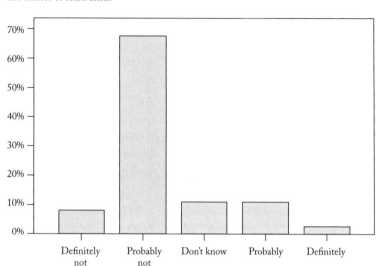

Irish had it not been for the Gael-Linn course. Eight per cent were 'definite' about this, while 68 per cent believed they 'probably' would not have had the opportunity. Only 14 per cent took the opposite view: members of the small Catholic contingent were most likely to believe that they could have had the chance to learn the language without the enrichment programme but even here they were in the minority.

Asked if they thought that learning Irish had helped them understand their culture and heritage better (Figure 26), almost half the respondents (47 per cent) agreed to some extent, while 34 per cent disagreed/strongly disagreed and 19 per cent didn't know. The variable is probably best considered in the context of an earlier questionnaire item in Section A, the statement 'Irish is an important part of my culture'. There, only 29 per cent of attenders agreed that it was, so Figure 26 could be interpreted as showing that while many felt their cultural understanding was enhanced by doing the course they did not necessarily regard it as being an important part of *their* personal social capital. But it might be too much to expect that such a short course should lead to a dramatic change.

Figure 26: Learning Irish has helped me understand my culture and heritage better

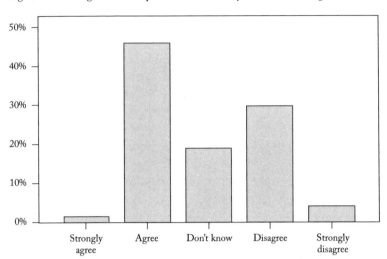

Figure 27: Do you feel you have benefited from doing the course?

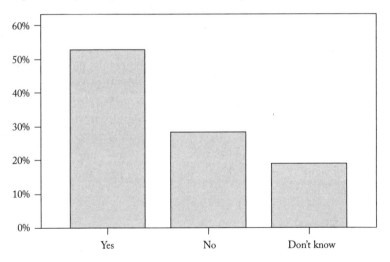

Evaluating the course is not something that can easily be done in one question, as so many separate factors come into play, but Figure 27 does provide an overall measure of its value as perceived by Gael-Linn's 'clients'. Fifty-three per cent believed that they had

Figure 28: People who do not know anything about Irish are missing out

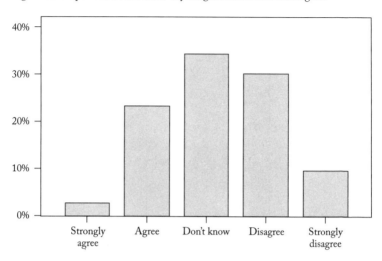

benefited, although 28 per cent felt they had not, with 19 per cent unsure.

The 'Missing out' variable (Figure 28) is a codicil to the course evaluation sequence and allowed attenders to look at Irish in a more 'global' way. Many respondents who rated the course positively and saw the benefits of a greater understanding of the Irish language were not necessarily convinced that those who did not have exposure to it were in any way disadvantaged. This again appears to firmly situate the perceived value of Irish in a purely personal context. As seen earlier, the popularity of course items such as place names and Gaelic surnames would seem to indicate an interest in Irish at a local rather than global level.

Future intentions

To what extent course-attenders were motivated by the programme to continue their contact with the language and culture was assessed by a short sequence of variables on future intentions. Firstly, they were asked if they would consider learning *more about Irish* (in the broader cultural sense) – 41 per cent ticked 'Yes' and 39 per cent ticked 'No', with 20 per cent undecided. A second question asked if they would consider learning *more Irish* and the percentages show a marked shift (Figure 29).

The percentage who replied yes on this occasion increased to 47 per cent, while the 'No' component fell to 34 per cent. The 'Don't know' category remained stable, dropping by only one point. This might be interpreted as further evidence of the popularity of the language element in the Gael-Linn programme but the most important finding is that almost half of all attenders expressed a desire to at least consider learning more Irish in the future.

Those pupils who answered 'Yes' in Figure 29 were then invited to indicate in what way they would most like to further their knowledge of the language. Precisely half the sample said they would be content to 'study informally' on their own, while the remainder were split between studying to GCSE/A Level (26 per cent) and joining a learners' group (24 per cent). No one said they would like to study Irish at university level.

The responses at least indicate a willingness to explore the language further but another question then probed their potential commitment level by asking students if they would consider going

Figure 29: Would you consider learning more Irish in the future?

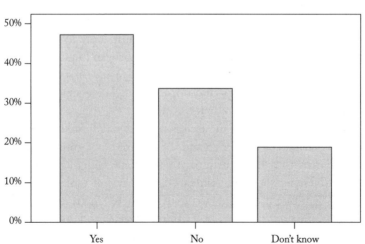

elsewhere to pursue their study if no classes were available locally. A large majority (64 per cent) were not prepared to go outside their locality and 19 per cent were unsure, with 17 per cent saying they would consider the elsewhere option. The answers to the previous two questions might at first glance be construed as indicating a lack of interest or commitment on the part of respondents, in that 'study informally on my own' and an unwillingness to travel elsewhere to learn Irish are effectively the lines of least resistance.

SUMMARY OF OTHER FINDINGS

Statistical testing[61] was used to look more closely at variables and attempt to confirm or rule out links between them. A lengthy section on the logic of testing, followed by the presentation of many percentages and statistical measurements, would be technical and turgid for the non-statistician, so for convenience and ease of reading what follows is a summary of the findings, concentrating on the more interesting trends and observations from the data.

Religion

Church of Ireland respondents were much more likely to describe their political views as 'Other/None' when compared to other Protestant groupings. Presbyterians were slightly more likely to label themselves as 'unionist/loyalist'. Religion did play an important – and statistically significant – role regarding attendance, respondents from a Church of Ireland background, for example, being more likely to have attended than their Presbyterian peers.

Further examination of the Religion variable (adjusted to include Church of Ireland, Presbyterian and Other Protestant groups only) in conjunction with a range of attitudinal variables highlighted some notable differences between religious categories. For example, 50 per cent of Church of Ireland respondents were 'interested' in the language, compared to 35 per cent of Presbyterians and 36 per cent of Other Protestants.

In terms of cultural importance, Church of Ireland respondents again took a more positive view than their peers – 29 per cent agreed that it was an 'important part of my culture', with 22 per cent Presbyterian and 16 per cent Others. As for the statement that everyone should have the chance to learn Irish, a majority of all groups were in favour, Church of Ireland respondents noticeably more so at 71 per cent (Presbyterian, 62 per cent; Other Protestant, 52 per cent).

It quickly became clear that Church of Ireland students were most likely to support 'positive' statements about Irish and to reject 'negative' statements (such as 'Irish is a dead language') in equal measure. Although many items produced broad agreement across all three groups, an obvious pattern emerged, with Church of Ireland respondents most sympathetic to Irish, Presbyterians much less sympathetic and Other Protestants varying from question to question. This broader pattern is seen in 'Agree' responses to the statement that Irish is 'too closely associated with republicans' (Church of Ireland, 71 per cent; Presbyterian, 84 per cent; 'Other', 76 per cent).

Church of Ireland respondents had a noticeably higher average encounter level (i.e. ways in which they had come across Irish) when compared to the Presbyterian and Other Protestant categories and, at 55 per cent, were most likely to agree that learning Irish had given them a better understanding of 'my culture and heritage', compared to 45 per cent of Presbyterians and 38 per cent of Other Protestants. However, when asked simply if they felt they had benefited from the course, a majority of Presbyterians (52 per cent) and Other Protestants (63 per cent) believed they had – only 45 per cent of Church of Ireland respondents agreed.

These figures appear to be contradictory but the wording of the statement may be a factor: Presbyterians and Others could have been more reluctant to look upon Irish as being part of '*my* culture and heritage', but still felt they had benefited from the course. On the other hand, Church of Ireland respondents, already more sympathetic towards Irish, might have felt they had less to learn and consequently 'benefited' less.

Gender

Gender did not play a significant role in determining whether or not respondents did the course and was found not to be an important factor in attitudes towards Irish.

The picture across the attitude variables tested was not a clear one, although females seemed to be generally more positive towards the language. They were, for example, more likely to be 'interested' in Irish and less likely to associate it with Catholics. Asked if everyone should have the chance to learn Irish, females were more positive at 71 per cent than males at 56 per cent. A greater proportion of females (35 per cent-v-24 per cent) wished they had had the chance to learn Irish earlier in their education. It cannot be ruled out that the issue of earlier female maturity is a factor in these differences and it should also be added that male responses were marginally more positive in a small number of other attitude variables.

Age

Given the small age-spread of 16–18, it was thought unlikely that this variable would be an important factor in determining attendance. However, analysis showed that 18-year-olds were less likely to have been attenders than their 17-year-old counterparts, while those in the 16-year-old group were evenly split.

It became quickly apparent that age was also a factor in other ways. It is interesting that younger respondents scored higher on recognition level, with averages of 5.23 for 16, 4.76 for 17 and 4.63 for 18. Age produced significant results across all tested variables. The most interesting finding was that the younger respondents appeared to be more sympathetic towards Irish across every component of the range subjected to statistical testing.

In relation to feelings on encountering Irish, for example, analysis showed that 62 per cent of 16-year-olds were 'Interested', compared to 50 per cent of 17-year-olds and 25 per cent of 18-year-olds. Similarly, on the cultural importance item, the 'Agree' level was 39 per cent at 16, 30 per cent at 17 and 10 per cent at 18. When asked if 'everyone should have the chance to learn Irish', the 'Agree' level was 85 per cent at 16, 71 per cent at 17 and 50 per cent at 18.

The pattern was a highly consistent one. Even when the comparatively small number of 16-year-olds was filtered out of the testing procedure, the difference between 17- and 18-year-olds remained significant. The reverse pattern might even have been predicted, working on the hypothesis that older respondents would take a more 'mature' attitude towards what is still a sensitive issue in Northern Ireland.

Politics

Perhaps unsurprisingly, those describing themselves as unionist or loyalist were less likely to have attended the course than their 'Other/None' counterparts, while those who described their politics as nationalist or republican registered a higher average encounter level than their peers.

After condensing the variable (unionist/loyalist and Other/None, with republican/nationalist filtered out) it was clear that politics was a key attitudinal factor. For example, when cross-tabbed with feelings on encountering Irish, it showed a fairly strong link between the variables: 67 per cent of unionists/loyalists were 'Disinterested', compared to only 21 per cent of Other/None.

On the question of who Irish 'is primarily for', the contrast was even clearer. Seventy-eight per cent of unionists/loyalists felt it was for Catholics and only 6 per cent believed it belonged to everyone. On the other hand, 41 per cent of Other/None respondents answered Catholics and 55 per cent thought it belonged to everyone. The 'Irish is a dead language' item showed, as we might now expect, high unionist/loyalist agreement (71 per cent), compared to 29 per cent for Other/None.

The strong link between politics and perceptions was found across all tested variables and unionists/loyalists consistently demonstrated a much 'darker' view of Irish, whereas the Other/None group tended towards a more positive view.

THE ULSTER-SCOTS QUESTION

While essentially on the periphery of this study, the items on Ulster-Scots are worth summarising briefly. Almost 90 per cent of all respondents had heard of Ulster-Scots but only 9 per cent claimed reading or speaking ability, while 15 per cent said that family members could read or speak it.

Asked if they themselves would like to learn Ulster-Scots, 46 per cent replied No, 17 per cent Yes and 37 per cent Don't Know. Almost half the sample (46 per cent) was of the opinion that Ulster-Scots is 'genuinely a language', but 28 per cent did not agree. A majority of all respondents (64 per cent) did not believe that Ulster-Scots 'is only for Protestants and unionists', although 16 per cent took the opposite view. On the issue of equal status and promotion for Ulster-Scots and Irish, a majority (53 per cent) agreed, 18 per cent disagreed and 28 per cent didn't know.

All of the statistical tests applied to the main questionnaire data could also be applied to the Ulster-Scots segment but only two variables, Religion and Politics, were used to try to establish if respondents' views were defined by these items. The figures above have already shown that, even though a relatively small minority expressed a desire to learn it, a majority felt it should be on an equal footing with Irish in terms of status and promotion. Of course, attaching value to something does not always involve a desire to become personally involved: during the Troubles, some may have expressed pride in different paramilitary groups, but that did not mean they wished to engage personally.

With Catholics and None filtered out, Presbyterians appeared to be the most aware of Ulster-Scots issues, 95 per cent having 'heard of it', compared to 75 per cent for the Church of Ireland group. While few claimed ability in the language, Presbyterians were most likely to answer Yes and also to say that they had family members able to read or speak Ulster-Scots. Almost 50 per cent of Presbyterians believed it 'is genuinely a language' (Church of Ireland, 29 per cent; Other Protestant, 57 per cent). Thirty-five per cent of Presbyterians, on the other hand, believed that it was not (Church of Ireland, 10 per cent;

Other Protestant, 22 per cent). This result was significant but heavily skewed by a large Church of Ireland 'Don't Know' component of 62 per cent. Presbyterians, at 60 per cent, were most likely to say that Ulster-Scots and Irish should be given equal status (Church of Ireland, 48 per cent; Other Protestant, 50 per cent).

Cross-tabulation of Politics and the Ulster-Scots items produced some statistically significant results. Unionists and loyalists appeared to be more 'in touch' with Ulster-Scots, either as speakers/readers themselves, or by claiming to have family members with such ability. A majority of unionists/loyalists believed Ulster-Scots is 'genuinely a language' (51 per cent), compared to 43 per cent for Other/None, but this did not translate into any great apparent hunger for learning Ulster-Scots – 21 per cent of unionists/loyalists and 12 per cent of Other/None expressed interest in doing so. Unionists/loyalists were significantly more likely to believe Ulster-Scots was 'only for Protestants and unionists', with 34 per cent compared to just 4 per cent of Other/None, although a higher proportion of both groups (unionist/loyalist, 48 per cent; Other/None, 72 per cent) disagreed. Finally, there was general agreement among both groups that Ulster-Scots and Irish should be given equal status and promoted equally (unionist/loyalist, 51 per cent; Other/None, 59 per cent).

CONCLUSIONS

Some findings were perhaps predictable but others were surprising, such as the apparent significance of age in relation to attitudes. Religion saw the emergence of a very distinct pattern that seems to indicate that members of different denominations have different views on Irish. The difference between Church of Ireland respondents and their Presbyterian counterparts is fascinating and a larger questionnaire sample would almost certainly have revealed equally intriguing differences in relation to the smaller Protestant denominations.

Gender turned out to be of no real significance, but politics appeared to play a very important role in determining attitudes, as was expected. That younger respondents surveyed were demonstrably more sympathetic towards Irish than their older counterparts is one of the most interesting findings. It might suggest that, as the Troubles recede into memory, they did not bring the same 'baggage' with them to the debate as their older counterparts. Perhaps the 18-year-olds studied had more vivid recollections of the Troubles than 16-year-olds because they were more aware of paramilitary violence and its effects when they were young children, even if this was only observed on television. If that is the case, the age factor offers much optimism for the future.

7

LEARNING THE LESSONS

INTRODUCTION

The aim of this work is to contribute to our understanding of young Protestants' views on the Irish language in Northern Ireland. Such an understanding is important, given that this is a post-conflict society coming to terms with a violent and disruptive past which discouraged individuals from exploring aspects of culture that were 'off-limits'. For Protestants, the Irish language was something that very few would openly take part in and be seen to enjoy. Those few Protestants who did engage with Irish were exceptions to the rule and often had, or at least felt they had, to pursue their interests in a clandestine manner.

While research has previously been conducted on the attitudes of adults to language issues, I hope that this book, by addressing the specific views of young people, is well-timed, given the planned changes in the education system in Northern Ireland. Although it is not possible to examine these plans in any detail because of their fast-changing nature, education reform will present new challenges and new opportunities. What is clear, though, is that even in the changed atmosphere of post-Troubles Northern Ireland, the question of language remains a significant faultline between the two communities.

SUMMARY AND OVERVIEW

Reviewing the fieldwork

To an extent, there was a difference between questionnaire information and focus group information that is inherently a part of the quantitative-v-qualitative dichotomy: in the groups, respondents had more clearly defined views on all issues. But this can be easily explained in that focus groups – unlike questionnaires – provide 'no place to hide'. It is easy to tick the 'Don't know' box in a questionnaire but, with a face-to-face question, that option all but disappears. Focus group dynamics remove the 'easy option' of neutrality as an automatic response – unless that 'Don't know' position is genuine and strongly held. The interviewee is under pressure to come up with a defensible position.

Careful focus group management, by identifying the 'quieter ones' and gradually bringing them into the process, encouraged them to think about the substantive issues, weighing them up as the debate proceeded before gently coaxing them to express their views. These views, hopefully, are an amalgam of subconscious ideas and careful consideration of the arguments they have listened to during the session. After all, the issues being discussed were often matters that the participant had never had to think about before and formulating an opinion takes time. We have already seen that even some of those with clearly defined views slightly moderated their positions at several stages in the process.

A well-designed questionnaire has statistical validity; a focus group, as qualitative data, does not. But it can provide reinforcement of key findings and is the ideal partner to the questionnaire in multi-strand research. In the case of this work, the groups fulfilled that brief and it is worth noting that virtually all of the issues and discourses raised in the groups had already been mentioned in the open-ended sections of the questionnaire.

Reflections and reflexivity

Looking back on the fieldwork is an important exercise that helps lead to an understanding of one's own possible impact on the project, as well as a certain degree of soul-searching. As mentioned in the introduction, I had to ask myself: 'Did I, the researcher, in any way influence the outcome of the research?' This is where reflexivity can be an important part of the qualitative methodology. A 'general principle', according to Coolican (2004:235), is to take 'methodological precautions' which alert readers to your 'own role in constructing what they are reading and of your own possible "stake" and so on'. In social sciences research, it is becoming increasingly difficult to avoid reflecting on one's personal relationship to the research process.

The questionnaire is an impersonal instrument and once it is completed the students leave the room, presumably looking upon it as merely another part of the school day. Every attempt was made to produce a questionnaire that was neither biased nor 'leading'. The qualitative element is different, as I was, to an extent, intruding on their personal lives. This is where there may have been a danger of my own feelings affecting outcomes. I was curious about participants' views and it is reasonable to assume that they were curious about *my* views. Why, they may have asked, did I want to know how they felt about Irish or Ulster-Scots. Did they feel there might have been 'right' answers and 'wrong' answers? It was important, therefore, that I gave no clue as to what was 'right' and what was 'wrong' and allowed focus group dynamics to take their course.

Most of the ethical issues which arose only became apparent on location. Had they been anticipated beforehand, appropriate coping strategies could have been devised, yet most were entirely unpredictable. It was essential that I did not become an active participant in the process, yet the temptation was always there. I had to make a conscious effort not to counter what I considered unsustainable arguments because the statement may have been totally tenable and true for the person who made it. As an independent researcher, I could not rule someone's opinion 'out of order' or 'off the wall'. I had to leave my own personal bias to one side.

The beauty of the focus group is that, once the process has taken on its own life and energy, the researcher becomes a mere observer/facilitator, while the subjects themselves argue the points. Occasionally, however, the tables are turned, and a participant will ask the researcher a question. I was asked, for example, what the difference between Irish and Scots Gaelic is and felt I had to respond, explaining the shared heritage of both. Thankfully, such questions were rare and my response to that particular question was unlikely to be interpreted as a direction.

As the groups came to a close, there was an end-game in that, having elicited their opinions, it was only natural that they should want to find out a little about me. The data had been collected by this stage and I revealed myself to be a Protestant Irish speaker.[62] For some, it was a pleasing dénouement, as they realised they had been talking to someone who they may have felt was sympathetic to their opinions. Not all may have shared this view, but the formality of the groups gave way to a friendly banter, some students asking me to translate various English words, phrases and even insults into Irish.

At this stage, I had the freedom to become an active participant post-event, knowing that the data had been collected with minimal direct personal intervention and that whatever I said now would not have any bearing on the quality of the focus group interactions. For some social scientists in the past, reflexivity may have been a 'problem' or something to be evaded but is now 'one of the strong currents within most qualitative approaches' (Coolican, 2004:234) and a valuable means of ensuring that one's own potential to become an active agent (as opposed to neutral observer – the perhaps unattainable 'ideal') is acknowledged and placed in perspective.

Significant findings

The questionnaire was very successful in ascertaining the views of students. The consistency of responses, plus high statistical correlation of positive/positive and negative/negative answers, indicates that the subjects took the enquiries seriously. The dataset opens a window on their general feelings about Irish and reveals many interesting points, some expected and some unexpected.

Denomination (i.e. types of Protestantism) was a statistically significant factor in determining attendance and it quickly became clear that Church of Ireland respondents were more positive towards the language than their Presbyterian counterparts, often by quite a margin in percentage terms. Might this mean that Church of Ireland respondents have a 'more Irish' sense of identity?

Politics, not unexpectedly, proved to be an important attitudinal factor, with those labelling themselves as unionist or loyalist much less likely to express positive views towards the language than those who described themselves as Other or None. Differences were often statistically significant when 'target' variables were analysed by politics, and unionist or loyalist respondents undoubtedly adopted a 'darker' view overall towards Irish.

Worth noting in itself is that so many described their politics as 'None', possibly indicating their lack of interest in the subject or, alternatively, feeling reticent or even embarrassed about labelling themselves. That so many chose 'None' might be an indicator of increasing political agnosticism on the part of young people in Northern Ireland.

The most encouraging finding of all, perhaps, was definitive evidence that the students had no objection to the provision of opportunities to learn Irish and indeed felt it desirable that everyone should have this choice in school. Over 70 per cent of attenders and 52 per cent of non-attenders agreed that Irish should be an optional subject, although there was less support for making it available to people of *all ages*. The difference, though, may be one of context, as the second question introduced other factors. The research has shown that compulsory Irish would be a turn-off for most and the word 'choice' was one used frequently in the focus groups.

There was certainly no appetite for education through the medium of Irish but, positively, few believed that Irish was being 'forced' on Protestants and unionists. Furthermore, the statistics show that the perceived unionist fear of Irish 'turning' learners into Catholics, nationalists or republicans is a nonsense for young people.

The discovery that age was a positive factor is something that offers hope for the future. Younger students were more favourable towards Irish (significantly so, in statistical terms) than their older counterparts and this might be an indication that attitudes are mellowing as memories of the Troubles fade among young people in Northern Ireland. The 'children of the ceasefire' factor is something that can be built upon.

Dealing specifically with course-takers, did the programme achieve its aims? There was a clear and measurable difference between how takers and non-takers scored on the number of 'Irish' items they recognised. However, while we can show statistically that attenders recognised more items on average, we cannot say that being course-takers made them more aware. It is a tempting – if dangerous – conclusion which could only be proven with more complex regression analysis techniques that are beyond the scope of this book. The possibility that attenders were already more aware of Irish beforehand must not be discounted, however alluring it might be to do so.

Given that the course approached Irish from a 'standing start', in that the vast majority of participants had had no pre-experience of Irish, the fact that 53 per cent overall felt they had benefited is encouraging. Even when this figure is broken down by various key variables, the results are still around the 50 per cent mark. Allowing for an often sizeable 'Don't know' component, this has to be interpreted as success.

The 'standing start' factor provides one reason why attenders did not see Irish on a par with 'mainstream' languages. Asked if they would be able to understand Irish in its written or spoken form, only ten attenders ticked 'Yes': technically all could have done so (albeit with a highly qualified 'Yes'). It seems apparent that most did not feel they had 'learned' enough to claim even a basic knowledge of Irish. Naturally, a course that lasts between eight and ten weeks cannot be expected to work miracles. After all, 'standard' language teaching takes place over many years.

Worth noting is how different religious groups rated the course by context. Presbyterians, for example, showed greater approval on the straightforward 'benefit' item, but less approval when the course was expressed in terms of '*my* culture and heritage'. Church of Ireland respondents may have been more in tune with Irish overall, yet it was Presbyterians and Other Protestants who seemed to derive the most 'benefit' from Gael-Linn's EPGS.

It is clear that the course opened new doors to the pupils, most believing that they would probably not have had the chance to learn Irish otherwise. The percentages of all participants who said that they would be willing to either learn more about Irish or learn more Irish were also heartening, although when probed further relatively few seemed prepared to commit themselves in the direction of formal learning.[63]

Again, other factors come into play: further formal study at their schools was not an option for respondents and to even attempt to undertake a recognised qualification in the subject would have demanded a major commitment at a time when pupils were at a defining moment in their academic lives; upcoming exams were an understandable priority. The reluctance to travel elsewhere to learn Irish cannot be dismissed as 'laziness' or lack of commitment, because the political geography of Northern Ireland must be considered – most Irish-language classes are still held in areas where Protestants and unionists might not feel comfortable, peace process or not.

Rejection of Scots Gaelic

The focus groups showed decisively that Scots Gaelic is not the way ahead in Northern Ireland. There was little appetite for learning it and even those opposed to Irish believed it was still preferable to and more relevant than Scots Gaelic. Colmcille (previously Iomairt Cholm Cille) might create ties between mainly Protestant Scots Gaelic speakers and mainly Catholic Irish speakers, but these contacts will probably not initiate any greater understanding of either language among Northern Ireland Protestants and unionists.

Thousands of Scots come to Northern Ireland each year to participate in the Twelfth celebration, while the fanaticism with which local fans follow Celtic and Rangers underlines old associations and rivalries (see Bradley, 2006). Glasgow remains in many ways a curious mirror image of Ireland a century ago, as evidenced by the eternal rivalry between 'Protestant' Rangers and 'Catholic' Celtic.[64]

In this way, the link is still there, but it is based on sociocultural ties, not linguistic ones. While history may prove that many Northern Ireland Protestants can trace some of their roots to Scots-Gaelic-speaking ancestors, this does not mean any special affection for that language. Gael-Linn appeared to recognise this at an early stage in its course development, by dropping the class on Scots Gaelic, as outlined previously.

MAKING IRISH RELEVANT

'Living Irish'

The popularity of certain course items should be a matter of reflection for Gael-Linn, but also has broader implications for Protestant understanding of and sympathy towards the Irish language. Interest was highest in terms of what I have described as 'living Irish'. The approval ratings for the language element, surnames, place names and the musical tradition show a thirst for more information about Irish in a primarily contemporary context and – especially – how it relates to the students' own lives.

The questionnaire showed what pupils want from the course and Gael-Linn must be attentive to their requirements as consumers by cashing in on the curiosity factor. A constant re-evaluation of the elements offered will make sure that the EPGS remains relevant. The course seems to be at its most successful in making students aware of the Irish that is all around them in a positive way they can appreciate.

The historical elements of the course did appear to be less appealing for most students, but it must be added that a few participants expressed a particular interest in this aspect of the enrichment programme. Nevertheless, the 'living Irish' element was always to the fore. Questionnaire-wise, music was very popular and many regarded that lecture as a highlight of the course. As for the focus groups, the music element was also highly rated but students were more inclined to mention contemporary 'Irish' pop bands rather than traditional musicians. That is not surprising as they would have had little opportunity to become acquainted with the traditional scene and consequently lump 'genuine' folk and contemporary 'Irish' music together.

Teaching materials

If the situation arises where young Protestants are to be introduced to Irish in formal education, much thought should be given to course structure and focus, as what works for Catholics might not hold for Protestant pupils.

The Gael-Linn programme could be of much help in developing suitable methods and resources for the dissemination of Irish across the spectrum. A course with too much emphasis on historical elements might be unappealing for most Protestant students, whereas one that is focused on 'practical' Irish could bring the subject to life in an inspirational way.

Neutrality in terms of teaching materials is essential and Gael-Linn's excellent resource pack proves that the right balance can be found – unfortunately, it was not available to all students. One could find fault with the Gael-Linn pack in that it uses old-fashioned cassette tapes and it is to be hoped that the planned reissue is based on more up-to-date media. Introductory courses such as Hughes's *Bunchomhrá Gaeilge* (2002) are neutral in tone and make use of CDs to set Irish in a conversational context (using native speakers). New technology, such as interactive DVDs, computer programs and even downloadable 'podcasts', offer a way into Irish for the iPod generation. Every use must be made of the technologies with which young people identify.

Overall, there does already seem to be a general trend towards more secular textbooks, with less emphasis on an idealised 'Catholic' lifestyle, involving priests, hurling and the like. Neutrality must never mean censorship, but the suitability of works such as Ó hEaráin's *An Focal Gafa* (1996), which appears to eulogise republicanism by using illustrations[65] that would enrage most Protestants and unionists, might usefully be questioned in any teaching environment.

Employment opportunities

The research showed that pupils did not feel that knowledge of Irish had any relevance in today's job market. This is another reason why a contemporary emphasis is important and takes the 'relevance' issue to its logical conclusion. One focus group participant, for example, thought that making Irish available in Protestant schools would create teaching jobs for Protestants in those schools – but little else. He obviously overlooked the possibility that Catholic teachers would be immediately equipped to take on the role! After all, where are the potential Protestant Irish teachers?

The general point is interesting, though, as few of the respondents would be aware of the flourishing Irish-language job market. Catholic pupils studying Irish will be aware that a wide variety of opportunities awaits those with qualifications in Irish, but young Protestants, who have little or no contact with Irish, can hardly be expected to know what the Irish-language sector offers in terms of career options.

Opportunities exist in the media, translation, administration and other fields. Another salient point is that fair employment legislation in Northern Ireland means applicants from 'under-represented' sections of the community are, as job advertisements often point out, 'especially welcome'. This is true of the Police Service of Northern Ireland, where applicants from the Catholic community are 'especially welcome', to counter inherited imbalances. The converse is true in the Irish-language sector and those from the Protestant community should expect to receive the same treatment in this area, where few are employed.

Employment opportunities must be flagged up as an incentive. Language economics is a relatively new academic discipline with evolving paradigms but Protestant Irish speakers with the appropriate qualifications could have a distinct advantage in the Northern Ireland context, although it would be preferable if self-advancement were not the sole motivation. François Grin, who has made a huge contribution to our understanding of language economics, reminds us that it is important not to lose sight of a language's 'non-market' value, which can offer much enjoyment in itself by providing, for example, access to other cultures (2003:para. 2). Nevertheless, Protestants have to be made aware of the employment possibilities at as early a stage as possible and introduced to Irish before it is too late. Realistically, once a student has chosen his/her GCSEs, it probably is too late.

'A language for old people'

Another interesting point from the focus groups was that many participants saw Irish as a language of 'old people'. This was the case for decades but today, with the growing Irish-medium education sector and wider knowledge of Irish generally in places where it has been 'extinct' for many many years, the language has many young speakers. Unfortunately, because of the political divisions in Northern Ireland, young Protestants are unlikely to come into contact with those who do use Irish, because they are from 'the other side'.

They are unaware that Irish is vibrant, energetic and a valid means of communication, just as up-to-date in terms of 'techno-speak' as any other European language. As Northern Ireland moves into a new and peaceful era, it is to be hoped that one of the benefits will be increased contact between young people from both traditions. Formal initiatives will probably continue to be an important part of that process for the foreseeable future, but exchanges between Protestant schools in Northern Ireland and schools in Gaeltacht areas could have positive outcomes in relation to Irish.

CHALLENGES, CHANGES AND OPPORTUNITIES

Globalisation

The globalisation discourse used by many students in the focus groups suggested that, in a fast-changing 'global village', Irish is redundant as a language of daily communication. This discourse, as applied by the students, ignores increasing interest in minority languages around Europe. Coulmas (2005:13) notes the 'contradictory' spread of major European languages: while these are responsible for reducing linguistic diversity globally, linguistic diversity is increasing in their home countries. More specifically, Solymosi draws attention to the growing awareness of identity among minorities in Hungary (2006:40) as just one of many examples. Yet in 'Protestant' schools in Northern Ireland, most students are encouraged to think globally, with languages such as French or Spanish perceived as being important in terms of commerce throughout the EU and beyond. Business French and even Japanese were alternatives to the Gael-Linn course in some schools.

However, another language matter only became a factor during the lifetime of this research. The questionnaires were administered before the implications of EU enlargement had become apparent, but Northern Ireland has since seen an influx of migrant workers from what are termed the 'Accession States'. They have brought their own languages with them. Crystal astutely predicted the linguistic complexities that EU expansion would mean years ago (1994:36), as did Stork and Widdowson even farther back, in the days when it was still called the Common Market (1974:168). Hayes, more recently (2003:175), recognised that the relocation of other groups here would be 'one of the greatest tests'.

Jarman (2006:47) notes how patterns of migration to Northern Ireland have changed. Initially, a 'substantial number' of Portuguese and Filipino workers arrived but the biggest change is that involving nationals from the so-called 'A8' Accession States which joined the EU in 2004. Only the UK, the Republic of Ireland and Sweden gave freedom of employment rights to the newly admitted Eastern European countries. Jarman (ibid:50) says that Northern Ireland appears to be attracting a proportionately larger number of A8 nationals than other UK regions and the pattern differs from previous models, in that incomers are moving to smaller towns and villages. National Insurance number applications in Northern Ireland used by Jarman show that, between April 2003 and January 2006, Poland (12,020), Lithuania (4,987) and Portugal (3,605) were the top three applicant countries. The real figures are probably much higher.

This introduces the question of language shift but, as any shift among the migrants is likely to be in the direction of English,[66] it need not detain us here. For our purposes, young Protestant people are now much more likely to come into contact with Polish, Lithuanian and Portuguese than they are with Irish. As the questionnaire showed, most had encountered Irish in indirect ways (on TV/radio and in place names, for example) but few had heard it spoken at first hand. In towns around Northern Ireland today, however, they hear Polish, Lithuanian or Portuguese in shopping centres, cafés and from neighbours. The possibility of them encountering Irish in the same environments is slight.

While immigration is a phenomenon whose social effects have still to be fully understood in Northern Ireland, it could be to the detriment of Irish. The concept of 'useful languages' could change, with young people much more likely to hear Polish or Lithuanian than French or German, never mind Irish. If Irish falls farther down what I term the 'linguistic league table', it could become harder to inspire young Protestants to learn Irish, as its relevance is again questioned. Unionist politicians are likely to employ statistics on the use of ethnic minority languages as part of their argument against funding or special status for Irish. Chinese[67] has often been used by unionists in this way.

Migration may have huge implications for Northern Ireland and there is a need for research into the many questions it raises, not least the increase in racist attacks (NICEM, 2006:5). Other disciplines and scholars are better placed to answer these questions. From the perspective of this work, migration presents a new difficulty for those trying to promote Irish as a language for all. However, there is the possibility that it could help move things in the opposite direction as young people, noting the easy bilingualism of migrants, feel some sort of need to find out more about culture closer to home. At its crudest level this could even become distilled into one simple question: 'They've got *their* language that I don't understand. Why don't I have a language that *they* don't understand?'

Ulster-Scots

The Ulster-Scots question has admittedly been given less attention than it deserves in this research, but the title of my book explains why – I am primarily concerned with attitudes towards Irish among young Protestants and other researchers are doing more focused work in this area. This is right and proper, for young people's attitudes towards Ulster-Scots deserve full investigation. In my work, the issue was introduced as a means of bias elimination in the research package.

However, there are important issues which could impact on the acceptability of Irish to young people. The questionnaire data revealed highly polarised views on Ulster-Scots and I was taken aback by the unexpected energy and liveliness of the focus group debates on what was meant to be a brief question *en passant*. That some young people said they would be prepared to learn Ulster-Scots 'if Irish continues to be a big thing' smacked of a 'them and us' approach, placing the issue firmly in the rights discourse arena and revealing that language issues continue to touch a raw nerve.

The danger is that Ulster-Scots becomes entrenched as the *de facto* 'Protestant language'. This would overlook (a) the fact that it is not spoken in all parts of Northern Ireland, including the capital city Belfast, and (b) that many Catholics in some of its 'heartlands' use it with the same fluency as their Protestant neighbours.[68] The worst outcome could be that young Protestants are directed towards Ulster-Scots as 'theirs alone' and denied the chance to explore their Irish heritage. Careful management, however, could promote mutual understanding and respect for others' cultures and show that diversity can be a source of enjoyment.

Attitudes to the GAA

A number of students clearly had problems with the Gaelic Athletic Association (GAA). The issue of sport had not been factored into the questionnaire but came to the fore in the focus groups. That this should have been the case when the discussion framework was concerned with language – not sport – is significant and reflective of highly negative Protestant perceptions of the association. It would not be stretching a point to say that the GAA is often regarded by Protestants and unionists as part of a broader pan-nationalist agenda. For many years the ban that prevented members of the security forces in Northern Ireland playing its games was proof for unionists that the body was not just steeped in the republican tradition but was an active player in promoting an anti-British mindset among Northern nationalists.

This is an important matter. It arose in the focus groups but was flagged in other ways. In Chapter Two it became clear that adult Protestant learners of Irish felt uncomfortable when the GAA was raised in peripheral class interactions. At coffee-break times, for example, Catholic speakers might discuss weekend club matches,

All-Ireland semi-finals and so on, joking about the merits or otherwise of particular county teams, using a lot of 'in-group' jargon which seems to exclude Protestants. As GAA-speak is common currency among many Catholics it would be unfair to attach any malevolent intent to this phenomenon – particularly as they may have assumed that all fellow-learners would naturally share their view of the world (Bradley, C., 2008).

Yet the GAA is an issue for Protestants of all ages. In Chapter Three Ó Ciaráin mentioned that lecturers found themselves fielding 'broad questions' about the organisation. The GAA is probably a *bête noire* for unionists but some focus group participants expressed a curiosity about the organisation, even to the extent of wishing that they had had the opportunity to play its sports.

The GAA's relationship with Northern Ireland Protestants has always been difficult, and most unionists view the organisation with some suspicion and no little distaste. Recent years have seen significant changes that have altered 'anti-British' regulations in its constitution. Rule 21 – which prevented members of the security forces in Northern Ireland from playing Gaelic games – was dropped in 2001 as the peace process led to the replacement of the Royal Ulster Constabulary (disliked by most nationalists) with the Police Service of Northern Ireland. In April 2005 the GAA's long-standing ban on the playing of 'foreign games' at its Croke Park headquarters in Dublin was set aside to accommodate the Irish rugby and soccer teams while their national ground was being rebuilt.

Both moves generated tremendous debate and soul-searching for the GAA. The first, vis-à-vis the security forces, might be interpreted as a daring investment in the peace process. The second, vis-à-vis 'foreign games', is seen by some as a coming to terms with the 'new Ireland' where cultural pluralism is the keystone, although cynics might say that the GAA sold out its nationalist roots to cash in on the temporarily homeless soccer and rugby teams.

Other developments have kept the GAA in the spotlight. In 2007, a Protestant County Fermanagh Gaelic footballer quit the game after receiving sectarian abuse from opposing fans and competitors. The player, who had lost a number of relatives, including his father, because of republican violence during the Troubles, resumed playing after the County Board assured him that such intolerance would not be countenanced. More positively, the GAA appeared to tentatively extend the hand of friendship to the Protestant community in 2007 when it helped progress the development of a hurling team which brought together young people from both sides of the sectarian divide in north Belfast (probably one of the most polarised areas in all of Northern Ireland). Two Catholic and two Protestant schools were involved in this initiative.

In reality, the GAA and Irish are two separate issues but unionists tend not to make the distinction. The GAA's 'Irishness' operates on a variety of levels (stadia signage, ground announcements, etc) but the language of day-to-day business is really English. To many unionists the GAA will remain a focus of suspicion for the foreseeable future but the organisation at last appears to be becoming more conscious of a need to engage with Protestants.[69]

In a thoughtful essay, Fermanagh footballer Colm Bradley called on the GAA to 'disentangle itself from the political baggage that its rulebook carries' and do much more to reach out to the unionist community (2008). Urging the organisation to overcome a 'paralysis of real action' and drop the 'political language', he may have taken the first step towards opening a meaningful debate which could overcome Protestant/unionist reservations about Gaelic sport by leaving politics to the politicians. The GAA may have a more significant role to play in changing Protestant attitudes towards 'the other side' than could ever have been imagined – not just in terms of sport or language.

Visibility of Irish

Curiously, given that so many respondents were fascinated by place names, the vast majority did not want to see Irish become 'more visible'. In some ways, Irish has been enjoying a higher profile. Information sheets and advertisements from some government departments carry logos in English and Irish (the inclusion of Ulster-Scots in some instances may have sweetened a potentially bitter pill). In October 2007 the Ulster Unionist Health Minister Michael McGimpsey reversed departmental policy to place advertisements and issue press releases in Irish as well as English. He maintained that the money spent on translation could be better spent on services. The tri-lingual logo on letterheads and press advertisements would remain but requests for Irish translations of documents would only be fulfilled if they met certain criteria.

It is interesting that the minister used the 'value for money' argument, a common discourse in the focus groups, where even respondents who were not hostile to Irish felt strongly that money should not be wasted on translation. Nevertheless, there has also been an increased realisation that Northern Ireland is a multilingual society and government information leaflets frequently include messages in other ethnic minority languages. A 2006 circular about changes in the rating structure had a 'further information' section in around ten languages, reflecting the diversity of cultures in contemporary Northern Ireland. The multilingual approach, perhaps, has watered down the hostility that might be provoked were these moves centred on Irish alone. But it cannot be denied that hostility does remain.

At a more local level, street signs are now appearing which also give the townland name, e.g. 'Sloan Street, Townland of Aughnacloy'.[70] Even though the signs are in English, the townland name provides a direct link to a hidden Irish background. Older people (from both traditions) are usually aware of their townland names; younger people less so.[71] But this brings Irish to life in a relevant way and has provoked no protest. These are positive developments which show in a low-key manner that Irish, whether or not the reader understands the townland name's Irish meaning, is part of the history of the area.

'New' place names differ from the Irish signage of republican areas erected during the 1980s when the language was at the forefront of the cultural 'struggle'. By giving recognition to the 'hidden' Irish of place names, the language gains currency in a non-confrontational manner. After all, place names are relevant to everyone, pre-dating modern divisions and conflicts. Furthermore, they could even invoke the curiosity factor, prompting people to seek a translation.

The Northern Ireland Placenames Project, based at Queen's

University Belfast, has enjoyed great success in taking 'place names on tour' with an exhibition that has given many from both sides of the community an understanding of their townland names. Local history societies, which bring together people of all backgrounds, have been keen consumers. The project's work is based on rigorous academic research but succeeds in making place names accessible and approachable for everyone.

History and role models

There is nothing wrong in playing up the role of Northern Protestants in the nineteenth-century Irish-language renaissance, but these pre-Partition pioneers cannot be twenty-first-century role models. As Adair (2000:145) asserts:

> Yesterday's achievements may be interesting and worthwhile, but these shouldn't be allowed to embargo current or future possibilities. Whilst we cannot function without a recognisable past, we are paralysed unless we seek to change and enlarge upon it.

The fact that the Cultúrlann in 'republican' west Belfast, a centre of the current language revival, is partly named in honour of Robert Shipboy MacAdam, the prominent nineteenth-century Protestant language revivalist, is not a key selling point. MacAdam and other revivalists bring nothing to a contemporary debate where Irish has been located firmly in a political milieu. An appreciation of this 'hidden history' is perhaps something that will only come with maturity. Even the loyalist paramilitaries who learned Irish in prison in more recent times are unlikely to serve as exemplars for a different generation. Seen through the eyes of 16-, 17- and 18-year-olds, they too are simply figures from history, linked to a loyalist 'cause' they neither identify with nor understand.

Could young Protestants benefit from Irish-speaking role models? Possibly, but there are no speakers with the 'street cred' required. Holmes (2001:56) says that role models for children include pop and sports stars who don't speak the minority language: the majority language has the glamour and power. To an extent, the youthful presenters of TG4 have disproved this by making the language appealing and trendy; a few respondents had already discovered the station, most notably because of its pop music output. Certainly, TG4 is not regarded as a 'politicised' factor and the station plays a very useful role in fostering the language in general, with even some appeal for those young Protestants who had discovered it.

In a way, minority languages can seem unglamorous in a contemporary cultural context. They need to be marketed, and in the Republic there are occasional advertising campaigns to promote Irish. That said, young Catholics were learning Irish in Northern Ireland long before this 'trendification', with boys in particular seemingly inspired by the 'macho' image of republican prisoners speaking Irish in jail (Pritchard, 2004:19/20). Macho republican 'glamour', however, cannot possibly be regarded as an inspiration of any sort for young Protestants or unionists.

Education reforms

The results of this study provide a cross-section of opinion across the grammar sector but education reforms will undoubtedly affect all schools, although there is no way of accurately predicting what the outcomes will be for young Protestants as regards Irish. There are some scenarios which might make it more difficult to facilitate engagement with the language but – simultaneously – there are other scenarios which might see Irish gently and uncontentiously nudged onto the curriculum for young Protestants.

The teachers interviewed agreed that modifications to the education system have had a damaging effect on the availability of elective modules, as schools struggle to cope with the demands of AS Level. This almost wiped out enrichment programmes and only a small number of institutions were able to retain them.[72] With the ultimate shape of post-primary arrangements still unclear, it remains to be seen how grammar schools will deal with this new world and whether or not they will continue to offer enrichment programmes such as Gael-Linn's.

One reason for optimism, however, is that post-primary schools are now expected to offer a wider range of subjects at GCSE and A Level and it is believed that this will lead to a pooling of resources, whereby students from a particular school may be able to study subjects not available in their 'home' institution. Falling enrolments and empty desks in both Protestant and Catholic schools are part of the equation, with economic necessity becoming a driving force for change in all sectors. Financial constraints could overcome barriers that previously seemed insuperable in Northern Ireland during the Troubles.

The 'Entitlement Framework' presents opportunities to provide previously unimaginable choices – for example, if School X offers German but not Spanish, while School Y offers Spanish but not German, resource-sharing will let students, if they wish, study both. This would enable Protestant pupils to do GCSE courses in Irish in nearby Catholic or integrated schools where it is taught. Advances in technology, too, have opened up new possibilities for distance learning, whereby a single lecturer can address multiple classrooms in different schools.

If this does become a reality, there are those who would balk at any such notion of 'mixing' (even in cyberspace) and one can expect concerted resistance from some politicians – and some parents – who might regard it as integrated education by the back door. Naturally, community relations on the ground in a given area could be an important factor.

The framework will not 'prescribe the courses that pupils should follow' (DENI, 2006b:4) and the combination of courses taken 'should reflect pupils' and parents' choices', so it seems unlikely that Irish would become a compulsory subject. Nevertheless, this scenario might put 'formal' Irish on the curriculum for Protestant pupils for the first time and would do it in the best possible way – by making it an option, not compulsory. Learning Irish would be a deliberate choice, not a timetabling imperative.

'DEPOLITICISATION' – A REALISTIC AIM?

This research suggests strongly that many believe 'depoliticisation' is an important component in any attempt to make Irish attractive to those from Protestant/unionist backgrounds, as the following focus group comments show:

I think you need to take the politics out of it. And ... if you take the politics out of it there are so many people who could feel that they could be able to learn it.

I think it's not really the politics or the people. It's just the extreme views of the politicians or whatever that make people wary. Just calm down a wee bit, and people will be more up for it.

The feeling that Irish is too closely associated with republicans underlines the 'image problem' the language faces among Protestants of all ages; whether it is possible to change this stereotypical view and shed the 'green' tinge unfortunately attached to the language remains to be seen.

I have already flagged up my personal discomfort with the concept of 'depoliticisation'. It requires careful consideration. Pupils wanted to see a scenario in which the 'politics were taken out of the language', but how realistic is this and what, indeed, does the word even mean? As seen in Chapter Two, English can be used in a contentious way but no one would suggest that it be 'depoliticised'.

Does 'depoliticisation' mean that republicans should stop using Irish? That's not a terribly realistic prospect, nor is the idea that Irish should only be used in a non-inflammatory way, as no one can prescribe the manner in which a language is spoken or written.

Republican slogans such as *'Tiocfaidh Ár Lá'* ('Our Day Will Come') are clearly antagonistic in the eyes of unionists and will remain so.[73] The desire for 'depoliticisation' as a precursor for Protestant re-engagement with Irish, then, is awkward. The alternative is an acceptance that while the language can be used to express republican sentiments it can equally be used to articulate a unionist viewpoint, as in *'Ní Thiocfaidh Bhur Lá'* ('Your Day Will *Not* Come'). Taken to the extreme, this could be described as 'antidote Irish', a way of sucking what unionists would view as the republican 'poison' out of the language. At the very least, it demonstrates forcefully that Irish is 'just a language'.

The concept of 'multi-politicisation' is entirely rational but may be hostage to the fact that unionist politicians will not be rushing to use Irish in the Assembly chamber or any other forum. Indeed, the reverse is possibly true, as unionists tried to outlaw the use of Irish in the conduct of some Stormont proceedings when a UUP MLA proposed a motion – unsuccessfully – to that effect in October 2007.

Even if a depoliticisation strategy were within the realms of broader political possibility, it is most unlikely that Sinn Féin would be an immediately amenable partner, for it made a less-than-useful contribution to the cause of linguistic harmony in March 2008 by naming a new Irish-language *cumann* (branch) in west Belfast after a dead IRA volunteer. This 'wonderful venture', according to Doherty (2008), was part of 'Sinn Féin's policy to continue to make Irish the daily working language of the party'. That the volunteer 'was a *Gaeilgeoir* and an inspirational figure who had an immense love for the language' (ibid) is not necessarily helpful in winning Protestants over to the Gaelic cause.[74]

The move was part of a Sinn Féin initiative to develop branches conducting business in Irish all over Ireland but hints at a continuing battle for the hearts and minds of other nationalists, rather than the old 'war' with unionists. When the epic struggle for nationalist supremacy was at its height, the SDLP held many of the trump cards in the Irish-language arena, as it had an authenticity that Sinn Féin could not rival. Bríd Rodgers, for example, was a native Gaeltacht speaker and other senior members had near-native fluency. Sinn Féin's speakers, by comparison, were derided by unionists, who mocked the inelegance of their delivery (most notably in the case of Gerry Adams, as seen above).

This brings several fascinating new dimensions into focus. Adams, from the city, was one of many politicised urban republican *Gaeilgeoirí* who could not compete with an authentic native speaker such as Rodgers, at least not on the fluency front. Sinn Féin's competition with the SDLP, therefore, has not been based on linguistic competency, but couched in a 'who's doing most for the language?' context.

Sinn Féin has undoubtedly externalised the debate by taking the 'fight' for language rights to unionists but at the same time has internalised the issue in a battle for the hearts and minds of nationalism, missing no opportunity to state what it has done, can do and will do for the language.

This can also be seen in the siting of Irish-language murals. These rarely appear on the outskirts of nationalist areas or at interface flashpoints, but seem to be concentrated in the inner republican heartlands where the message is not going to be seen by Protestants. Anyone can spray *Tiocfaidh Ár Lá* on whatever wall happens to present itself as a convenient canvas for aerosol rhetoric, but the more sophisticated and decorous offerings seem to be aimed at an internal nationalist audience, not an external unionist one. Sinn Féin's language battle is being fought on two fronts.

All of which takes us back to 'depoliticisation'; a soft and uncertain term for something that defies accurate definition. A much better strategy would be to discard the language of political correctness and adopt a 'real-life' approach based on the immediacy of Irish in all our lives. Politics, after all, is really quite a nebulous thing in itself. It's less a case of 'taking the politics out of Irish' and more about putting the language back into the real world.

Fact-based strategies can be more usefully employed to widen the appeal of Irish. Gael-Linn's course shows students that the language can mean something to them as individuals, helping them to see Irish outside the political sphere and make them aware of how they interact with it at a personal level. This is more likely to make a genuine difference than some vague aspiration that might seek to lay down arbitrary rules on where the use of Irish in a public-facing context is considered 'acceptable' or 'legitimate'.

EVALUATING THE 'NEW ENGAGEMENT'

Gael-Linn's enrichment course has not been the only attempt to bring young Protestants into contact with Irish over the years. Ó Glaisne (1981:36-37) recalls an experiment at Methodist College Belfast[75] in the early 1970s when sixty Sixth Formers participated in a six-week project to increase awareness of Anglo-Irish culture and, perhaps, provide a stimulus to 'reconsider, critically, their social attitudes and beliefs'. Some students' comments recorded by Ó Glaisne are like a mirror image of those encountered in this research. One wrote: 'I have learned about the great influence of the Irish language today, and before the Project began I never knew anything about it.' Significantly, respondents mentioned place names in favourable terms, a distant echo of this research's findings.

That course took place over thirty years ago. In June 2007, students at a grammar school in County Londonderry – or Derry – took part in a Lá Gaelach (Irish Day), with emphasis on basic language, surnames, place names, song, the Protestant Irish tradition and dancing. It was organised by a local community group and the school, with help from the Ultach Trust. Questionnaires were distributed after the event and returns indicate a favourable response.[76]

However, these are 'one-offs': Gael-Linn's programme has been well-directed, successful and, most importantly, sustained. In other words, Gael-Linn is pioneering a 'new market', taking Irish into areas where it otherwise would not have gone, set back only by the timetable strictures of AS Level. Despite minor faults, the course has indicated a way ahead. It has shown that young Protestants are willing to take a closer look at Irish, a vital first step. There is much to be learned from the approach, particularly as it is in so many ways breaking new ground with an objective and accurate introduction to Irish.

As Northern Ireland society matures and hopefully puts the dark years of the Troubles behind it, however, the issue of young Protestants and Irish may move onto a bigger stage, meaning that other actors could come into the equation, official agencies progressing the issue in schools. That remains to be seen but it has been demonstrated that there is a young Protestant audience prepared to find out more about Irish – if they are given the chance to do so.

Sociolinguistics, history, education and politics have all been factors in this study but what really matters is that there appears to be a latent curiosity about Irish that can provide an opportunity to introduce young people from the Protestant/unionist community to a language that is as much a part of their environment as it is of their Catholic and nationalist neighbours. The problem is that it is less possible for Protestants to be curious about something if they are unaware of its existence in anything other than a political context. Irish has now been put on the agenda for some young people who might otherwise never have given it a second thought.

People are naturally curious about the world around them and this is, in my opinion, the way to open the door to a greater understanding of Irish. The fascination of students with place names and surnames shows that the language has some relevance for them. Political perceptions are an unfortunate and significant confounding factor, yet the course has proven that even those who might be wary of 'anything Irish' are still curious about it. Furthermore, Irish dancing has been seen to traverse the divide in an enjoyable, harmless way and is accessible to both communities.

Making Irish available is a start. Optional 'formal' Irish would be the ideal outcome but, in the absence of that, Gael-Linn, having established a tried and tested formula that seems to work well, must be encouraged to expand its course and again reach a wider audience. Whatever happens in terms of education reform, efforts should be made to find curriculum space to ensure that enrichment studies are once more generally available.

Naturally, not everyone will want to do such a course. Naturally, not everyone who does such a course will be inspired to follow it through to a higher level. Yet everyone who does such a course has the chance to see that it is not the fault of Irish that it has become pigeonholed by the politics of Northern Ireland. After all, Irish is a language, like any other, with scope for use and misuse. As I said in my introduction, one can curse the Pope in Irish just as easily as one can curse the Queen in English.

With every course, there will be those who refuse to take part and there will be those who drop out after a few weeks, yet many pupils will have been introduced to the language in a way that demonstrates its relevance to all in Northern Ireland. Those who reject Irish will nonetheless have seen a different dimension to the language: even if it is impossible to entirely eliminate their prejudices, they will (unknowingly, perhaps) have benefited and taken a small step forward. Encouragingly, only a handful showed a level of hatred for Irish on a par with the depressing results of the Kerr research in the mid-1990s, a sign, perhaps, that attitudes are already changing. The word 'Taig' was not mentioned once.

Young Protestants have the right to enjoy the language and must be offered the opportunity, but the 'O' word – optional – is central. Imposition is not an option.

Much depends on the stability of Northern Ireland's new political arrangements and the ability of the politicians to ensure that they can 'deliver the peace'. While this is true of every aspect of life in Northern Ireland, in terms of the language issue public confidence that peace is 'for real' could help transform the situation. It is possible that (a) more 'neutral venue' classes will appear, (b) there will again be classes in Protestant areas, as was the case with McCoy's working-class learners, (c) Protestant learners will have fewer reservations about crossing ethno-religious boundaries to find classes, and (d) the religious beliefs and politics of the learner will cease to become a matter for conjecture or suspicion.

In coming years, the results of other long-term factors will also be seen: these include increasing confidence that the peace is 'for real', the gradual secularisation of society, the impact of equality legislation and changes to the policing and judicial systems in Northern Ireland. The EU has recognised that borders are no longer barriers, while encouraging cultural diversity. Figures from the 2001 census prove that more Protestants are becoming acquainted with Irish, even if the numbers are relatively small.

Opening minds is the key. Those inspired by the EPGS will go forward with a mindset that augurs well for the future – if they have enjoyed learning even a little Irish it is unlikely that they will object in later years if their own children are offered the chance to do 'formal' Irish. Perhaps the most realistic role models are not sports or pop stars but simply parents who have themselves learned that Irish is a language, not a threat. Such role models in future might be some of the teenagers surveyed in this research.

I believe I have shown that a little education *can* make a positive difference. The challenge now for schools, education authorities and society itself is to ensure that the opportunity to learn Irish is available to all. Politicians of all colours also have a role to play, by helping moderate the debate and bringing about the circumstances where Protestant engagement with Irish becomes a real possibility.

I fervently hope that Protestants and unionists will no longer see Irish as the language of the enemy. Place names, surnames and even the way we use English prove that both sides have rather more in common than they might like to believe. Irish is not a battle for hearts and minds: it's simply a matter of everyone taking ownership of something that belongs to us all.

APPENDIX 1
THE QUESTIONNAIRE

LANGUAGE ATTITUDES SURVEY

SCH: ❑❑❑/❑❑

Your cooperation in completing this questionnaire is appreciated. All responses will be treated in the strictest confidence. We would like to find out about your views on the following.

Section A

This section to be completed by everyone. Tick **ONE** *box only for each question,* **except where stated otherwise.**

1 **Did you attend the Gael-Linn course?**
  Yes ❑
  No ❑

2 **Age (write in):** _____

3 **Gender**
  Male ❑
  Female ❑

4 **Do you regard yourself as belonging to any particular religion?**
  Yes ❑ → Go to Question 4(a)
  No ❑ → Go to Question 4(b)

4(a) **What religion, religious denomination or body do you belong to?**
  Church of Ireland ❑
  Presbyterian ❑
  Methodist ❑
  Roman Catholic ❑
  Other (write in) ❑ _____

(b) **What religion, religious denomination or body were you brought up in?**

     Church of Ireland   ❏

     Presbyterian   ❏

     Methodist   ❏

     Roman Catholic   ❏

     Other (write in)   ❏ _____

5 **Do you speak any other languages? Tick ALL that apply.**

     French   ❏

     German   ❏

     Spanish   ❏

     Other (write in)   ❏ _____

6 **Have you heard of Ulster-Scots?**

     Yes   ❏ → Go to Question 7

     No   ❏ → Go to Question 13

7 **Can you read or speak Ulster-Scots?**

     Yes   ❏

     No   ❏

8 **Can anyone in your family read or speak Ulster-Scots?**

     Yes   ❏

     No   ❏

9 **If you don't already speak it, would you like to learn Ulster-Scots?**

     Yes   ❏

     No   ❏

     Don't know   ❏

10 **Do you believe Ulster-Scots is genuinely a language?**

     Yes   ❏

     No   ❏

     Don't know   ❏

11 **Do you believe Ulster-Scots is only for Protestants and unionists?**

     Yes   ❏

     No   ❏

     Don't know   ❏

12 **Should Ulster-Scots and Irish have equal status and be promoted equally?**

    Yes   ❑

    No   ❑

    Don't know   ❑

13 **Have you come across the Irish language in ANY form? Tick ALL that apply.**

    (a)   in language classes   ❑

    (b)   in other classes at school   ❑

    (c)   in Irish programmes on TV/radio   ❑

    (d)   on street/road signs   ❑

    (e)   in place names   ❑

    (f)   in Gaelic surnames   ❑

    (g)   in conversation   ❑

    (h)   in relation to music   ❑

    (i)   as used by politicians   ❑

    (j)   on official documents   ❑

    (k)   in advertising/newspapers   ❑

    (l)   in Other Ways (please specify)   ❑ _____

14 **Would you understand Irish in its spoken or written form?**

    Yes   ❑

    No   ❑

15 **What do you feel when you encounter the Irish language?**

    Totally disinterested   ❑

    Mildly disinterested   ❑

    Indifferent   ❑

    Mildly interested   ❑

    Strongly interested   ❑

16 **Irish should be made available as** *an optional subject* **for every school pupil in Northern Ireland** *regardless of religion.*

    Strongly agree   ❑

    Agree   ❑

    Don't know   ❑

    Disagree   ❑

    Strongly disagree   ❑

17 **Greater efforts should be made to make Protestants and unionists of all ages more aware of the Irish language.**

     Strongly agree   ❑

     Agree   ❑

     Don't know   ❑

     Disagree   ❑

     Strongly disagree   ❑

18 **Do you feel that learning Irish would help turn Protestants and unionists into Catholics, nationalists and republicans?**

     Strongly agree   ❑

     Agree   ❑

     Don't know   ❑

     Disagree   ❑

     Strongly disagree   ❑

19 **If I was a parent I would be happy to send my children to an Irish-medium school (i.e. where all teaching is conducted in Irish).**

     Strongly agree   ❑

     Agree   ❑

     Don't know   ❑

     Disagree   ❑

     Strongly disagree   ❑

20 **Which of the following terms best describes your political outlook?**

     Loyalist   ❑

     Nationalist   ❑

     None   ❑

     Republican   ❑

     Unionist   ❑

     Other (write in)   ❑ _____

21 **In general, what are your opinions of the Irish language?**

     Strongly negative   ❑

     Somewhat negative   ❑

     No opinion   ❑

     Somewhat positive   ❑

     Strongly positive   ❑

22 **Who do you feel the language is primarily for?**
Tick ONE only.

Catholics	❏
Protestants	❏
Everyone	❏
No one	❏

23 **Do you feel that you have been excluded from the Irish language and culture?**

Yes	❏
No	❏
Don't care	❏

How do you respond to the following statements?
Tick ONE box for each.

	Strongly Agree	Agree	Don't Know	Agree	Strongly Disagree
24 'I wish I had had the chance to learn Irish at an earlier stage in my education.'	❏	❏	❏	❏	❏
25 'The Government should not be spending taxpayers' money on the Irish language.'	❏	❏	❏	❏	❏
26 'Irish is an important part of my culture.'	❏	❏	❏	❏	❏
27 'Irish is a dead language.'	❏	❏	❏	❏	❏
28 'Everyone should have the chance to learn Irish.'	❏	❏	❏	❏	❏
29 'Most Protestants and unionists would not want to learn Irish because they feel it is too closely associated with republicans.'	❏	❏	❏	❏	❏

30 'Irish is a useful
language and could   ❏   ❏   ❏   ❏   ❏
help me get a better job.'

31 'The Irish language is
being forced on   ❏   ❏   ❏   ❏   ❏
Protestants and
unionists.'

32 'The Irish language
should be made more
publicly visible.'
(e.g. on road   ❏   ❏   ❏   ❏   ❏
signs, public notices/
advertisements and in
official letters/documents)

33 No question! Please go to Section B

Section B

This section to be completed by course attenders only

34 Why did you decide to do the Gael-Linn course?
Tick ALL that apply.

I was curious	❏
My friends were doing it	❏
I was interested in Irish	❏
I like learning languages	❏
There are Irish speakers in my family	❏
I had nothing better to do	❏
Other reasons (specify below)	❏

_____

_____

_____

_____

_____

_____

35 **How did your family/friends react when they discovered you were learning Irish?**

        Hostile   ❑

        Amused   ❑

        Interested   ❑

        No reaction   ❑

36 **Did you find the resource pack which accompanied the course useful?**

        Yes   ❑

        No   ❑

37(a) **Do any of your relatives speak Irish?**

        Yes   ❑ → Go to Question 37(b)

        No   ❑ → Go to Question 38

(b) **If you answered *yes* above, please tick ALL that apply below.**

        Mother   ❑

        Father   ❑

        Aunt/Uncle   ❑

        Grandparent ❑

        Brother/Sister ❑

        Other (please specify below) ❑

38 **What aspects of the course interested you most? (*Tick two*)**

        Learning Irish ❑

        Place names ❑

        Hiberno-English ❑

        The Protestant Gaelic tradition ❑

        Gaelic surnames in English ❑

        Music and the two traditions ❑

        History of the Irish language ❑

        Other (specify below) ❑

39 **Would you consider learning *more about the Irish language* (i.e. its history, folklore and place names) in the future?**

        Yes   ❑

        No   ❑

        Don't know   ❑

40   **Would you consider learning *more Irish* in the future?**

      Yes   ❏

      No   ❏

      Don't know   ❏

41   **If you answered *yes* to the previous question, would you like to (tick ALL that apply):**

      Study Irish for GCSE/A Level   ❏

      Study Irish at university level   ❏

      Study informally on your own   ❏

      Join a learners' group   ❏

42   **If no classes/opportunities were available in your locality would you consider going elsewhere?**

      Yes   ❏

      No   ❏

      Don't know   ❏

43(a)   **Has learning Irish changed your political views?**

      A little   ❏

      A lot   ❏

      Not at all   ❏

(b)   **Has learning Irish made you more sympathetic to nationalist or republican views?**

      Yes   ❏

      No   ❏

      Don't know   ❏

44   **If you had not done the Gael-Linn course, do you think you would ever have had the opportunity to learn Irish?**

      Definitely not   ❏

      Probably not   ❏

      Don't know   ❏

      Probably   ❏

      Definitely   ❏

How do you respond to the following statements?
    Tick ONE box for each.

	Strongly Agree	Agree	Don't Know	Agree	Strongly Disagree
45 'Learning Irish has helped me understand my culture and heritage better.'	❑	❑	❑	❑	❑
46 'It is easier for my generation to get to know Irish than it was for my parents' generation.'	❑	❑	❑	❑	❑
47 'People who do not know anything about Irish are missing out.'	❑	❑	❑	❑	❑

48(a) **Do you have any opportunity to use Irish outside school?**
    Yes ❑
    No ❑

(b) **If you answered YES above, *where* do you speak Irish?**

_____

_____

49 **Do you wish there were more opportunities for you to use Irish?**
    Yes ❑
    No ❑
    Don't care ❑

50(a) **Do you feel that you have benefited from doing the course?**
    Yes ❑
    No ❑
    Don't know ❑

(b) **If you feel you have benefited, please explain in what way.**

_____

_____

_____

_____

_____

51 **Please make any other comments you have about the Irish language and Ulster-Scots. Use bullet points if you wish.**

_____

_____

_____

_____

_____

_____

_____

_____

_____

_____

_____

_____

_____

_____

_____

_____

_____

_____

BIBLIOGRAPHY
AND FURTHER READING

NOTES ON ELECTRONIC REFERENCES

In addition to traditional printed sources, many of the references in this bibliography relate to articles and resources on the worldwide web. These are available on specific 'pages', accessible by the *http://* address given in the references. Frequently, though, the location of pages changes, so a date, showing the last time I accessed the page at that address, is also given. A 'redirect' will lead to the new link, if one exists, but sometimes a previously accessed page will become permanently unavailable for a variety of reasons.

Occasionally, typesetting and justification requirements mean that the *http://* address cannot be shown 'as is' and may need to be 'broken' over several lines. In these instances, the full address (delineated by the < and > symbols) can be copied directly into the browser, but spaces should be removed. It is frequently not possible to give 'page numbers' in http documents, so an in-text citation will often just include the year.

Some electronic resources are downloadable in portable document format (.pdf). If there is an original document page number, that is cited (in the case of an e-journal, for example). When no original numbering is present, I give the page number of the pdf viewer, visible at the bottom of the viewer's window. Numbering is not always possible in the case of web pages in html format.

Adair, Mark. 2000. 'Boundaries, diversity and inter-culturalism: the case of Ulster Scots', pp.143–7 in Kirk, John M. and Ó Baoill, Dónall P. (eds), *Language and Politics: Northern Ireland, the Republic of Ireland, and Scotland*. Belfast: Cló Ollscoil na Banríona

Adams, G.B. 1964. 'The last language census in Northern Ireland', pp.111–46 in *Ulster Dialects: An Introductory Symposium*. Holywood: Ulster Folk Museum

Adamson, Ian. 1974. *Cruthin: The Ancient Kindred*. Newtownards: Nosmada Press

Andrews, Liam S. 1997. 'The very dogs in Belfast will bark in Irish', pp.49–94 in Mac Póilin, Aodán (ed.), *The Irish Language in Northern Ireland*. Belfast: Ultach Trust

——— 2000. 'Northern nationalists and the politics of the Irish language', pp.44–63 in Kirk, John M. and Ó Baoill, Dónall P. (eds), *Language and Politics: Northern Ireland, the Republic of Ireland, and Scotland*. Belfast: Cló Ollscoil na Banríona

ARK. 1999. 'Northern Ireland Life and Times Survey', 1999 [computer file]. ARK <http://www.ark.ac.uk/nilt> [distributor], June 2000 [accessed 11 December 2003]

Avery, Hilary and Gilbert, Andrea. 2006. 'First encounters with Ulster-Scots language, history and culture', pp.64–8 in Ó Riagáin, Dónall (ed.), *Voces Diversae: Lesser-Used Language Education in Europe*. Belfast: Cló Ollscoil na Banríona

Bardon, Jonathan. 1992. *A History of Ulster*. Belfast: Blackstaff Press

Barnard, T.C. 1993. 'Protestants and the Irish language, c. 1675–1725', pp.243–72 in *Journal of Ecclesiastical History*, vol. 44 no. 22. Cambridge: Cambridge University Press

Barnier, Alan. 2003. 'The identity game: sport and national identity in Northern Ireland and Scotland', pp.54–60 in Longley, Edna, Hughes, Eamonn and O'Rawe, Des (eds), *Ireland (Ulster) Scotland: Concepts, Contexts, Comparisons*. Belfast: Cló Ollscoil na Banríona

BBC. 2005a. 'Pair unhurt in petrol bomb attack'. <http://news.bbc.co.uk/go/pr/fr/-/1/hi/northern_ireland/4632745.stm> [accessed 29 June 2005]

——— 2005b. 'NI religious gap closes'. <http://news.bbc.co.uk/1/hi/northern_ireland/2588251.stm> [accessed 11 October 2005]

——— 2005c. 'Playwright "driven out by idiots"'. <http://news.bbc.co.uk/1/hi/entertainment/4551870.stm> [accessed 4 August 2006]

Beckett, J.C. 1969. *The Making of Modern Ireland 1603–1923*. London: Faber & Faber

BICO (British and Irish Communist Organisation). 1973. *'Hidden Ulster' Explored: A Reply to Padraig Ó Snodaigh's 'Hidden Ulster'*. Belfast: Athol Books

Bilger, Cordula. 2002. 'War zone language: language and the conflict in Northern Ireland', pp.318–26 in Kirk, John M. and Ó Baoill, Dónall P. (eds), *Language Planning and Education: Linguistic Issues in Northern Ireland*. Belfast: Cló Ollscoil na Banríona

Blaney, Roger. 1996. *Presbyterians and the Irish Language*. Belfast: Ulster Historical Foundation/Ultach Trust

Bradley, Colm. 2008. 'GAA still a cold house for Protestants', in *Gaelic Life*. 4 April 2008. <http://www.nwipp-newspapers.com/GL/free/315474080962843.php> [accessed 9 April 2008]

Bradley, Joseph M. 2006. 'Sport and the contestation of ethnic identity: football and Irishness in Scotland', pp.1189–208 in *Journal of Ethnic and Migration Studies*, vol. 32, no. 7, September 2006

British and Irish Communist Organisation *see* BICO

Brown, Terence. 1992. 'Identities in Ireland: the historical perspective', pp. 33–45 in Lundy, Jean and Mac Póilin, Aodán (eds), *Styles of Belonging: The Cultural Identities of Ulster*. Belfast: Lagan Press

———— 1995. Cited, p.28, in *Giving Voices: The Work of the Cultural Traditions Group 1990–1994*. Belfast: Cultural Traditions Group of the Northern Ireland Community Relations Council

Bryan, Dominic and Gillespie, Gordon. 2005. *Transforming Conflict: Flags and Emblems*. Belfast: Institute of Irish Studies, QUB <http://www.research.ofmdfmni.gov.uk/flags.pdf> [accessed 28 July 2006]

Buchanan, R.H. 1995. 'Chairman's report', p.3 in *Giving Voices: The Work of the Cultural Traditions Group 1990–1994*. Belfast: Cultural Traditions Group of the Northern Ireland Community Relations Council

CCEA. 2005a. 'Northern Ireland Curriculum'. <http://www.ccea.org.uk/> [accessed 27 April 2005]

———— 2005b. 'Purpose of Transfer Tests'.
<http://www.ccea.org.uk/> [accessed 27 April 2005]

CCRU (Central Community Relations Unit). n.d. *Evaluation of Gael-Linn's Enrichment Programme in Gaelic Studies.*
Belfast: CCRU

Chrisafis, Angelique. 2005. 'Loyalist paramilitaries drive playwright from his home', in the *Guardian.* <http://www.guardian.co.uk/uk/2005/dec/21/arts.northernireland> [accessed 22 February 2008]

Christian Brothers, The. 1995. *New Irish Grammar.* Dublin: C.J. Fallon

Cohen, Louis and Manion, Lawrence. 1994. *Research Methods in Education* (4th edn). London: Routledge

Comhairle (na Gaelscolaíochta). 2005. 'About Us – What We Do?' <http://www.comhairle.org/english/aboutus.asp?Action=Start> [accessed 27 April 2005]

Coolican, Hugh. 2004. *Research Methods and Statistics in Psychology* (4th edn). London: Hodder & Stoughton

Corkery, Daniel. 1942. *What's This About the Gaelic League?* Baile Átha Cliath: Conradh na Gaeilge

Cosgrove, Brian. 2003. 'Not cricket?', pp.61–4 in Longley, Edna, Hughes, Eamonn and O'Rawe, Des (eds), *Ireland (Ulster) Scotland: Concepts, Contexts, Comparisons.* Belfast: Cló Ollscoil na Banríona

Coulmas, Florian. 2005. 'Changing language regimes in globalizing environments', pp.3–15 in *International Journal of the Sociology of Language*, no. 175/176

Coulter, John. 2004. 'Reclaiming Irish', in *The Blanket: A Journal of Protest and Dissent.* <http://lark.phoblacht.net/phprint.php> 27 December 2004 [accessed 6 June 2005]

Craig, Patricia. 2007. *Asking for Trouble: The Story of an Escapade with Disproportionate Consequences.* Belfast: Blackstaff Press

Cronin, Michael. 1996. *Translating Ireland: Translation, Languages, Culture.* Cork: Cork University Press

Crozier, Maurna. 2003. 'Devolution and cultural policy', pp.44–9 in Longley, Edna, Hughes, Eamonn and O'Rawe, Des (eds),

Ireland (Ulster) Scotland: Concepts, Contexts, Comparisons. Belfast:
Cló Ollscoil na Banríona

Crystal, David. 1994. *The Cambridge Encyclopedia of Language* (repr.)
Cambridge: Cambridge University Press

CTG (Cultural Traditions Group). 1995. *Giving Voices: The Work of the
Cultural Traditions Group 1990–1994*. Belfast: Northern Ireland
Community Relations Council

Cultúrlann. 2006. Clár Ealaíon, Iúil–Meán Fómhair/Arts
Programme, July–September. Belfast: Cultúrlann MacAdam
Ó Fiaich

DCAL (Department of Culture, Arts and Leisure). 2007. 'Proposed
Irish Language Legislation: Consultation on Equality Impact
Assessment'. <http://www.dcalni.gov.uk/19_january_2007.pdf>
[accessed 21 February 2008]

de Brún, Fionntán. 2006. 'The Fadgies: an "Irish-speaking colony"
in nineteenth-century Belfast', pp.101–13 in de Brún, F.
(ed.), *Belfast and the Irish Language*. Dublin:
Four Courts Press

Delargy, Mary. 2001. 'Linguistic diversity education project',
pp.61–5 in Kirk, John and Ó Baoill, Dónall P. (eds),
*Linguistic Politics: Language Policies for Northern Ireland,
the Republic of Ireland, and Scotland*. Belfast: Cló Ollscoil
na Banríona

DENI (Department of Education Northern Ireland). 2005a.
<http://www.deni.gov.uk/about/d_ed_system.htm>
[accessed 22 April 2005]
———— 2005b. <http://www.deni.gov.uk/about/d_history_2.htm>
[accessed 22 April 2005]
———— 2005c. <http://www.deni.gov.uk/2005_18-entitlement_
framework-initial_guidance.pdf> [accessed 4 August 2006]
———— 2006a. <http://www.deni.gov.uk/index/22-
postprimaryarrangements-new-arrangements_pg.htm>
[accessed 4 August 2006]

Department of Culture, Arts and Leisure *see* DCAL
Department for Education and Skills *see* DFES
Department of Education Northern Ireland *see* DENI

Devine, Paula and Schubotz, Dirk. 2004. 'Us and Them?: Research Update No. 28'. Belfast: ARK Social and Political Archive <www.ark.ac.uk/publications>

DFES (Department for Education and Skills). 2005a. <http://dfes.gov.uk/qualifications/mainSection.cfm?sID= 43&ssID=124> [accessed 29 April 2005]

——— 2005b. 'GCE A level: A2'. <http://dfes.gov.uk/qualifications/mainSection.cfm?sID=43&ssID=136> [accessed 29 April 2005]

Doherty, Pearse. 2008. <http://www.sinnfein.ie/news/detail/26047> [accessed 19 March 2008]

Dolan, T.P. 2002. 'Language policy in the Republic of Ireland', pp.144–56 in Kirk, John M. and Ó Baoill, Dónall P. (eds), *Language Planning and Education: Linguistic Issues in Northern Ireland, the Republic of Ireland and Scotland*. Belfast: Cló Ollscoil na Banríona

Dunbar, Ciarán. 2005. 'An Péindlí Deireanach/The final Penal Law', pp.8–10 in *An tUltach*. iml. 81, uimh. 7 (vol. 81, no. 7) [July 2005]

Dunleavy, Janet E. and Dunleavy, Gareth W. 1991. *Douglas Hyde: A Maker of Modern Ireland*. Berkeley: University of California Press

Dunn, Seamus, Morgan, Valerie and Dawson, Helen. 2001. *Establishing the Demand for Services and Activities in the Irish Language in Northern Ireland*. Belfast: Policy Evaluation and Research Unit for DCAL's Linguistic Diversity Branch

Edmund, John. 2002. 'Ulster-Scots language and culture', pp.175–82 in Kirk, John M. and Ó Baoill, Dónall P. (eds), *Language Planning and Education: Linguistic Issues in Northern Ireland*. Belfast: Cló Ollscoil na Banríona

Edwards, Viv. 2006. 'Education and the development of early childhood bilingualism', pp.16–24 in Ó Riagáin, Dónall (ed.), *Voces Diversae: Lesser-Used Language Education in Europe*. Belfast: Cló Ollscoil na Banríona

Ewart, Shirley and Schubotz, Dirk et al. 2004. *Voices Behind the Statistics: Young People's Views of Sectarianism in Northern Ireland*. London: National Children's Bureau

Fenton, James. 2000. *The Hamely Tongue: A Personal Record of Ulster-Scots in Country Antrim*. Belfast: Ullans Press
——— 2000. *Thonner and Thon: An Ulster-Scots Collection*. Belfast: Ullans Press
Fishman, Joshua. 1972. *Language and Nationalism: Two Integrative Essays*. Rowley, MA: Newbury House
Fitzduff, Mari. 2000. 'Language and politics in a global perspective', pp.75–80 in Kirk, John M. and Ó Baoill, Dónall P. (eds), *Language and Politics: Northern Ireland, the Republic of Ireland, and Scotland*. Belfast: Cló Ollscoil na Banríona
Fitzsimons, J. 1949. 'The official Presbyterian Irish language policy in the eighteenth and nineteenth century', pp.255–64 in *The Irish Ecclesiastical Record*, vol. 72
Foley, Nadette. 2000. 'Discrimination and the Good Friday Agreement', pp.101–5 in Kirk, John M. and Ó Baoill, Dónall P. (eds), *Language and Politics: Northern Ireland, the Republic of Ireland, and Scotland*. Belfast: Cló Ollscoil na Banríona
Ford, Alan. 1999. 'Bedell, William', p.41 in Connolly, S.J. (ed.), *The Oxford Companion to Irish History*. Oxford: OUP
Foster, R.F. (ed.). 1992. *The Oxford History of Ireland*. Oxford: OUP
Gael-Linn. 1988. *Irish in the Northern Education System: A Plan For Development*. Dublin: Gael-Linn
——— 2005a. 'About Gael-Linn'. <http://www.gael-linn.ie/aboutgaellinnhome.aspx?Lang=EN> [accessed 13 May 2005]
——— 2005b. '1950'.<http://www.gael-linn.ie/aboutGaelLinn/history.aspx?lang=En> [accessed 13 May 2005]
——— 2005c. '1960'. <http://www.gael-linn.ie/aboutGaelLinn/history.aspx?lang=En&decade=1960> [accessed 13 May 2005]
——— 2005d. '1970'. <http://www.gael-linn.ie/aboutGaelLinn/history.aspx?lang=En&decade=1970> [accessed 13 May 2005]
——— 2005e. '1980'. <http://www.gael-linn.ie/aboutGaelLinn/history.aspx?lang=En&decade=1980> [accessed 13 May 2005]
——— 2005f. '1990'. <http://www.gael-linn.ie/aboutGaelLinn/history.aspx?lang=En&decade=1990> [accessed 13 May 2005]
Gallagher, Frankie. 2006. Quoted in '£3.3m going to replacing

murals'. <http://news.bbc.co.uk/1/hi/northern_ireland/
5163170.stm> [accessed 14 July 2006]

Gallagher, Tony. 2001. *Culture and Conflict in Northern Ireland.*
Strasbourg: Council of Europe

Garipov, Yagfar and Solnyshkina, Marina. 2006. 'Language reforms
in Tatarstan's education system', pp.131–7 in Ó Riagáin, Dónall
(ed.), *Voces Diversae: Lesser-Used Language Education in Europe.*
Belfast: Cló Ollscoil na Banríona

Garland, Roy. 2001. *Gusty Spence.* Belfast: Blackstaff Press

Gergen, Kenneth J. and Gergen, Mary M. 1991. 'Towards reflexive
methodologies', pp.76–95 in Steier, Frederick (ed.), *Research and
Reflexivity.* London: SAGE Publications

Gilbert, Andrea. 2003. 'Ulster-Scots in education in Northern
Ireland: the history of the language', pp.78–87 in Ó Riagáin,
Dónall (ed.), *Language and Law in Northern Ireland.* Belfast: Cló
Ollscoil na Banríona

Gilligan, Chris and Lloyd, Katrina. 2006. 'Racial Prejudice in
Northern Ireland: Research Update No. 44' (June 2006). Belfast:
ARK Social and Political Archive. <http://www.ark.ac.uk/
publications/updates/update44.pdf> [accessed 2 September 2006]

Goldenberg, Lisa. 2002. *The Symbolic Significance of the Irish
Language in the Northern Ireland Conflict.* Dublin: The
Columba Press

Good Friday Agreement. 1998. *The Agreement: Agreement Reached in
the Multi-Party Negotiations.* Belfast

Görlach, Manfred. 2000. 'Ulster-Scots: a language?', pp.13–32 in
Kirk, John M. and Ó Baoill, Dónall P. (eds), *Language and
Politics: Northern Ireland, the Republic of Ireland, and Scotland.*
Belfast: Cló Ollscoil na Banríona

Gray, Peter. 1999. 'Davis, Thomas', p.137 in Connolly, S.J. (ed.), *The
Oxford Companion to Irish History.* Oxford: OUP

Greene, David. 1972. 'The founding of the Gaelic League', pp.9–19
in Ó Tuama, Seán (ed.), *The Gaelic League Idea.* Cork:
Mercier Press

Grin, François. 2003. 'About language learning and labour market
rewards: summary of keynote speech', delivered at Language

Works Conference, 28 March 2003. <http://66.249.93.104/
search? q=cache:nmqiegDvMegJ:www.icc-europe.com/Olten
_page_201202-Dateien/Publication/Francois%2520Grin/
Article%2520Grin.doc+Francois+Grin&hl=en&gl=uk&ct=
clnk&cd=8> [accessed 20 August 2006]

Hanson, David. 2006. Quoted in '£3.3m going to replacing murals'.
<http://news.bbc.co.uk/1/hi/northern_ireland/5163170.stm>
[accessed 14 July 2006]

Hayes, Bernadette C. and Dowds, Lizanne. 2006. 'Social contact,
cultural marginality or economic self-interest? Attitudes
towards immigrants in Northern Ireland', pp.455–76 in
Journal of Ethnic and Migration Studies, vol. 32, no. 3,
April 2006

Hayes, Maurice. 1995. 'Whither cultural diversity?', pp.8–9 in
*Giving Voices: The Work of the Cultural Traditions Group
1990–1994*. Belfast: Cultural Traditions Group of the Northern
Ireland Community Relations Council

———— 2003. 'Closing address: language and law in Northern
Ireland', pp.173–5 in Ó Riagáin, Dónall (ed.), *Language and Law
in Northern Ireland*. Belfast: Cló Ollscoil na Banríona

Henry, Alison. 1995. *Belfast English and Standard English: Dialect
Variation and Parameter Setting*. Oxford: OUP

Holmes, Janet. 2001. *An Introduction to Sociolinguistics*. Harlow:
Longman/Pearson

Horsbroch, Dauvit. 2001. 'A twalmonth an a wee tait forder',
pp.123–33 in Kirk, John M. and Ó Baoill, Dónall P. (eds),
*Linguistic Politics: Language Policies for Northern Ireland, the
Republic of Ireland, and Scotland*. Belfast: Cló Ollscoil na
Banríona

Hudson, R.A. 2004. *Sociolinguistics* (2nd edn). Cambridge:
Cambridge University Press

Hughes, A.J. 1997. 'Hiberno-English or English as spoken in
Ireland', pp.38–45 in *Aspects of a Shared Heritage*. Armagh:
Gael-Linn

———— 2002. *Bunchomhrá Gaeilge: Basic Conversational Irish*.
Belfast: Clólann Bheann Mhadagáin

Hume, David. 1986. 'A sad case of cultural neglect', pp.11–12 in *Young Unionist*, November 1986.

——— 1990. 'Ulster Protestants and the Gaelic Language', pp. 19–20 in *New Ulster: The Journal of the Ulster Society*, issue 11, Summer 1990

ICC (Iomairt Cholm Cille). 2006. 'Aims'. <http://www.colmcille.net/content.asp?id=10&lang=1> [accessed 3 August 2006]

IHT (International Herald Tribune). 2008. 'Ireland's leaders call for alcohol restraint during St Patrick's Day'. <http://www.iht.com/articles/ap/2008/03/17/europe/EU-GEN-Ireland-St.-Patricks-Day.php> [accessed 22 March 2008]

Jackson, Kenneth H. 1969. 'The Irish language and the languages of the world', pp.1–10 in Ó Cuív, B. (ed.), *A View of the Irish Language*. Dublin: Stationery Office

Jarman, Neil. 2006. 'Diversity, economy and policy: new patterns of migration to Northern Ireland', pp.46–61 in *Shared Space*, issue 2. Belfast: Community Research Council for Northern Ireland

Katzner, Kenneth. 1995. *The Languages of the World* (new edn). London: Routledge

Kennedy, Jane. 2004. Quoted in: '11-plus to be abolished'. <http://news.bbc.co.uk/1/hi/northern_ireland/3429541.stm> [accessed 3 May 2005]

Kernohan, Harry. 1995. 'A General Introduction on Education in Northern Ireland'. <http:www.batod.org.uk/index.php?id=/batod/regions/northernireland.htm> [accessed 27 April 2005]

Kerr, David. 1990. 'ANALYSIS: the place of the Irish language today' in *Ulster Nation*. <http:www.ulsternation.org.uk/place_of_the_irish_language.htm> [accessed 2 July 2005]

Kerr, Eddie. 1994. *Our Common Heritage: A Study into Attitudes and Perceptions of the Unionist Community Relating to the Irish Language*. (For Kudos on behalf of Naíscoil na Rinne, Derry) [unpublished]

Kiberd, Declan. 1993. *Idir Dhá Chultúr*. Dublin: Coiscéim

Kirk, John M. (ed.). 2001. *Language Links: The Languages of Scotland and Ireland*. Belfast: Cló Ollscoil na Banríona

———— 2000. 'Two Ullans texts', pp.13–32 in Kirk, John M. and
Ó Baoill, Dónall P. (eds), *Language and Politics: Northern Ireland,
the Republic of Ireland, and Scotland*. Belfast: Cló Ollscoil
na Banríona

Kirk, John M. and Ó Baoill, Dónall P. (eds). 2000. *Language and
Politics: Northern Ireland, the Republic of Ireland, and Scotland*.
Belfast: Cló Ollscoil na Banríona

———— (eds). 2002. *Language Planning and Education:
Linguistic Issues in Northern Ireland*. Belfast: Cló Ollscoil
na Banríona

Kramsch, Claire. 1998. *Language and Culture*. Oxford: OUP

Laird, John (Lord Laird of Artigarvan). 2001. 'Language policy of
the Ulster-Scots Agency', pp.37–41 in Kirk, John M. and
Ó Baoill, Dónall P. (eds), *Linguistic Politics: Language Policies for
Northern Ireland, the Republic of Ireland, and Scotland*. Belfast:
Cló Ollscoil na Banríona

Lambkin, B.K. 2001. ' "Boundary-awareness": language, migration
and the introduction of citizenship education to schools in
Northern Ireland', pp.195–209 in Kirk, John (ed.), *Language
Links: The Languages of Scotland and Ireland*. Belfast: Cló Ollscoil
na Banríona

Lee, J.J. 1989. *Ireland 1912–1985: Politics and Society*. Cambridge:
Cambridge University Press

Long, Naomi. 2006. 'Unionists' cold feet only chill factor for 2006
St Patrick's Day'. Belfast: Alliance Party of Northern Ireland
<http://www.allianceparty.org/news/1815.html?PHPSESSID=
6cc219594e9486424f9de52da81ae3b9> [accessed 10 July 2006]

Longley, Edna. 1992. 'Writing, revisionism and grass-seed: literary
mythologies in Ireland', pp.11–21 in Lundy, Jean and Mac Póilin,
Aodán (eds), *Styles of Belonging: The Cultural Identities of Ulster*.
Belfast: Lagan Press

———— 1995. Cited, p.27 in *Giving Voices: The Work of the Cultural
Traditions Group 1990–1994*. Belfast: Cultural Traditions Group
of the Northern Ireland Community Relations Council

Loughlin, James. 1999. 'Butt, Isaac', p.65 in Connolly, S.J. (ed.),
The Oxford Companion to Irish History. Oxford: OUP

Mac an Fhailigh, F. and Ó Ciaráin, R. 1997. 'Introduction', p.1 in
Aspects of a Shared Heritage. Armagh: Gael-Linn
Mac Aodha, Breandan, S. 1972. 'Was this a social revolution?',
pp.20–30 in Ó Tuama, Seán (ed.), *The Gaelic League Idea*. Cork:
Mercier Press
Mac Corraidh, Seán. 2006. 'Irish-medium education in Belfast',
pp.177–83 in de Brún, Fionntán (ed.), *Belfast and the Irish
Language*. Dublin: Four Courts Press
MacDonagh, Oliver. 1993. *States of Mind: A Study of Anglo-Irish
Conflict 1780–1980*. London: George Allen & Unwin
Mac Giolla Chríost, Diarmait. 2000. *Planning Issues for Irish
Language Policy: 'An Foras Teanga' and 'Fiontair Teanga'*.
<http://cain.ulst.ac.uk/issues/language/macgiollachriost00.htm>
[accessed 18 March 2004]
MacKinnon, Kenneth. 2003. 'Celtic languages in the 2001 census:
how population censuses bury Celtic speakers', pp.250–61
in Kirk, John M. and Ó Baoill, Dónall P. (eds), *Towards
Our Goals in Broadcasting, the Press, the Performing Arts and
the Economy: Minority Languages in Northern Ireland,
the Republic of Ireland and Scotland*. Belfast: Cló Ollscoil
na Banríona
Mac Nia, Seán. 1997. 'Bunchúrsa Gaeilge', pp.53–77 in *Aspects of a
Shared Heritage*. Armagh: Gael-Linn
Mac Póilin, Aodán. 1990. *The Protestant Gaelic Tradition* (pamphlet).
Belfast: Ultach Trust
——— 1992. *Léacht ar [The] Protestant Gaelic Tradition*
[unpublished]
——— 1997. 'Gaelic surnames in English', pp.20–6 in *Aspects of a
Shared Heritage*. Armagh: Gael-Linn
——— 1999. 'Language, identity and politics in Northern Ireland',
pp.108–32 in *Ulster Folklife*, vol. 45
——— 2000. 'Taig talk', pp. 88–95 in McCoy, Gordon with Scott,
Maolcholaim (eds), *Aithne na nGael: Gaelic Identities*. Belfast:
Institute of Irish Studies and Ultach Trust
——— 2002. Speaking on *Eorpa*. BBC Scotland (TV).
19 November 2002

———— 2006. 'Irish in Belfast 1892–1960: from the Gaelic
League to Cumann Cluain Ard', pp. 114–35 in de Brún,
Fionntán (ed.), *Belfast and the Irish Language*. Dublin:
Four Courts Press

Magee, John. 1988. 'The Neilsons of Rademon and Down:
educators and Gaelic scholars', pp.63–75 in *Familia*,
vol. 2, no. 4

Maguire, Gabrielle. 1991. *Our Own Language: An Irish Initiative*.
Clevedon: Multilingual Matters

Malcolm, Ian. 1996. 'Unionist argues case for Irish classes', pp.14–15
in *News Letter*, 12 January 1996

———— 1999. 'It's a tongue – so stick it out', p.13 in *News Letter*,
9 April 1999

———— 2006. 'Cuirimis stampa na Gaeilge ar ghnó na tíre seo',
pp. 4–5 in *Lá*, 18 July 2006

McAllister, Ian. 2005. 'Driven to Disaffection: Religious
Independents in Northern Ireland: Research Update No. 41'.
<http://www.ark.ac.uk/ publications/updates/update41.pdf>
[accessed 28 November 2005]

McCafferty, Kevin. 2001. *Ethnicity and Language Change: English in
(London)Derry, Northern Ireland*. Amsterdam: John Benjamins
Publishing Company

McCone, K. et al. (eds). 1994. *Stair na Gaeilge*. Magh Nuad: Roinn
na Sean-Ghaeilge, Coláiste Phádraig

McCoy, Gordon. 1997a. *Protestants and the Irish Language in
Northern Ireland*. Unpublished PhD thesis, QUB

———— 1997b. 'Protestant learners of Irish in Northern Ireland',
pp.131–70 in Mac Póilin, Aodán (ed.), *Irish in Northern Ireland*.
Belfast: Ultach Trust

———— 2006. 'Protestants and the Irish language in Belfast',
pp. 147–76 in de Brún, Fionntán (ed.), *Belfast and the Irish
Language*. Dublin: Four Courts Press

McCoy, Gordon with Scott, Maolcholaim. 2000. 'Introduction',
pp.1–18 in McCoy, Gordon with Scott, Maolcholaim (eds),
Aithne na nGael/Gaelic Identities. Belfast: Institute of Irish
Studies, QUB and Ultach Trust

McCoy, Gordon and Ní Bhaoill, Róise. 2004. *Protastúnaigh an lae inniu agus an Ghaeilge/Contemporary Protestant Learners of Irish.* Belfast: Ultach Trust

McDowell, David. n.d. 'Ulster culture – the theft of our past', pp. 8–9 in *Ulster Review*, issue 5. Belfast

McGimpsey, Christopher. 1994. Untitled article, pp.7–16 in Mistéil, Pilib (ed.), *The Irish Language and the Unionist Tradition.* Belfast: Ulster People's College/Ultach Trust

McGugan, Irene. 2002. 'More progress for Scots in the twenty-first century', pp.23–6 in Kirk, John M. and Ó Baoill, Dónall P. (eds), *Language Planning and Education: Linguistic Issues in Northern Ireland.* Belfast: Cló Ollscoil na Banríona

McKay, Patrick. 1999. *A Dictionary of Ulster Place-Names.* Belfast: Institute of Irish Studies, QUB

McKee, Vincent. 1997. *Gaelic Nations: Politics of the Gaelic Language in Scotland and Northern Ireland in the 20th Century.* London: Bluestack Press

McKendry, Eugene. 2001. 'Modern languages education policies and Irish in Northern Ireland', pp.211–22 in Kirk, John (ed.), *Language Links: The Languages of Scotland and Ireland.* Belfast: Cló Ollscoil na Banríona

McMinn, Joe. 1992. 'Language, literature and cultural identity: Irish and Anglo-Irish', pp. 46–53 in Lundy, Jean and Mac Póilin, Aodán (eds), *Styles of Belonging: The Cultural Identities of Ulster.* Belfast: Lagan Press.

Meek, Donald E. 2000. 'God and Gaelic: the Highland churches and Gaelic cultural identity', pp. 28–47 in McCoy, Gordon with Scott, Maolcholaim (eds), *Aithne na nGael: Gaelic Identities.* Belfast: Institute of Irish Studies, QUB and Ultach Trust

Miller, Robert L. 2005. *The Quantitative Perspective in Social Research.* [Class notes from seminar, QUB]

Miller, Robert L. and others. 2002. *SPSS for Social Scientists.* Basingstoke: Palgrave Macmillan

Milroy, Lesley. 1987a. *Language and Social Networks* (2nd edn). Oxford: Blackwell

———— 1987b. *Observing and Analysing Natural Language*. Oxford: Blackwell

Milroy, Lesley and Gordon, Matthew. 2003. *Sociolinguistics: Method and Interpretation*. Oxford: Blackwell

MORI (Market and Opinion Research International) (Ireland). 2006. *Promoting the Irish Language – Qualitative Research. Report prepared for Foras na Gaeilge*. Dublin: MORI

Moutray, Stephen. 2004a. 'Moutray blasts Irish language proposals', p.6 in *Lurgan Mail*, 22 April 2004

———— 2004b. 'Praise for Ulster Scots movement', p.6 in *Lurgan Mail*, 29 April 2004

Mullen, Brian. 1997. 'Music and the two traditions', pp.33–7 in *Aspects of a Shared Heritage*. Armagh: Gael-Linn

Neilson, Rev. William. 1808 (repr. 1990). *An Introduction to the Irish Language*. Belfast: Ultach

Nic Craith, Máiréad. 1995. 'The symbolism of language in Northern Ireland', pp.11–46 in Kockel, Ullrich (ed.), *Landscape, Heritage and Identity: Case Studies in Irish Ethnography*. Liverpool: Liverpool University Press

NICEM (Northern Ireland Council for Ethnic Minorities). 2006. *Annual Report 2004–2005*. Belfast: NICEM

NICIE (Northern Ireland Council for Integrated Education). 2005. *IE Movement: Taking the Fear Out of Difference*. <http://www.nicie.org/aboutus/> [accessed 26 April 2005]

Nic Leoid, Anna. 2002. Presenting *Eorpa*. BBC Scotland (TV), 19 November 2002

Nig Uidhir, Gabrielle. 2006. 'The Shaw's Road urban Gaeltacht: role and impact', pp.136–46 in de Brún, Fionntán (ed.), *Belfast and the Irish Language*. Dublin: Four Courts Press

NISRA (Northern Ireland Statistics and Research Agency). 2005a. 'Household Form'. <http://www.nisra.gov.uk/census/pdf/Householdform.pdf> [accessed 2 October 2005]

———— 2005b. 'Knowledge of Irish'. <http://www.nisra.gov.uk/census/metadata/glossary.html#Knowledge%20of%20Irish>

———— 2005c. 'Community Background and Religion'. <http://www.nisra.gov.uk/census/pdf/Communitybgrel/.pdf> [accessed 30 September 2005]

———— 2005d. 'Northern Ireland Census 2001 Output Disclosure Control'. <http://www.nisra.gov.uk/census/censusmethodology/ disclosure.html> [accessed 11 October 2005]

Ní Uallacháin, Pádraigín. 2003. *A Hidden Ulster: People, Songs and Traditions of Oriel*. Dublin: Four Courts Press

Novak-Lukanovič, Sonja. 2006. 'Minority languages in education in Slovenia', pp.113–25 in Ó Riagáin, Dónall (ed.), *Voces Diversae: Lesser-Used Language Education in Europe*. Belfast: Cló Ollscoil na Banríona

Nowlan, Kevin B. 1972. 'The Gaelic League and other national movements', pp.41–51 in Ó Tuama, Seán (ed.), *The Gaelic League Idea*. Dublin: Mercier Press

Ó Baoighill, Pádraig. 2002. 'The Irish language in Tyrone', pp.665–96 in Dillon, Charles and Jefferies, Henry A. (eds), *Tyrone History and Society*. Dublin: Geography Publications

———— 2003. 'Gael-Linn i gCúige Uladh: 1953–1973', pp.8–10 in *An tUltach*, Samhain 2003, vol. 80, no. 11

———— 2004a. 'Gael-Linn i gCúige Uladh: 1953–1973, Cuid III', pp.6–9 in *An tUltach*, Eanáir 2004, vol. 81, no. 1

———— 2004b. 'Caoga Bliain ag Fás', pp.12–13 in *Ireland's Own*, 23 January 2004

O'Brien, Eileen. 1995. *Modern Ireland, 1868–1966: History Essays for Leaving Cert*. Dublin: Mentor Publications

O'Brien, Flann. 1942. *An Béal Bocht*. Dublin: An Preas Náisiúnta

Ó Broin, Colm and Ó Conghaile, Tomaí. 2006. 'Cás cinniúnach Gaeilge le tosú', p.1 in *Lá*, 19 July 2006

Ó Buachalla, Breandán. 1982. 'Arthur Brownlow: a gentleman more curious than ordinary', pp.24–8 in *Ulster Local Studies*, Summer 1982, vol. 7, no. 2

———— 1994. Untitled article, pp. 34–44 in Mistéil, Pilib (ed.), *The Irish Language and the Unionist Tradition*. Belfast: Ulster People's College/Ultach Trust

Ó Byrne, Cathal. 1946 (repr. 1982). *As I Roved Out: A Book of the North*. Belfast: Blackstaff Press

Ó Cadhain, Máirtín. 1965. Extract from *Mr. Hill: Mr. Tara*, quoted in <http://www.searcs-web.com/ocadh.html> [accessed 13 June 2005]

Ó Cairealláin, Gearóid. 2002. Interviewed on *Eorpa*. BBC Scotland (TV), 19 November 2002

Ó Ciaráin, Réamonn. 2004. Based on interview with subject held in Gael-Linn's Armagh office, 29 January 2004

———— 2005. Based on follow-up e-mail correspondence with subject in June 2005

Ó Cuív, Brian. 1969. 'Irish in the modern world', pp.122–32 in Ó Cuív, Brian (ed.), *A View of the Irish Language*. Dublin: Stationery Office

Ó Duibhín, Ciarán. 2003. 'A comment on the presentation of the Irish language question in the 2001 census of Northern Ireland', pp.262–4 in Kirk, John M. and Ó Baoill, Dónall P. (eds), *Towards Our Goals in Broadcasting, the Press, the Performing Arts and the Economy: Minority Languages in Northern Ireland, the Republic of Ireland and Scotland*. Belfast: Cló Ollscoil na Banríona

Ó Fiaich, Tomás. 1969. 'The language and political history', pp.101–11 in Ó Cuív, Brian (ed.), *A View of the Irish Language*. Dublin: Stationery Office

Ó Glaisne, Risteárd. 1981. 'Irish and the Protestant tradition', pp.33–44 in Kiberd, Declan (ed.), *The Crane Bag*, vol. 5, no. 2

———— 2005. *Eagarthóir*. Binn Éadair: Coiscéim

Ó Grianna, Séamus. 1979 (repr.). *Nuair a Bhí Mé Óg*. Cork: Cló Mercier

Ó Gruagáin, Micheál. 1998. *An Ghaeilge/The Irish Language: A Paper by Micheál Ó Gruagáin, Chief Executive of Bord na Gaeilge*. Dublin: publisher unknown <www.bwrdd-yr-iaith.org.uk/download.php/pID=4542.4> [accessed 10 July 2006]

Ó hAilín, Tomás. 1969. 'Irish revival movements', pp.99–100 in Ó Cuív, Brian (ed.), *A View of the Irish Language*. Dublin: Stationery Office

Ó hEaráin, Séamas. 1996. *An Focal Gafa*. Belfast: publisher unknown

Ó hEithir, Breandán. 1991 (repr.). *Over the Bar*. Dublin:
Poolbeg Press

Ó Huallacháin, Colmán. 1994. *The Irish and Irish: A Sociolinguistic
Analysis of the Relationship Between a People and their Language*.
Dublin: Irish Franciscan Friars Provincial Office

Oideas Gael. 2006. 'About Us'. <http://www.oideas-gael.com/
Leathanacha/oideas_gael.html> [accessed 3 August 2006]

Ó Liatháin, Concubhar. 2004. '"Teanga na Leipreachán" á labhairt
ag an DUP', p.1 in *Lá*, 5 April 2004

Ó Mainnín, Mícheál. 1997. 'Irish placenames', pp.3–8 in *Aspects of a
Shared Heritage*. Armagh: Gael-Linn

Ó Máirtín, Mícheál. 1997. 'A short history of the Irish language',
pp.9–19 in *Aspects of a Shared Heritage*. Armagh: Gael-Linn

Ó Múilleoir, Máirtín. 2006. Speaking on *Good Morning Ulster*, BBC
Radio Ulster, 1 August 2006

Ó Murchú, Máirtín. 1971. *Language and Community/Urlabhra agus
Pobal (Occasional Paper 1)*. Dublin: Stationery Office

Ó Neill, Seamus. 1966. 'The hidden Ulster: Gaelic pioneers of the
North', pp.60–6 in *Studies: An Irish Quarterly Review of Letter,
Philosophy and Science*, vol. LV, Spring. Dublin: The Talbot Press

O'Reilly, Camille, 1998. *The Irish Language in Northern Ireland: The
Politics of Culture and Identity*. Basingstoke: Macmillan

Ó Riagáin, Dónall. 2006. 'Introduction', pp.1–8 in Ó Riagáin, Dónall
(ed.), *Voces Diversae: Lesser-Used Language Education in Europe*.
Belfast: Cló Ollscoil na Banríona

Osborne, Bob, Smith, Alayne with Hayes, Amanda. 2006. *Higher
Education in Northern Ireland: A Report on Factors Associated with
Participation and Migration*. University of Ulster, Social & Policy
Research Institute <http://www.research.ofmdfmni.gov.uk/
highereducation.pdf> [accessed 20 June 2006]

Ó Snodaigh, Padraig. 1995. *Hidden Ulster: Protestants and the Irish
Language* (3rd edn). Belfast: Lagan Press

Ó Torna, Colm. 2003. 'Agallamh na Míosa: Bill Boyd – Ministir
Preispitéireach', p.4 in *Saol*, Nollaig 2003

Parsley, Ian. 2001. 'Ulster-Scots: politicisation or survival?',
pp.177–80 in Kirk, John M. and Ó Baoill, Dónall P. (eds),

Linguistic Politics: Language Policies for Northern Ireland, the Republic of Ireland and Scotland. Belfast: Cló Ollscoil na Banríona

Peover, Stephen. 2002. 'The current state of Irish-medium education in Northern Ireland', pp. 124–30 in Kirk, John M. and Ó Baoill, Dónall P. (eds), *Language Planning and Education: Linguistic Issues in Northern Ireland.* Belfast: Cló Ollscoil na Banríona

Pritchard, Rosalind. 2004. 'Protestants and the Irish language: historical heritage and current attitudes in Northern Ireland', pp.62–82 in *Journal of Multilingual and Multicultural Development*, vol. 25, no. 1

Quinn, Cosslett. 1994. Untitled article, pp.24–33 in Mistéil, Pilib (ed.) *The Irish Language and the Unionist Tradition.* Belfast: Ulster People's College/Ultach Trust

Rannut, Mart. 2006. 'The role of education in reversing language shift: the Estonian experience', pp.78–88 in Ó Riagáin, Dónall (ed.), *Voces Diversae: Lesser-Used Language Education in Europe.* Belfast: Cló Ollscoil na Banríona

Rees, D.G. 1996. *Essential Statistics* (3rd edn). London: Chapman & Hall

Robb, John. 2004. *New Ireland: 30 Years On.* Coleraine: New Ireland Group

Robinson, Philip. 1997. *Ulster-Scots: A Grammar of the Traditional Written and Spoken Language.* Belfast: The Ullans Press

Rodgers, Bríd. 2004. As guest presenter on *Talkback*, BBC Radio Ulster, 7 September 2004

Rosenberg, Lisa. 2002. *The Symbolic Significance of the Irish Language in the Northern Ireland Conflict.* Dublin: Columba Press

Sapir, Edward. 1957. Mandelbaum, David G. (ed.), *Culture, Language and Personality: Selected Essays.* Berkeley: University of California Press

Schiller, Rina. 2001. *The Lambeg and the Bodhrán.* Belfast: Institute of Irish Studies, QUB

Seery, James. 1991. 'Dr Neilson's Irish grammar', pp.2–10 in *The Bulletin of the Presbyterian Historical Society of Ireland*, vol. 20 (March 1991)

Sinn Féin. 1984. *Learning Irish: An Information and Discussion Booklet*. Belfast: Sinn Féin

Smith, William. 1994. Untitled article, pp.17–23 in Mistéil, Pilib (ed.), *The Irish Language and the Unionist Tradition*. Belfast: Ulster People's College/Ultach Trust

Smyth, Marie and Goldie, Roz. 2001. *Two Reports on Children, Young People and the Troubles in Northern Ireland*. Belfast: Community Conflict Impact on Children. <http://www.conflictresearch.org.uk/archives/ccic_two_papers.pdf> [accessed 28 July 2006]

Solymosi, Judit. 2006. 'Accommodating linguistic diversity in Hungary's education system', pp.40–6 in Ó Riagáin, Dónall (ed.), *Voces Diversae: Lesser-Used Language Education in Europe*. Belfast: Cló Ollscoil na Banríona

Stork, F.C. and Widdowson, J.D.A. 1974. *Learning About Linguistics*. London: Hutchinson

Suurenbroek, Frank and Schrover, Marlou. 2005. 'A separate language, a separate identity? Organisations of Frisian migrants in Amsterdam in the late nineteenth and early twentieth centuries', pp. 991–1005 in *Journal of Ethnic and Migration Studies*, vol. 31, no. 5, September 2005

Sweeney, Kevin. 1988. *The Irish Language in Northern Ireland: Preliminary Report*. Belfast: Policy Planning and Research Unit, Statistics and Social Division

Tannahill, Anne. 1995. 'Reflecting our place and time', pp.12–13 in *Giving Voices: The Work of the Cultural Traditions Group 1990–1994*. Belfast: Cultural Traditions Group of the Northern Ireland Community Relations Council

Thomson, Alwyn. 2000. 'Evangelicalism, culture and the Gaelic tradition in Ireland', pp.48–52 in McCoy, Gordon with Scott, Maolcholaim (eds), *Aithne na nGael/Gaelic Identities*. Belfast: Ultach Trust/Institute of Irish Studies, QUB

Trask, R.L. 1999. *Language: The Basics* (2nd edn). London: Routledge

Ulster Nation. 2005. 'Our task – a role for radical Ulster-Nationalists' in *Ulster Nation*. <http://www.ulsternation.org.uk/ index.html> [accessed 2 July 2005]

Ultach Trust. 2006. 'Background'. <http://www.ultach.dsl.
pipex.com/english/index_en.htm> [accessed 16 March 2006]
———— 2008. 'Frequently-Asked Questions about the Irish
Language'. <http://www.ultach.org/> [accessed 21 February
2008]
UMS (Ulster Media Surveys). Commissioned by McCann-Erickson
Belfast. Published in *Belfast Telegraph*, 5 April 2000
UYUC (Ulster Young Unionist Council). 1986. *Cuchulain: The Lost
Legend, Ulster: The Lost Culture?* Belfast: UYUC
Walsh, L. 1844. *The Home Mission Unmasked … in a Series of Letters.*
Belfast: publisher unknown
Watson, Mike. 2002. 'Towards a language policy for Scotland',
pp.27–34, in Kirk, John M. and Ó Baoill, Dónall P. (eds),
*Language Planning and Education: Linguistic Issues in Northern
Ireland.* Belfast: Cló Ollscoil na Banríona
Welch, Robert. 1996. 'Ó Cadhain, Máirtín', pp.405–6 in *The Oxford
Companion to Irish Literature.* Oxford: OUP
Williams, N. 1999. 'Irish language', pp.268–270 in Connolly, S.J.
(ed.), *The Oxford Companion to Irish History.* Oxford: OUP
Wilson, Sammy. 2002. Speaking on *Eorpa.* BBC Scotland (TV),
19 November 2002
Zwickl, Simone. 2002. *Language Attitudes, Ethnic Identity and Dialect
Use Across the Northern Ireland Border: Armagh and Monaghan.*
Belfast: Cló Ollscoil na Banríona

NOTES

1 'The Plantation' is the name given to the comprehensive colonisation of large parts of the province of Ulster by English and Scottish settlers – the 'Planters' – who began to arrive in considerable numbers in the early seventeenth century. Of all the provinces, Ulster had been the most resistant to English 'manners'. See e.g. Bardon (1992:115–147) for a detailed account.

2 Emancipation was the process whereby restrictive laws and statutes against Catholics were gradually relaxed and repealed (often following agitation) during the late eighteenth and early nineteenth centuries. See e.g. Beckett (1969:284–335).

3 Ó Glaisne, a County Cork Methodist, also came under fierce attack from BICO. He is discussed at length in Chapter Two.

4 To be more precise, it is the term unionist politicians favour; many 'ordinary' Protestants call it 'Derry' as well. Indeed, one of the Loyal Orders is called 'The Apprentice Boys of Derry'.

5 Belfast's population is sharply divided. East Belfast is 'more Protestant' and west Belfast 'more Catholic', although communities from 'the other side' live in both areas.

6 No attempt will be made to discuss the history of Northern Ireland since Partition, other than with regard to the language's

fortunes, but for an introduction to the period see e.g. Bardon, 1992; Foster, 1992; Gallagher, 2001; Lee, 1989.

7 The current education system in Northern Ireland is discussed in the following chapter.

8 The term 'Gaeltacht' describes an area where Irish is the daily means of communication for a majority of inhabitants. Nowadays, these are exclusively in the Republic of Ireland, primarily in Counties Donegal, Galway and Kerry.

9 Ó Glaisne incurred the wrath of the British and Irish Communist Organisation for his appeals to Protestants to become acquainted with Irish (BICO, 1973:45–48).

10 In reality, the language had become part of the republican political agenda at the Gaelic League Ard Fheis in 1915 (see Chapter One), but in the 1970s and 1980s attitudes towards Irish assumed an even greater importance in the Northern Ireland political arena.

11 *Gaeilgeoir* is a term for users of Irish, normally used to indicate non-native-speaking activists who are often learners. Native Gaeltacht speakers would not regard themselves as *Gaeilgeoirí*.

12 Ulster-Scots is regarded by some as the Protestant/unionist 'antidote' to Irish, viewed as a response to the apparent success of the Irish-language movement. See later in this chapter.

13 An exposition of the 'hijacked' -v- 'surrendered' dichotomy, discussed later.

14 'Jailtacht' is a pun on the Gaelic word '*Gaeltacht*', coined as a nickname for republican compounds in the prison where inmates communicated in Irish.

15 The Red Hand Commando group was allied to the larger UVF, and its name was sometimes used as a flag of convenience by the main organisation.

16 The Fáinne is a small circular pin badge worn by some Irish speakers to denote their level of fluency and indicate to others that they have the language.

17 Fianna Fáil is the largest political party in the Republic and prides itself on being Ireland's 'republican party'. Sinn Féin would dispute this claim, which might explain why IRA prisoners took umbrage at 'Fianna Fáil Gaelic', a variety based on southern – not northern – Irish.

18 Moutray's volte-face ended with a paragraph in 'fluent' Ulster-Scots – even though his district has no tradition or history as an area where the *leid* was ever spoken.

19 Interviews from the research have been cited by many scholars to summarise highly negative Protestant attitudes to Irish. Some respondents referred freely to 'Taigs' and 'Fenians' – grossly disparaging references to Catholics – and one interview had to be terminated after eleven minutes because the researcher 'received a lot of vitriolic abuse

from the respondent', who declared that all Irish speakers 'were in the IRA'.

20 Northern Ireland Statistics and Research Agency.

21 Please note that all figures in this section are produced using tables from NISRA, available on the census 2001 website or the NICA Census Analyser.

22 The number of those claiming knowledge of Irish but either stating that they had no religious affiliation or not stating any religious affiliation increased from 9,831 in 1991 to 14,110 in 2001.

23 'Depoliticisation', as mentioned in the introduction, is frequently used in the language debate, but defining it is difficult. I examine the term and all that it implies in Chapter Seven.

24 A staunch unionist friend, an accomplished uilleann piper, tells me that during the 1960s/70s he played folk music in a west Belfast club; only when a balaclava-wearing gang hijacked the stage to make an announcement on behalf of the IRA did he feel that it was time to find other venues.

25 I began learning Irish at just such a course in Queen's and was subsequently inspired to study Celtic at BA level.

26 <http://www.ulsterscotsagency. com/wordulsterscot17.asp> [accessed 9 November 2007]

27 'Strongly disagree/Disagree' and 'Strongly agree/Agree' categories have been compressed in this section.

28 'Council for the Curriculum
Examinations and Assessment',
since rebranded as CEA.
29 The fishing town of Kilkeel is a
mainly Protestant enclave in
predominantly nationalist south
Down.
30 A civil service department
charged with formulating,
reviewing and challenging
government policies to address
issues of equality and improve
community relations. It
subsequently became the CRU
(Community Relations Unit).
31 More detailed information on
evaluation of the course is
provided below.
32 In Northern Ireland grammar
schools, Sixth Form equates to
the two years of A Level
study.
33 Paramilitary groups were highly
active in south Armagh during
the Troubles, leading to deep-
seated distrust and bitterness
between the two communities.
34 Crossmaglen, in south Armagh, is
a republican town close to the
border, seen by unionists as an
IRA 'stronghold'. Harryville, in
County Antrim, is staunchly
loyalist and the scene of sectarian
protests outside the local church
as Catholics went to mass during
the late 1990s.
35 In a BBC Radio Ulster interview
on 18 February 2005, the then
Ulster Unionist Party leader
David Trimble, while conceding
that he did not speak Irish,
expressed an interest in the Ulster
dialect and appeared to suggest
that if Protestants were to learn

Irish, this would be the natural
choice.
36 Again, Irish-speaking Protestants
in Gaeltacht areas would be no
strangers to Gaelic sports.
Northern Ireland perceptions,
however, are different. See
Bradley, C. (2008) for a personal
view of how those involved in
GAA activities – particularly those
from Northern Ireland – are
perceived.
37 See Chapter Two.
38 The 'sash' is an item of regalia
worn by members of the Orange
Order at parades which include
the Twelfth of July, a celebration
of King William's triumph at the
Battle of the Boyne in 1690. As
such, it is a definitive 'Protestant'
symbol.
39 The other group, however, did
not share these sentiments and
made no negative comments.
40 This was the school which had
reintroduced the course in the
year of research.
41 As later chapters show, a
substantial proportion of students
nominated the language content
as their favourite part of the
course, so this 'criticism' must be
placed in the broader context.
42 This, conveniently, was the school
with the smallest number of
course-takers.
43 This is not to downplay the
effects of parental influence and
other environmental variables,
but it does show the importance
of politics as a factor *the pupils*
considered significant.
44 Until the 2002 suspension of the
Northern Ireland Assembly,

Bairbre de Brún of Sinn Féin was Minister for Health, Social Services and Public Safety. She insisted that all departmental job advertisements appear in both Irish and English, a policy which drew considerable opposition from unionists.

45 This interviewee was incorrect, as the security forces ban had been lifted by this stage.

46 See Ewart et al. (2004) but note that in 2008 an Ulster Unionist Belfast Lord Mayor took part in the city's St Patrick's Day celebrations (IHT, 2008).

47 This ties in well with research which shows that even those who do not have Irish-language skills can be drawn into watching TG4. In the case of sport (and music), the viewer can rely on visual elements rather than language facility (MORI, 2006:22).

48 The Republic's 'Irishness' might be relatively visible in terms of traffic signage, bilingual shop-fronts and pre-recorded public announcements in Irish, yet much of this is purely cosmetic (Malcolm, 2006). Officially, it is now supposedly 'easier' to deal with public organisations *as Gaeilge* but Gaeltacht residents have found that the exercising of their rights in this regard is not so straightforward in practice (MORI, 2006:34).

49 'Slag', in this context, is a colloquial term for gentle ribbing. Milroy (1987:58) notes its use in Belfast, but it is a fairly universal Northern Ireland term.

50 This is a reference to marching bands, which are heavily identified with loyalist culture and take part in parades associated with the Loyal Orders.

51 His point might be true in much of the country but would not apply in some parts of western Scotland and Glasgow, where one's religious beliefs can be rather important. Sectarian tensions, reflecting the Northern Ireland divide, still run high.

52 This group was organised in an area which is part of the Ulster-Scots heartlands.

53 This does not mean any over-arching dislike for Irish *per se*. Students everywhere have their 'favourite' and 'most-hated' subjects.

54 A reference to the 'séimhiú' in Irish, where initial mutation, indicated by the letter 'h', softens the sound.

55 A friend who taught Irish to an adult group on the loyalist Shankill Road in Belfast reported that surnames and place names were of 'very significant interest' to attenders. He felt they may have been engaged in 'a search for real roots, rather than anonymous Britishness'.

56 Upper Sixth is the final year of possible formal education for A Level students in grammar education in Northern Ireland.

57 There were two versions of the final questionnaire, a short version for non-attenders and a long version for attenders. The long version is in Appendix One.

58 Allow for rounding up/rounding down.

59 Statistical testing confirmed that the number of languages known did not translate into greater likelihood of attendance.

60 From a Presbyterian respondent.

61 Tests on the data mainly involved the Chi-Square statistic, although the t-Test, ANOVA and Spearman's rho correlation were also employed. SPSS (Statistical Package for the Social Sciences) was used for the analyses.

62 I could not have done this after the questionnaire sessions as some of the respondents went on to take part in the focus groups.

63 There is anecdotal evidence that some EPGS 'graduates' have gone on to study beginners' Irish at university.

64 At one time it was taken for granted that only Catholics played for Celtic and only Protestants played for Rangers. Today, winning is all that matters and the religious affiliations of players are of less importance than was once the case. Many fans, however, still look upon Celtic-v-Rangers matches as having more import than mere sport and people have been killed for wearing the 'wrong' shirt.

65 I don't wish this to be interpreted as an attack on the author – it is possible, given the ways of publishing, that the illustrations were chosen independently and without his knowledge.

66 Coulmas (2005:13) posits that migrants who acquire the requisite 'new' language will not necessarily give up their native languages, and refers to 'new

multilingual urban environments where they settle in compact communities'. This appears to be the case – thus far – in Northern Ireland.

67 Chinese, of course, is not one monolithic language but 'shorthand' for a number of languages.

68 A former presenter of BBC Northern Ireland's weekly Ulster-Scots programme *A Kist o' Wurds* is a Catholic.

69 In late 2007 the then Northern Ireland Culture Minister, Edwin Poots of the DUP, addressed a GAA conference in Belfast and urged the organisation to make efforts to persuade Protestants to embrace the sport and culture. During his speech, the Minister – who had controversially decided not to proceed with legislation for an Irish Language Act earlier in the week – acknowledged the importance of the language to many people in the GAA and promised that he would do nothing to inhibit their enjoyment of it.

70 This example is from Lurgan, County Armagh. The practice is now common in many parts of Northern Ireland.

71 In March 2008 I gave a talk on place names to a senior citizens' group in Lurgan. They were delighted when I translated names they had grown up with and lamented the fact that few young people seemed to use them any more.

72 It seems ironic that the Department of Education has

itself hinted at the value of enrichment courses (DENI, 2005c:7), while helping to make their implementation more difficult.

73 Pupils at a Protestant school in which I gave a talk in 2007 told me that pupils from a neighbouring Catholic college would often shout '*Tiocfaidh Ár Lá*' as pupils gathered in the town centre while waiting for buses. Some found this provocative and insulting.

74 That said, Sinn Féin branches are almost always named after expired 'heroes' of the republican cause. That an Irish-speaking 'cumann' should be named after an Irish-speaking 'patriot' is incidental.

75 Irish classes had been available at this school in the 1960s.

76 Since conducting the initial fieldwork for this book, I have continued to collect data.

INDEX

This index covers the main body of the text but not the notes and bibliography. The terms Protestant/unionist/loyalist and Catholic/nationalist/republican are used in overlapping contexts in the text: references in the index are grouped according to the terminology of the text with cross-references to other relevant information. The author's own research is listed under the term 'EPGS research'.